T0149900

Journey to the Heart of the Maker

Journey to the Heart of the Maker

KELLY RIVERA

Gateways Books
Nevada City, California

Distributed by Gateways Books and Tapes
P.O. Box 370
Nevada City, CA 95959
1-800-869-0658

http://www.idhhb.com
http://www.gatewaysbooksandtapes.com
ISBN Softcover: 978-0-89556-147-3

Seven poems* from The Soul of Rumi: A New Collection of Ecstatic Poems
Translated by Coleman Barks
Copyright © 2001 by Coleman Barks. Reprinted by permission of Harper Collins Publishers
*Essence is Emptiness (61), The Creek and the Stars (14), Wooden Cages (21), Fourteen Questions (25), The Battered Saucepan (24), A Way of Leaving the World (15), The One Thing You Must Do (prose)

Reprinted by permission of Random House / Broadway Books:
Excerpts from: The Illuminated Rumi, © 1997 Coleman Barks and Michael Green
Reprinted by permission of Samuel French:
Excerpt from the Ron Harwood play The Dresser

Library of Congress Cataloging-in-Publication Data

Rivera, Grace Kelly, 1956-
Journey to the heart of the Maker.
    p. cm.
ISBN 978-0-89556-147-3
1. Conduct of life. 2. Gold, E. J. I. Title.
BJ1581.2.R58 2011
204'.4--dc23
                        2011035448

This book is dedicated
to all
who heed the call
to come home.

Contents

Death in the Garden
Grace Kelly Rivera
Mixed Media on Prepared Arches Paper 30"x22"
© 1989 Grace Kelly Rivera

Introduction

My Teacher once described our first encounter as a moment of pure intimacy. It is a perfect description. I was among a large group of seekers at a Zendo in New York City that morning, being led through some unusual movements as we awaited E.J. Gold's arrival. He walked in and past a few rows of people and came to stop where I was standing. Our eyes locked and the most incredible thing happened within — it was as though an invisible zipper unzipped me and a soundless voice offered the contents saying, this is what there is to work with. I knew instantly he was the one. He has said that at that moment all the doors were open to me.

Moments of such clarity are a delightful treat to folks who walk around as criminally bewildered as I do. Bewilderment is just part of a mystic's life. Bewildering events started happening from very early childhood. I grew accustomed to strange phenomena and knew an active lucid dream life in which I experienced astral projection. There was one such event involving the energetic configuration many call Mary, as in the Blessed Mother, that is of particular interest here.

It was a hot night in the middle of July, summer of 1981. After the initial uncomfortable sensations of separation, my body of awareness hovered over the physical body. I felt myself being inexorably pulled in the direction of the window. Outside was a scene that did not correspond to the physical reality I normally knew — a courtyard of an apartment building on 96th street and Madison Ave. in New York City. Just outside my window seemed now to be on Fifth Avenue somewhere in front of Central Park. It was snowing. Mary was surrounded by people I didn't recognize. Her arms were folding and unfolding, and my awareness seemed to zoom into this repeated motion when her voice — more than that, her energy — beckoned me to "Come, come be with E.J. and the community."

At that time I had no clue who or what an E.J. is. It wasn't until two years after this lucid experience that I met him. The significant culmination of the many "pointed" events that unfolded in those two years was the "discovery" of what I later came to know as Prayer Absolute, a form of prayer that is done for the benefit of the Absolute, rather than as a supplication. It is a path that leads to the assumption of the cross of time and space where one catches an eternal glimpse of creation from the Creator's perspective. It is a path in which I found myself taken up, *as if* by a gigantic hand one fateful night. Within two weeks of the experience I found myself in the company of the only person I know of on the planet to have described this form of prayer in his writings. Obviously there were many factors prior to and certainly after meeting Mr. Gold and joining him in California that indicated a connection outside of this time and place.

The decision to join him in California was a no-brainer, meaning that yes, I was out of my mind, and yes, it just had to be. There was simply no question, from the point of meeting him, as to whether or not I would work with him. That was nearly three decades and countless lifetimes ago. One thing about this path that is as sure as rain — there will be many deaths, many hearts grown and thrown into the sun.

A first big taste of the quality of purifying fire that the Teacher provides came about around the issue of communication. We were at a different workshop still in New York, and there was a marvelous talk on the idea of bringing the Creation to life. He was making a specific subtle point that at this moment is lost to me, but at the time I seemed to understand well. However, when I was asked by E.J. to communicate my understanding, it was clear I lacked the skill to convey it effectively, and he lit into me for lacking the compassion to pass on to others what I knew. It was a stunning moment, he had delivered a shock, the taste of which lasts to this day. Gratefully so, for it helped me formulate the sincere wish to learn how to communicate well and compassionately about this Work that answers my heart's deepest calling.

I think this body would be dead by now had I not joined the caravan back Home. Well, perhaps I am dead, in a way. In fact, when a lot of extracurricular events happened at the time of 9/11, I assumed that the precognizant vision, vivid voyaging, lucid dream experiences of falling, informing others we were dead — I assumed these reflected my connection to the event through having worked at Windows on the World on top of World Trade Center Tower 2. But I was informed by an impeccable authority — E.J. Gold — that in fact I was among the missing. Even with all my bewildering past, this would seem impossible to believe were it not for direct experience with parallel world personae I've had. All of this to say I am very much indebted to that Agency that has shown me the great mercy of expanding my perceptual capability beyond the confines my conditioning would have me stay in, and the compassion to lead me to where I might be given some explanation. For whatever reason, it seems I was pre-destined to have a life that pushed out beyond the box in which it was given conception. Lots of unpleasantness, but the rewards are literally out of this world.

Before encountering alternative ideas that put me in search of a Teacher, the bewildering events only fueled my sense of isolation, and the knee-jerk response to this was to crave normalcy. Normalcy on this planet often seems to involve a lot of drama. What extraordinary capability I have shown in this game of "hide and seek" where I bury myself in phenomena then long for the uncovering. Not for nothing I'm an actress. Well, actually, in fact, it is for Nothing I am an actress now.

My skills as an actress, combined with visionary capabilities, helped to produce the profound inner theater space that allowed me to enact the ascension onto the cross of time and space through Prayer Absolute. An electrical experience like Prayer Absolute seems to have the side effect of *compelling one to evolve so that one might be of greater service.* Just one facet of the Situation can be likened to a little kitten stuck up in a tree, frightened. A person growing a soul feels compelled to help when she sees this. Prayer Absolute puts one in a position of seeing. It becomes a little more painful not to evolve than it is to stay complacent in the false security of normalcy as we normally see it.

But for every action there does seem to be an equal and opposite re-action, and the impulse to evolve will meet with resistance. For me, the evolutionary path is a lot about making friends with that resistance. In making friends, I've become a better student of Compassion. In the process of unraveling the false reality structures I have the talent for cre-ating, there has developed a sense of wonder over the incredible creative power at our disposal. There is also developed a gratitude for the Great Work that offers us the possibility of liberation from the prison that we tend to make with this creative power and guides us to participate in Cre-ation at a much greater scale.

But as Rumi would remind me, this path of Love requires that I be tricked first. I have been tricked into trying to maintain the identity that seems to emerge time and again from the rubble of the previous incar-nation. Eventually, from all the death and rebirth, there seems to have emerged something that speaks to the permanence that we crave, a per-manence that reflects the state of constant flux of the primordial being. It is an ever-minimizing identity structure that develops the ability to live multi-dimensionally.

We do kiss a lot of princes along the way to the king though, don't we? As indicated, it was clear from the beginning of my work with E.J. that I had some obligation to learn how to communicate about these ideas effectively. But I had to undergo a lot of demolition work before the one who is capable of fulfilling this obligation was given the space to emerge and develop. Each step along the way has revealed a different nuance of the habit to substantiate the outer world through a process of identifica-tion. The demolition work takes place within the constructs of daily life in an evolutionary school. Intentionally created, conditions trigger de-fense mechanisms against awakening at the same time we are given the reminding factor and force of a living Guide to inspire our efforts. The Guide is adept at bringing one to the brink of expansion and helping one take the leap.

After much repetition of this wind and water way — death, rebirth, changes profound and subtle — one begins to see the miraculous art and craft behind the creation of evolutionary school conditions and how this has been magnificently applied in one's relationship to the Guide. The extraordinary skill and method and compassion — these begin dawning on one as the medicine one takes restores the Voyager's vision. The heart is opened further by the confoundingly delightful fact that Much Ado must take place about Nothing in order to witness this beauty unfold. One stands in awe — speechless, yet something pries my mouth open to speak.

This is how Dear Oobe came about — or so it seems to me at this moment. A forum needed to be created through which I could realize another level of my quest to learn how to communicate effectively about this Work. After the establishment of the online E.J. Gold's Gorebagg/JustinTV channel and my completion of a show based on his book, which deals with the ideas around Dear Oobe and Objective Prayer, a Dear Abby type show around Work ideas seemed like the way to go. This seed evolved into the regular noon to one Pacific Time, Sunday show called *Dear Oobe*.

This book uses, as its basis, a collection of scripts for the Dear Oobe shows. I should explain that the title "Dear Oobe" came from E.J., OoBE standing for Out of Body Experience. The show basically consists of readings of writings — my own and others — that treat topics on matters of voluntary evolution and practical work on self. Questions and topic suggestions were given by audience members. Eventually I was asked about my writings, and thankfully my dear Work buddy, Jewel McInroy, helped to see that this book was written.

I am fortunate to have received a lot of help. This, like any Work endeavor around this school, involves many; it is a group project. To produce the Dear Oobe show requires the work of a dedicated staff, as does the production of this book. I am honored to be in the company of my compatriots here, and ever grateful for the opportunity to work with and be supported by a committed group of individuals.

But there is one individual who stands out greatly, for without him, none of this cooperative work would be possible. E.J. once described our relationship by saying that he is my mother, father, brother, teacher, friend, lover, uncle and sister. When he said this so many years ago I sensed the truth of what was being said, but couldn't begin to fathom the depth of its meaning, a depth that continues to reveal itself. This sacred relationship contains all relationships within it. As indicated, his role has been that of resisting force to my unconscious habits, until, with his incredible skill and grace, enough obstruction was removed to help me stop resisting his resistance so much.

With this "making friends with resisting force," a growing gratitude is but one effect. How does one possibly express her gratitude for the profound gift of life given by such an enlightened rascal as E.J. Gold? On a very rare occasion, we happened to be taking a stroll alone, and he told me that all he ever wants from anyone is *the truth*. It is my sincere hope that this book is in keeping with his fundamental wish, reflecting a love that I find to be the only true response to a Teacher's magnanimous and constant call To Be.

Moon / Branches
Grace Kelly Rivera
Mixed Media on Prepared Arches Paper, 16"x20"
© 2004 Grace Kelly Rivera

Ascension
Grace Kelly Rivera, oil on canvas, 48" x 40" © 2011 Grace Kelly Rivera

Topic One

Verification and Objectification on the Transformational Path

By what means can one tell (verify) that one is indeed working and/or achieving transformation? Without some type of feedback, how can one assess one's own progress in the Work? Through our various subjective lenses, how can we learn to objectify our progress?

We objectify our progress to the degree that we can objectify our daily experience of life. If we are living objectively, objectivity is a natural part of our life. I'll offer this little picture: one's self-awareness is expressed as the whole and the particular at once. The individualized expression of oneness, we are functions within the contextual awareness of the whole, and we are the whole gestalt. To the degree we are able to function in this manner which is naturally impartial, it seems we will be able to objectify our progress. Given this state of being, one might be more inclined to live a life that is obliged to evolve for the greater good. In the realm of service, one is given an opportunity for objective assessment.

Transformation will tend to beget more transformation. This transformation has much to do with the removal of obstacles to awakening. The more obstacles, the more likely we are to be caught up in those subjective lenses instead of catching the Moments of Freedom where objectivity can be experienced. Given more momentum on the side of transformation, we can better see ourselves in relationship to the whole. Accumulated waking state experience that reveals the Work will give us points of reference that might satisfy a bit the wish for feedback.

Points of waking state reference might offer us standards against which to measure our progress. I use the word progress a little reluctantly because this implies something linear while the growing of a soul is not within the realm of the linear. At the same time, we live in a realm that includes time and the experience of progress along a transformational path, with signposts along the way. But with transformation, there is change that renders points of reference limited in their usefulness. In this realm the human idea of duplication will fail us. However, one thing seems to hold true no matter what the path looks like — it goes to Philadelphia, the City of Brotherly Love. We might see how far or near we are to the goal of true brotherly love. This describes a condition made possible when one has the quality of consciousness described, with a living ongoing awareness of the whole and the part that contains the whole.

The ability to tolerate the negative manifestations of others toward ourselves and others without reaction is considered a benchmark of self-completion, a minimal requirement. There may be the impulse present to activate compassion, but there is no manifestation of personal reaction to the unpleasantness. Focus has been transformed away from the personal because one has ceased to have the quality of identity that emphasizes separation and organic significance.

Each seed for a soul will require food, light and water
for growth, but to varying degrees according to its
intrinsic nature.

There are different levels and categories to consider in addressing the issues of verification of our progress. We have Work on self, Work for others, and Work for the Work — a veritable smorgasbord of Work categories. A sign of progress seen at one point of the path will not necessarily mean the same thing when seen again. What is good nourishment at one phase is sheer poison at another. Each seed for a soul will require food, light and water for growth, but to varying degrees according to its intrinsic nature. Discernment will take on new meaning also as our faculties expand their capacity to process the increased input and corresponding energy that comes with greater degrees of obligation and service. There is work so impartial and intrinsic to the very core of "Being," one ceases to have a separate identity to know or not know, one knows because one is. That knowledge can best be held in the vast space of silence. The moment we move into description of that knowledge, we invite ourselves back into a more limited realm of separation where there is question and the need for verification.

I remember in New York there was one very potent talk E.J. gave during which someone asked about a person he knew who was supposed to be in the Work. The response E.J. gave was sparklingly crystalline in its mood. For a moment it seemed as though we were in a vast field that at the same time was a contained space within which he spoke with great tenderness. He asked if this "Work" person had ever been known to deliberately brush by a leaf, or . . . and he mentioned some small ordinary seeming activities that are lost to me now. What I do remember is that these reflected an exquisitely subtle quality about the nature of the Work. I caught a glimpse of what was being described as he spoke, not from the words said so much as the mood created in the space. I suddenly flashed on the following little scene from prior to meeting him that seemed to whisper the same fragrance.

The event took place when I was rather down and out in New York City — jobless, confused, carrying around a heavy burden of broken dreams. Fortunately, I loved to walk and this often would change my state, so on this particular day I proceeded to take a familiar route from my apartment on 96th and Madison, crossing Central Park down around 86th and then over to Central Park West at 72nd Street, across from the Dakotas — old apartment buildings where the likes of John Lennon lived and near where he died. By this point in my life I knew to periodically "Stop the World." Stopping the world meant putting a stop to the ordinary life's concerns that involved my survival in the world and devoting my attention instead to the calling of the moment. Giving up my job hunt and worrying, I was free to drink in all the deliciousness around me.

The day was glorious — spring and a lush Central Park bustling full of friendly people, birds, squirrels — the sun was bright and warm and before long my mood couldn't help but lighten. I decided to stop and sit on a park bench there at Central Park West, along with several other folks who basked in the sunlight. Actually, there really was no decision about it; I found myself suddenly moved to sit. No sooner did I sit down when this big, beautiful Monarch butterfly hovered by, then rested on my right shoulder. It stayed there for at least three, possibly five full minutes — long enough to draw a small crowd of marvelous older women mostly, marveling over the Monarch with me as I sat perfectly still, honored to be its temporary throne. Then its majesty took off again, and I knew my mission was complete for the day. As I walked home I also knew something special had taken place there, but my mind could not grasp the deeper significance of this impression beyond remembering an old poster I once saw that said, "Happiness is like a butterfly; the more you chase it, the more it eludes you, but if you stay still, happiness, like the butterfly might come and softly rest on your shoulder."

It wasn't until I found myself within the context of a school that this impression was given fresh light, one my mind could not have conceived of prior to exposure to its influence. School experience gave new meaning to this event that contributed to my movement, even though I had no understanding of this at the time. Later, after I'd been working with E.J. for about a year or so, he told a story of having to travel across the country just to perform a very simple action that was Work-vital. I related to him my butterfly story, and he verified my growing understanding of this subtlety. There is not necessarily going to be foreknowledge to our movements in the Work, nor understanding as we normally understand it.

I recount the story to illustrate this unknowing quality of the journey, as well as the un-linear nature of the movement, with the reminder that at times the knowledge of whether or not we are walking our path might be unavailable. And this unavailability seems to be compassionate, lawful, and merciful. At the same time, given the advantage of hindsight, we all can see those times in our lives that contributed to or influenced our eventual seeking and perhaps learn to be open to all experience. We are asked to trust in the midst of bewilderment.

Bewildered surrender is a part of the Way.

Mystical experience can expose one to radiations that have a transformational effect, a part of which will be the increasing inclination toward transformation. But my mystical experiences involve no volition as I usually experience it — in fact, it feels as though some invisible and very large hand takes me by the scruff of the neck and the only real option is to surrender. There may be volition involved insofar as I have adopted habits that might better bring me to the conditions required for a revelatory experience, but revelation has its own timing.

What I'll call here the conscious self, who is able to communicate and navigate through the physical plane, has an established and developing relationship with whatever that Agency is that seems to take me up and put me onto an inexorable track. After enough of these voyaging and macrodimensional episodes, one gains maze brightness and the ability actually to drink these experiences in. "Drinking in" is more about opening up a bit wider than reaching for the cup — it is a movement that reflects surrender, yielding. I once heard a description of the Absolute, God, as being utter limpness, contrasted to the quality of rigidity that the wrathful God picture might paint. There is an unconditional yielding to beingness — all is given space to be. I am reminded of a state of profound, turning-inside-out-surrender that serves for me as a piece of authentic data reflecting the relationship between the Shekinah, the Bride of God, and His Endlessness Himself.

As indicated in my introduction to this book, there was intimation of my eventual meeting with E.J. in a lucid dream years before we actually met, and there were other signs along the way, with always this feeling of looking for someone whom I very much needed to spend time with. About two weeks before we met, an event took place for me of a completely different order, a new kind of mysticism from any I'd encountered in my voyaging life.

I was working at Windows on the World on top of the World Trade Tower 2. I came back to my apartment late as usual — it was around two in the morning. Wired, I went to my drawing table to work on a project I had going. My attention was keen and I saw, as I drew, that every stroke and breath counted. Pausing, I reflected for a moment on an experience of drawing at the Cloisters Museum, where I had previously worked. I'd been exploring different shading techniques with my pencil, creating gradations of tone randomly, when there suddenly seemed to emerge from the page a clear image of a gargoyle. I *as if* sculpted it out a little more, then the intensity of the electrical experience had me fearful it might animate, and I stopped before long. But it had put me on to a current of the Work, a new way of seeing that had been in development for some time.

So there I was now at my drawing table pondering all this and aware of the relentless knot of fear that I always seemed to feel. I broke from my table and sat on the edge of my couch/bed and asked myself the question, "What am I afraid of?" The space had a particular feeling to it — imminence with electrical crackle.

Thought at some point seemed to change its speed of transmission, and clearly I was functioning from a higher mental state. With lucidity, my mind conjured up a particular fear or set of fears, and *as if* walked through them systematically, releasing in a complete, three-centered (three-centered refers to the three distinct centers, or brains, that govern the intellectual, the moving-instinctive and the emotional functions.) way that thing I was clinging to that I feared losing, then finding another layer of fears representing attachments, conjuring them up vividly so as to release and reduce, and so on. It was as though a special theater had been set up especially for this process, and every aspect of it was vibrantly alive. The subtle internal movements were thunderously huge. Thought accelerated until there were no longer thought forms, but they were represented by geometric forms and then these gave way to an even greater objectivity. I moved against the wind and at the same time surrendered. Eventually I was brought to the realm of death, where I released and let go every consideration presented.

There was a profound shift into yet another level of being. Here I came upon eternity and existed for one eternal moment at the cross of time and space. With this, a flash of light that was accompanied by the thought form "God needs help/I am God," to all of which my entire body seemed to gasp involuntarily.

Two weeks later I met E.J. and found out that this experience was called Dear Oobe, I'd stumbled upon a form of it called The Great Gasp. At the time this happened, I knew something of a different order had taken place, and at the same time there was an unreal quality to it. Despite the fact that I'd by that point been exposed to Fourth Way material and Sufism, my Catholic conditioning was still very much in place.

Experiencing *God needs help/I am God* went deep against this grain and reflected nothing of what I would have considered my path. Nonetheless, something had shifted within that seemed to have a strong effect on the movement of my life from that point. Following this experience, until meeting E.J., I found myself quite detached from the things of my life at the same time experiencing a fresh sense of necessity about my inner work. On the day I saw the poster that brought me to his workshops in New York, I was carrying a copy of Ouspensky's *In Search of the Miraculous* in my hand and wrote the contact telephone number in pencil on the title page. I was carrying this book with me to remind myself as I rode the train downtown and during my break at work of the wish to self-complete.

It's only in hindsight that I can see how pivotal certain events, such as that one, were in my evolutionary path. Seems I am given grace when I least expect it. Hindsight is useful in showing us where we've been helped along the way and how we don't know. But if we want to hang out where grace might find us again, steeping ourselves in the present moment will better serve.

The evolutionary path requires us to learn how and when to yield as we relinquish our outer lives to serve our inner.

It is said that a universe changes into another universe by a process of absorption — the old being absorbed by the new. This way of morphing plays out in micro realms as well. Looking at the possible higher bodies that, when developed, sum up to Completed Being, their evolutionary movement is similar. The development of the astral body requires the outer physical world become resisting force to the active inner, pushing the energy normally used to feed the outer world reality toward the inner. It's as though the astral body swallows the physical through this reality pump reversal that, once complete, forms a new dynamic relationship to feed subsequent and more refined bodies. The old dissolves and is absorbed by the new, and our center of gravity changes away from the physical to more rarefied planes of existence.

As Rumi might put it, we break our jar and empty it out into the ocean so as to be one with it. The ocean of meanings will change as we evolve. Viewed from a Taoist place, perhaps this movement can be described as more Yin than Yang. The evolutionary path requires us to learn how and when to yield as we relinquish our outer lives to serve our inner.

The set of skills that develop around the surrender of our outer lives might be a good place to look at getting some feedback about one's work. There can be confusion due to the ferocity of purpose that we are at times called upon to muster just to keep walking our path and to take the opportunities for making super efforts that come our way. It can be easy to mistake this for a forcefulness that seems only to lead us astray. When we are overly identified with the quest to awaken, we merely have found another way to sleep. Our Work movement will have its seasons and nuances — the ability to discern and make voluntary the corresponding postures so that we are using momentum well would fall under this category of surrender.

Tai Chi shows us to work with the energy as it is flowing, to become one with it and then direct it as is wanted. So it is in our lives, those things considered adversarial to our purposes can become rich sources of evolutionary fuel. If we can gain enough of an impartial identity within, from this platform we may develop new habits of wakefulness, riding the force and momentum of our chronic defense reactions to the waking state to bring us to awakening. Then there may be times when inner work is dry, and it seems one is just treading water. Here, too, we can take this opportunity to be voluntary about what is happening in the season of our work life. We can sink into the moment's season from the platform of using the opportunity to experience this aspect of being in a human form. Allowing what is to be keeps muscles activated and at the ready to make use of work opportunity when it presents itself.

Using an art form as a means through which to apply work ideas gives us a great platform from which to witness the ability to surrender. By surrender I mean having the presence to be with what is. Spontaneity will be one quality that will be reflected in this ability, and with it artistic daring. When one is in a place of being surrendered to the moment, without any agenda, without anything left to lose, the moment becomes a big playing field of potential. The moment is the key to eternity, for God's sake. We tap into creative force when we are completely drowned in the present and able to express this force purely. This can be felt and seen in performance of all kinds as well as the visual arts.

I also refer to the ability to let go of what is dying, to know how to change form or track with the movement of the spirit. You surrender to a practice, to an activity, to the moment, and if you are a Lover, all of these are just different manifestations of your Beloved. I am borrowing from the Sufi metaphor here, as it reflects an ongoing experience I've had throughout my life. The Beloved is the one that has been beckoning me at the same time I've been seeking. This has been made very clear to me in my experiences of Dear Oobe. Annihilation is the cure to the disease of being in love with the Beloved like this. There is a longing I know about that, at first, had me seeking material means of satisfaction to no avail. Eventually, I came to see some of my spiritual pursuits as equally materialistic. Seeking satisfaction of that longing is no longer the aim. Surrender in the aimless bewilderment of the journey better describes the quest.

Be Melting Snow

Totally conscious, and apropos of nothing, you come to see me.
Is there someone here? I ask.
The moon. The full moon is inside your house.

My friends and I go running out into the street.
I'm in here, comes a voice from the house, but we aren't listening.
We're looking up at the sky.
My pet nightingale sobs like a drunk in the garden.
It's midnight. The whole neighborhood is up and out
in the street thinking, the cat burglar is somewhere in this crowd.
No one pays attention.

Lo, I am with you always means when you look for God,
God is in the look of your eyes,
in the thought of looking, nearer to you than your self,
or things that have happened to you
There's no need to go outside.

Be melting snow.
Wash yourself of yourself.

A white flower grows in the quietness.
Let your tongue become that flower.
                        (Barks, *The Essential Rumi*, page 12)

   Against the backdrop of that practice we are faithful to, we can see movement and change. Because we tend to be creatures of habit and subject to identification, it serves us well to carry on more than one practice, in accordance with the guidance we receive. The serious practice of multiple disciplines that address our evolutionary needs has many benefits. A healthy palette of activities will offer opportunity for the development of all centers, thus balancing any dominance we might have in the physical, emotional or intellectual. By applying oneself to multiple practices for evolutionary work, one attracts help in navigating around attachment to any one form. We also receive opportunity for distilling our basic skills of attention as we see them in different forums of application. In this light we can strengthen, develop and expand these skills. We learn *how* we learn and we learn how *to* learn.

   We can drink in those moments in our lives that are so saturated with Work purpose that the distinction between us and our work lives dissolves. Moments can be seen for the rich potential that they hold. Such impressions are vitally nutritional to our conscious lives. We can also be aware that at the same time they produce waste product. The way we eliminate some waste product of this nature is through talking. Talking has its place, but when it is abused, we starve spirit. Like what we know about nutrients and the alchemical factory of the human biological machine — we are nourished to the degree that the food is actually processed, converted into viable nutrients, then substances needed for the maintenance of different systems, provided they are not diverted elsewhere, converted to waste. We need to be able to digest food we eat, process nutrients and eliminate waste products to keep the machine operant.

   This is applicable to the ingestion, digestion and processing of impressions and what they feed. We know there are substances that, when taken in over a period of time, will produce cancer. It seems this can translate into work terms as well. When referring to ordinary nutrition, one of the signs of an allergy can be the craving for a particular food that then triggers a set of unhealthy reactions. Wheat allergies tend to work this way. So, likewise, if we find ourselves craving the same kind of experience over and again, chances are we have some imbalance that needs to be addressed. Gaining the objectivity to see that imbalance is the first step. For this we are likely to need help and guidance. Don't underestimate the ego's power to use what it can to feed its hungry necessity. Even the game of awakening can feed sleep. This is why it is useful to get help from a professional, one who has walked the evolutionary path and knows the terrain well enough to guide.

One of the things an evolutionary school provides is a set of activities that offer conditions for self-observation conducive to developing habits of impartiality. Objective activities, for example, those activities that render genuine service to the aims of the school, lend themselves to the necessary conditions, addressing the various needs of the participants. Perhaps, more important than the activity itself is the *how* of that activity — there is a way that an Expert will know to use seemingly ordinary activities — such as learning a musical instrument — for work purposes. The momentum of our tendencies toward the organic must be shifted to that of our awakening, and for this we are going to need objective help. But there are some things we can do to help create a quality of objectivity that is needed in our self-observation. This impartial self-observation is of the essence.

Journaling can be a helpful tool for gaining some objectivity. When you read back on journals after keeping them for a while, you can see where the attention has been focused most often, and patterns of thought and action that may contribute to repeated unwanted experience. Personally, I have found journaling invaluable, and have practiced it on and off throughout my adult life. When I started working with the play *Creation Story Verbatim* (3), E.J. asked me to keep a journal and to write *as if* speaking to others. Years ago, when I found myself stuck in a way that was reflected in my art studio work, I started a practice of writing three pages of stream of consciousness first thing in the morning.

I modified the technique of the morning page writing to suit my changing needs over time. One modification was to write a note at the

To study a subtle habit of unconsciousness as it plays out in multiple ways helps us to establish a relationship with our issues that better empowers us for wanted change.

points where I would find myself spacing out in the writing meditation. Seeing this, seeing where my attention falters repeatedly, enables me to see that same glitch translate in other realms of activity. For example, I noticed a connection between the way I would falter in the articulation of some of my flamenco dance movement and where my attention tends to falter and dissolve into the atmosphere in my writing meditation, and this was further shown in a particular kind of stroke of the paintbrush where I am not breathing with it to its completion. To study a subtle habit of unconsciousness as it plays out in multiple ways helps us establish a relationship with our issues that better empowers us for wanted change.

Another modification was in working out areas of stagnation specifically. Devoting a journal to writing out my imbalances intentionally, constructively and vigilantly, noting where stream of consciousness is interrupted, has been of great help to the process of release. Journaling can offer tangible proof of where we are focused, where we have moved, emotional postures and beliefs and the patterns and cycles that move us along our path.

It is said that Spirit is the art of making flow what once was blocked or frozen.

Is there movement? Not just any kind of movement, but do we see telltale signs of the deeper movement of spirit? Have we noticed a thawing of emotional postures? This can be seen in our most difficult relationship issues — when we examine our long term relationships and the inevitable sticking points, are these showing signs of change in habit? One thing to know here, what we usually consider to be emotions is better termed "moving center emotions" as they are experienced by sensation. Emotions that originate in our true emotional center, which requires a particular reversal of our intellectual and moving/instinctive functions to be activated, are radiant in nature. We can see the possibility of thawing our emotional postures by placing our attention on the sensations that form them, relaxing the tensions that keep them in place and keep us well identified with the dream. We have to really want to stop identification with the significance of our beliefs. The heat for thawing is received through our attention, and it behooves us to develop our attention to provide the light and heat we need for this inner transformative work.

Are we breathing life into our spirit or out of it? Are we taking our physical reality and feeding our inner world? In this process of reversing our reality pump so that the outer world feeds the inner, a lack of passion about things one may have felt strongly, a growing impartiality we may see. With growing impartiality comes space enough for tolerance. At the same time, there will be a new sense of obligation that is experienced as a form of passion, perhaps we can call it a passion without adrenaline. It is a passion to fulfill our work obligation and to evolve so that we might better serve.

To make flow what is stuck will require some form of dissolution. When we look at the model provided by Gold in *The Human Biological Machine as a Transformational Apparatus*, (later referred to as *HBM*), we can see the relationship between the human biological machine and the essential self as electrical fields bearing an affinity that binds them. The resulting relationship has the potential of producing evolutionary changes that can potentially serve the Absolute. This is possible only when the human biological machine is awake, operating as a transformational apparatus for the essential self in a process of mutual reciprocal initiation. One definition of an awakened human biological machine is that it becomes invisible and passive to the active essential self. The essential self is thus able to experience the life of the human biological machine firsthand, as it were, and undergo the kinds of electrical alterations necessary to its evolution. This is a very schematic representation of this model, but it serves our purpose here.

A malfunctioning transformational apparatus that is not correctly processing nutrients in the form of impressions can develop electrical field anomalies which can be further impacted by other electrical debris such as thought forms. A trauma will have a certain amount of electrical mass to it that will draw yet more resonant electrical mass if it is not discharged appropriately. In other words, negative electrical charge can beget more negative electrical charge. The combined effect is one of obstruction to energetic flow and an accumulation of this static energy that can be expressed as habitual fear reactions and other repeated behaviors. All of this serves to keep one rooted in the organic.

It is hard to point with pride at the nothingness we have "accumulated," so we do well to refrain from over-analysis of the evolutionary process in terms of linear progression.

Our awakening is cumulative in experience, but that accumulation has a lot to do with the dissolution of impediment to the waking state. In the waking state one is exposed as an essential self, unadorned in a realm of pure being. It is hard to point with pride at the nothingness we have accumulated, so we do well to refrain from over-analysis of the evolutionary process in terms of linear progression. If we are to view this progression at all, it seems wise to do so from a platform of overview and objectivity, that is, from an awakened place. Chances are we won't need to view this progression while in an awakened place; rather, one will, along the way, catch note of change, just as a by-product of the moment's work activity. I was once told, in response to a question I had based on misguided understanding of the awakening process, that there is no such thing as an anchor that keeps one enlightened, basically — there is constant flux. One works to develop habits that keep one moving in the general direction of evolutionary refinement for the purpose of fulfilling one's service and function.

It is so highly individual, this business of Work, and yet, at the same time, there are signs and indications that are universal, precise and unmistakable. How these signs and indications play out within the framework of one's relationship to the HBM will of course be individual. One universal sign seems to be a lessening of self-consciousness that occurs as the outer life is surrendered to the inner. The Tarot card of the Fool points to this aspect of the path. There is no longer the quality of self-concern that plagues us with fear and hesitation. Self-consciousness is partially a child of conditioning that established us as part of the herd, initiating us into consensus reality. Increasing ease of movement in life seems to accompany increase in one's sense of humor about one's own character — a good sign of objectivity. This sense of humor will be genuine and compassionate and will extend out to all. Tolerance has space enough for humor. Good humor will bridge distances and melt barriers.

It takes an Expert to be able to see and recognize the process as it is being expressed in the individual. Such an Expert will likely be adept at brinksmanship — recognizing when the being is on the brink of further unfolding and supporting or creating those conditions, whereby, the leap can be made. And of course there is likely to be resistance and discomfort involved in some of those conditions. That's in part why we need the objective help the school can provide in many areas, including that of gaining objectivity. The dissolution of one's own agenda for the benefit of the greater good needs an arena through which it can be played out, and in the playing out, one is given objectivity. Working to a greater good objectifies your function, presents before you the weaknesses and impediments in high relief, and this can be a great relief to one who experiences the pressure of needing to return the hospitality of the Absolute.

Ultimately, the Teacher is within, we are put in touch with this Source and our path is activated with the help of our outer Teacher's grace and guidance.

So periodically, the feedback might need to be straight from an Expert's mouth. But remember the Expert might shape-shift. The Expert can sometimes be speaking through the mouth of someone you don't particularly feel drawn to listen to, or in the form you might not admire. Developing our voyager attention and the corresponding objectivity is essential, so to speak. We also cultivate our Love for the Work so that we see things in relationship to this fundamental aspect of our lives. If one has a strong Work wish, what is necessary to one's Work will come with the wishing — our voyager attention helps us see and receive this grace. Ultimately, the Teacher is within, we are put in touch with this Source and our path is activated with the help of our outer Teacher's grace and guidance.

Because of the complex way we are put together, however, it does us no use to compare progress or to have expectation about work progression. To begin with, comparison and expectation are creatures of the head brain — the "formatory apparatus", as it is sometimes put, and this mode of thinking is beyond its range when used to approach such matters. One of the things we need to learn how to deal with is abstraction in this regard. At the same time, our abstract longing for work needs fertile ground to know actualization.

It serves to learn how to become as a child — embracing the wonder of the moment, without expectation. Our degree of fluidity in this realm is another good place to look for feedback about our work. Are we developing fluidity in our transactions? Can we quickly about-face or change tracks as indicated? Are we developing our shamanic abilities to shape-shift in accordance with the time, place and people? These are certainly signs of the way being traveled as they imply a lessening identification with the outer form and willfulness being replaced by alignment to Work Will.

None of this stuff seems to play in the neat way our conditioning might have us want to believe. But with practice, with the right kind of exposure to appropriate conditions, a different kind of conditioning begins to take place that develops our sensing. We begin to see this deep movement with a new kind of diffused vision. This quality of instinctive vision informs us where to look to see the signs we need from time to time, pointing us toward Philadelphia, the City of Brotherly Love. Because that is one thing that seems to hold true all the way around for Completed Beings, they've all been to *Philadelphia*.

A lot is hinged on our ability to separate ourselves from our own trip. Obligating oneself to something bigger than oneself, which benefits many under school conditions, and at the expense of personal wishes, can serve in this separation process, this objectification. Somewhere we need to find the crowbar that will extract us from our self-importance. When we have found ourselves able to tolerate the negative manifestations of others and interact well with all different types, then we will have transcended our own typicality. In a sense, we will have absorbed all typicality as self-completion implies the return of the parts to the whole.

Once we develop a set of habits that can allow this quality of objectivity, it becomes easier to see the signs that tend to be all around us, letting us know where we're at. Objectivity is the difference between seeing the Statue of Liberty from above and standing right in front of it. From a perspective above, you can see the relationship it has to its surroundings, while directly in front of it you would get a different perspective of that relationship altogether. When we are attached to certain patterns of thought and action, we naturally invoke a limited range of possibility and movement. Objectivity lets us see the playing field and range of possibility, the time, place and people.

There is a wonderful story of Rumi's that illustrates even a great man like Solomon can err, but given the habit of surrender, the error is readily corrected. Solomon was on his throne, rather irritated over certain matters in his kingdom. Suddenly his crown slid down over to the side of his head, sitting crooked. He adjusted it and again, it slid to the side — this happened once more, and finally, Solomon asked the crown what was up, why did it keep tilting over like that? The crown spoke, "I have to do that out of respect for you and with deepest humility to show you that you are not completely yourself." With that, Solomon realized that it was he who had been causing disruption to his kingdom with his thoughts and irritation. With that realization, the crown happily sat straight back up on his head.

We all have our inner relationship to our work and how we treat that relationship; how we honor it is a big indicator of where we are. Do you honor the relationship you have to your work? Do you honor in others their right to work? Do you experience gratitude for the opportunity to Work? It seems in part we are drawn to a school to learn something about developing this relationship such that we more readily cease to resist the demolition of matrix that is an inevitable part of voluntary evolution. Compassion grows in the refuse of this process.

Some of the data we require comes in the form of an exact quality of feeling. With repeated experience of this phenomenon, for which a school provides conditions, comes both an expansion and diffusion of awareness. It is said relative to Angelic Invocation that the experience of ecstasy is merely an indicator of penetration, of successful invocation. If one goes for that ecstasy directly, then what was angelic becomes demonic, what was white magic now taints toward black. With that in mind, it makes sense that our work will keep us moving along, not staying stuck in any one place, and that different needs will present themselves at different points of the journey.

Do you see an increase in work will, skill or obligation? Has your chronic defense mechanism against the waking state shown signs of dismantling? Again, the constant of certain practices and activities will give you some background against which you can see the movement of your Work.

There is also the scope of our work to consider. The movement is ever inward. But to a degree this inward movement will be reflected in the outer range of activity. There has been more than one source of wisdom to point out that we are blessed to the degree we can genuinely wish for others the goodness we wish for ourselves. Developing the ability to "work wish" is a skill in itself, and just as phenomena and the non-phenomenal are intricately woven together, the ability to wish for ourselves is intimately connected to our ability to wish for others.

Do you find yourself moving in a direction of external consideration over internal? When we are considering only ourselves and what benefit we can extract from experience, we show our station — we are babies not yet developed in our higher faculties. Like a baby, we are limited in what we can do in the world. As we grow we'll find need for new kinds of nourishment, and in part this nourishment comes through opportunity to serve a greater good. When we find ourselves taking to a new form of nourishment, this can be sign of movement in the right direction. Here is a Rumi poem that addresses this phenomenon:

The Creek and the Stars

*Spirit is so mixed with the visible world that giver, gift and beneficiary are one thing. You **are** the grace raining down, the grace is you. Creation is a clear, flat, fast — moving creek, where qualities reflect.*

Generations rush by, while the stars stay still without a splash. When you lose your appetite for food, you'll be given other nourishment.

There's well-being that is not bodily and beings that live on fragrance. Don't worry about losing animal energy. Go the way of love and ask provisions.

Love more the star region reflected, less the moving medium.

(Barks, *The Soul of Rumi*, page 72)

I was once told that Alchemy is actually like a map which tells you where you are — not a map that you follow to get from point A to point B. Landmarks — such as sublimation, coagulation, putrefaction — let you know where you are, but even that observation will effect minor change. My understanding of this is akin to what I have come to understand of the Russian actor Constantin Stanislavski's work — the man considered to be the founder of Method Acting. He observed great actors on stage as well as in their everyday environment and from his notes saw certain things they had in common. His intent was not necessarily to make a method, but out of his work a method, in fact, several methods, have been developed.

There are certain earmarks to look for in a great actor, and there are states in alchemy that one will note as occurring in a particular sequence, but following a method created from these observations will not necessarily take us where we want to go. How the various stages of the alchemical process are expressed when speaking of the alchemy of self-completion will be unique to the individual. There are definite stages and these are sequential in cumulative terms. However, when dealing with the alchemy of self-completion, there are many factors of complexity present in the set, setting and dosage of the transforming voyager. The state of being that might be akin to the alchemical stage of putrefaction will be expressed in one type of individual in a way that is distinct from another. An intentional shock to a person's Work octave might thus take the form of confrontation with an individual at one moment, then at another it will be non-action that delivers the goods.

Seeing a method from observation isn't without its wisdom. If you follow the trail until you gain enough momentum, you might eventually get to Philadelphia. If you act as if enough, you might eventually actualize. We are simply warned against over-emphasis of method over intuition. Different approaches will be found effective at different times. The medium can be an exercise or a practice done on a daily basis with which we develop an ongoing relationship that with time might grow impartial. Yet our relationship to our work practice will be profoundly intimate and will express our individuality.

I will offer my own experience of working with the play *Creation Story Verbatim* as a small example. E.J. told us when he first gave Robbert Trice, my acting partner, and I the Being Task of performing this play, that while initially the effects of this undertaking would benefit our work, eventually it would cease to be of benefit to the actors, who would serve as instruments for the benefit of a greater whole. Repetition of this theater piece, under at times extraordinary school conditions, has offered me a means to gauge change. And that change is largely in the form of a hollowing out that allows for greater flexibility of response to the moment onstage.

The quality of consciousness is different. Initially, the range of my interior concerns around the theatrical endeavor was limited by self-importance that narrowed my sphere of awareness. Over time and the wind and water of the way, this has opened out to a larger range of awareness that takes in the energetic configuration of the audience as a whole comprised of individuals. How the energy is moving, the effect of the communication on the space and a myriad of other factors take up the place that ego-based considerations left behind. It is still the same form of practice, but the practice seems to have changed its emphasis. When we practice in a way that serves others, it suggests that we are ready to work with a greater amount of energy and increased necessity — again a good sign of movement along the path.

When one is obligated to something outside of oneself, putting one's Work Wish to action, that involves more than oneself, the quality of energy and results to be obtained through one's efforts with that energy change exponentially. Because service is part of being in *Philadelphia*, if you have a service that you perform on a regular basis, then you are given opportunity to see many things about where you are sitting relative to your wish to work. You develop certain internal muscles that form the basis for further transformational work.

We are asked to know ourselves as others know us. What a sly way of gaining access to the path that transcends typicality. But the physical reality of it as expressed in working with a group toward the common goal of say, arriving at a decision on what to serve for lunch at the next workshop, hardly would betray that access point. The secret does keep itself. It is hidden in the physicality of it in part — the King is naked, we see this, but we think that we don't see it. We need a love for the Work that brings us to where our thirst for it might be quenched. The King, our Beloved, is naked here now as intimate with us as our breath. The quality of Love that gives us a glimpse of this is fierce; it burns like fire, cutting through our illusions like a knife. And it is what we ache for.

What do you feel obligated to, what does your Work obligation feel like? When you say "Work" what do you mean by that at this point in time? Do you see change in your understanding of what it is to Work? Are you connected to the longing to Work as it is in the heart? I have found it helpful to sit still and sense my longing to Work, affirming my wish to Work with a sincere prayer that I be guided in whatever way necessary to my transformation for greater service. Everyone has his/her method or methods — prayer, meditation, contemplation, affirmation... whatever is used, attitude will be a key factor. Attitude is a big key to breaking the self-hypnosis that keeps us from seeing the Garden of Eden. As is said, you simply stop not-seeing the Garden you are walking in.

I remember once, long ago, we were doing an all-nighter, preparing for a museum exhibit. E.J. was full of energy, and I wondered how that could be while I barely managed to keep awake enough to see the illustration I was drawing as part of the exhibit. I asked myself, as I watched him stride across the atrium with great intensity — how and why is this so incredibly important to someone that I knew to traverse worlds? And the answer came to me — he does this for the Absolute.

With that he looked at me, without question, having read my mind, beaming, and he sort of gushed at me, indicating emphatically that I was on track. I was given access to a new level of energy that transformed the activity I was doing and the way in which it was being done. There was a slight but profound shift that included a changed attitude of fertile possibility as opposed to limitation. With this shift I was able to access the living work artifact, my Teacher, as he worked before me.

Where are your priorities, really — do they reflect your Work Wish?

One description of the evolutionary process is that it is a series of trials out of which one emerges, having either gained a skill or lost an impediment or any combination thereof. Have you seen this quality of experience repeat in your life?

Do you see a changing relationship to people — to children, to animals, to things, to spaces? Are you on the side of the problem or the solution most often? Where are your priorities, really — do they reflect your Work Wish? Do you find your habits changing? Are you able to tolerate the negative manifestations of others toward yourself and others? Against the mark of this minimum requirement for the perfected individual, seems likely you might be given some feedback about where you are.

Sometimes a question requires other questions be asked before an answer presents itself. I've presented you here with some questions you might ask yourself, and there are, no doubt, others that will put your hand to the pulse of where you are living in your Work life and what might help this precious life flourish.

Here are some questions Rumi puts forth to fan your heart's fire.

Fourteen Questions

What if I broke off a whole branch of roses? What if I lost myself in the Friend? How would it be to have no faith? What if I picked a pickpocket's pocket?

Does it mean anything when a single basket is lost in Baghdad, when one wheat grain is missing from the barn? How long will this illusion last?

What remains when a lover sits quietly with the beloved for one second? Will it involve you at all if I say some unsayable things? Will my heart feel relieved doing that?

Something passed between lover and beloved. Are you part of these goings-on? What does the soul feel when Jesus heals the body?

This is the night when life decrees can change. If the moon came to visit me, would that affect other people?

Shams Tabriz, if I gave workers a holiday and if I turned the marketplace upside down, would that be a kind of image for how you love the world?

(Barks, *The Soul of Rumi*, page 116)

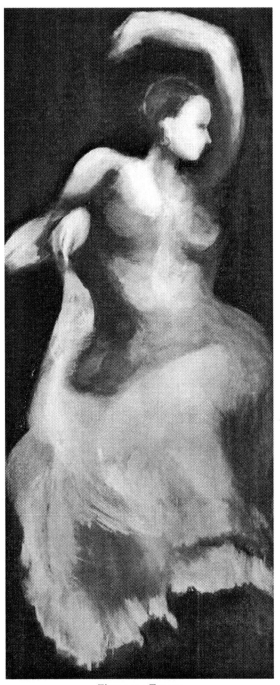

Flamenco Tangos
Grace Kelly Rivera
Acrylic on Canvas, 72"x36"
© 2006 Grace Kelly Rivera

Fire and Water
Grace Kelly Rivera, acrylic on canvas, 5' x 4' © 2011 Grace Kelly Rivera

Topic Two

Where is Center?

How do I find my True Center?

Our first topic responded to the question, "How do I know I'm on the Right Path?", which suggests travel. Here we have a wish to know about arriving at Center, suggesting stability, Source, the rock from which and toward which we move. Our longing for true center, especially when the platform for our reality seems to be crumbling, reflects the pull to unity from the illusion of separation that seems to be at the very core of being.

A small avalanche of images comes spilling forth at the provocation of the concept "True Center." First, I see a circle and then the emptiness within that circle. The fleeting image of a cup and I remember that it is the emptiness of the cup that is useful for filling with what quenches thirst and nourishes or intoxicates. The thought of wine brings me to the realm of the Beloved, and from there I see the Throne, at the center of all this adoration, expressed as sound vibration — choirs of angels that maintain its buoyancy. Did I mention that I have a fertile imagination?

Moving on, from this greatest of heights I free-fall back into the relative solidity of the three dimensional tactile hallucination I happen to be in. Given the luxury of memory, I remember that years ago I made a floor mat using canvas upon which I painted a design incorporating a version of one of E.J.'s female images/guides. When I showed it to him, he was prompted to pull out a beautiful book with images and text translating the Papyrus of Ani. It was written in hieroglyph, naturally, and illuminated by beautiful Egyptian paintings. E.J. explained of the flat dimensional images that, in fact, they represented the point of view of the time — the consciousness was experienced above the body to one side, I believe generally to the right. One can find description of this elsewhere, it is an experience I have had, and I've conversed with others that have tuned into this perspective as well. In all of this, I am gathering.

But there are distinctions to be made in this work of ours to transform so that we can become useful conscious participants in Creation. There is a particular kind of suffering the Creator suffers, as a result of being strapped into a creation that was involuntarily made — these concepts are distinctive on their own. In order to help alleviate this suffering and see the work to be done, one must be in an awakened state. Here we come upon another distinguishing factor of this school — the elucidation that the human biological machine is what awakens. So in this realm, the first distinction we will make is between being awake and asleep. All and everything, and every category therein, will differ based on this distinction alone, including the experience of True Center. The longing to find "Center" can perhaps best be seen in its various permutations when we look at the model of the afterlife experience and the unraveling of consciousness as described in the *American Book of the Dead*. We can readily see how unconscious habits around the longing to find "Center" in a sleeping machine might only serve as obstacle to the stated goal.

In the death experience, for which life offers much opportunity for practice, the Voyager's consciousness unravels to its primal components. The unraveling presents as a series of hallucinations, including guides, that offer cleansing radiations to clear away the tendencies and accumulations from organic life. At each stage is opportunity for liberation. We are cleansed of obstruction to liberation by bathing in the cleansing radiations, experienced as brilliant light of different colors. At the same time, as these brilliant lights present themselves, there will also be given the opportunity to hide from them into what appears as softer, dull lights. Unconscious rebirth will result when one is drawn toward the soft, dull light, out of fear, confusion and avoidance of the cleansing radiations.

**Chambers and Guides have their instructions, a part of which
is sincere prayer for our liberation, as we confront the cleansing
radiation.**

If, in our lifetime, we have developed strong unconscious habits of avoidance — even in the name of finding Center from chaos, this avoidance will translate correspondingly in the afterlife journey. Chambers and Guides have their instructions, a part of which is sincere prayer for our liberation as we confront the cleansing radiation. This quality of prayer and open confrontation seems like a good point of reference, if we can cultivate its experience, because this is what brings us toward liberation into the Clear Light of objective reality. If we can turn and face the music — or brilliant light — in the course of living, we begin to make voluntary the inevitable process of unraveling that accompanies our return.

I will refer to the Simurgh experience from time to time because it was such an extraordinary invocation, yielding many impressions and radiological factors that were transformative. The Simurgh refers to a brilliantly alive macrodimensional creature that, on rare occasion, can be invoked by an assembly of folks under the right set of conditions. It is the goal of the thirty birds that make the long journey in the wonderful allegorical tale, *Conference of the Birds.* (Note — for more indepth reading on the subject, *Life in the Labyrinth* by E.J. Gold has a chapter devoted to description of this vitally successful school experiment, as well as *Talk of the Month* #38 titled "The Simurgh.")

Robbert and I were asked to perform the *Creation Story Verbatim* play in an intimate setting intentionally created for the purpose of it being a vehicle for invocation. At a certain point in the journey, I experienced myself *as if* at the crown of what was an enormous bird-like creature of tremendous electrical aliveness. The experience of voyaging that evening, even prior to the point of the chamber of the Simurgh, was quite pronounced, and the morphology was obligingly fluid.

When all seemed to pause for eternity in the highly electrical reality of the Simurgh, it felt as though it were being breathed through me, through the entire assembly, where its massive wings rustled until they settled into place and it simply was there, extraordinarily present, breathing. As indicated, the perspective was *as if* from the crown, and the assembly of the audience that sat in semicircle around us formed the serpentine-like body. Being at the crown, I nevertheless felt as though at the very Center, breathing that creature to life. And all of this certainly did not take place while I felt myself to be what I would call my grounded Center within. Rather, I found myself, largely through conditions created by the Expert, helplessly without enough identity to form a Center as I might have wanted at the time.

Center is going to take on different meanings in accordance with one's identity, or lack thereof, at any given moment. I believe it is only in the fluidity of this changing meaning that we will find any semblance of true Center. A shaman is a person that has developed, among other traits and skills, the ability to awaken and return to relative sleep at will in accordance with necessity.

One of the first sacrifices we must make in this Work is that of comfort.

Sometimes getting to Center means having to sit right smack dab in the center of our off-centeredness. Sometimes when we are asking how we can get what we want, even if that is to be at Center, we might do better to ask how we can stop wanting something to get. We have the luxury now of time, space and the mental capacity for filtering all and everything so that it has some semblance of manageability. This luxurious position gives us opportunity to adopt habits that translate into confrontation of the real nature of our being. It is these habits that carry us through on our voyage in the Bardos or between-lives transit space, where we have no mind with which to respond to the rapid onslaught of impressions that will take place as consciousness unravels. From another angle, if we can catch a glimpse of frozen eternity and remember how fortunate we are to have phenomena for our transformational possibility, we're given inspiration for seizing the opportunity before us.

I had a small art studio at one of the group houses where I've lived within the community. I had been working intensely on a couple of different pieces, one of them being a Rembrandt portrait *après*. Working late into the night, everyone had already gone to bed in our crowded abode where a couple of folks slept out in the living room in sleeping bags. For some reason, I was brought to an awakened state. I found myself alone, utterly alone, and everything around me was alive with attention that was directed at me. In fact, there was nothing outside of me upon which to place attention — everything was me. I had the fleeting thought, in my agitation and discomfort, "Ah, I know, I'll get into Rembrandt"... but then realized that I was Rembrandt, there was nothing to get into, I was as into anything as could possibly be. With this came the symptoms of "earth sinking into water" and I nearly blacked out, falling to my knees from where I somehow managed to crawl out the door. I crawled down the small hallway to the living room where I saw one of the house members asleep, softly breathing. The blessed sight of human company was indescribably delicious and I took it in by the gulps.

It is this experience, along with others of equal discomfort, that give me a point of reference for the understanding of the suffering of the Absolute, as well as a hearty appreciation for phenomena and the passage of time. From this platform, I have begun to tear myself away from the dependency on good/bad and into a realm of objective science that allows me to more readily sit in human experience as it is. In bad times, if we can say to ourselves something like, "Okay, this is what it feels like to be in human form here now," appreciating the form, accepting the particular fixed tableau one finds oneself in, we begin to learn the alchemy that true human beings know well. Alchemy recognizes and uses the putrefaction and breaking down of elements as phases in the process of perfection. In a sense, we beat death by being at one with it, by voluntarily dying before we die. The moment we accept our situation completely, we *as if* absorb it and in the absorption find reflection of the primordial tendency pointed to in the phrase "Nothing stands before the Face of God and lives."

Gold offers an excellent model in the book, *The Human Biological Machine as a Transformational Apparatus*. Our lives can be viewed as a series of fixed tableaus, forming *as if* a tunnel through which the Essential Self traverses and emerges transformed when that tunnel is awakened. The human biological machine is that tunnel as well as the body in its set and setting that seems to carry one through these events. The machine is viewed as an electrical entity with which we, as an Essential

Self, also an electrical entity, have a particular affinity that caused us to fall into our particular tunnel/lifetime. One object of the game is to light up the entire tunnel through awakening. The human biological machine becomes a transformational apparatus for the essential self and a mutual reciprocal initiation process occurs between these two electrical fields that produces evolutionary change.

In looking at this model, we can see that Center can mean any number of things. It can mean the experience of the Essential Self. It can mean the Center of the life of the machine, which will include psyche, or the conditioned persona, and Essence. It can mean the Center of one of the fixed tableaus along the tunnel. It can mean the Center of all and everything. And all of these Centers will be applicable and right-action-compliant at different times along the way.

Like so many other matters in this work, it is highly individual and all is subject to the needs of the time, place and people. In doing the Face of God exercise, we diffuse the vision such that we have a patchwork quilt of undifferentiated form and color before us to the greatest extent of periphery. We then merge with that completely. Say we successfully get all the way to the point of merger — Center is going to be a completely different experience from what might be had doing tasks on a day-to-day basis. As a matter of fact, Center at that point would be pointless.

One thing upon which we all will likely agree is that the experience of True Center implies the presence of the path of Right Action. And right action may at times dictate us to engage in activity that may seem to create imbalance and throw us off center.

Relative to our work, right action may have us creating chaos out of the order that a sleep-dominant machine will have established. The human biological machine wants to know the fulfillment of being a transformational apparatus and does bring us to a school. But it also has the impulse to remain where it is and stabilize a situation, reach a steady state. Stabilization will not be something readily found in the afterlife transit experience — they don't call it transit for nothing. School conditions will provide ample opportunity to shake loose from unconscious habits created around the machine's tendency toward stability. Of course this shaking loose will have the simultaneous effect of activating that tendency at times to excruciating pronouncement.

But praise be to the machine, for without it, the possibility of evolution would not exist. The fact that we find ourselves in a human biological machine can be viewed as a reaction to endlessness. Creation is in effect a form of imbalance. By the fact of its existence, however, there is created the possibility of alleviation of the suffering inherent in the situation of the Absolute that is strapped to a sleeping creation. This trend of imbalance, creating conditions of potential transcendence, can be seen playing out in various ways. This is, in effect, how evolutionary change takes place. An imbalance is created by conditions that exist in the dynamic between the electrical fields of the essential self and the machine that must be equalized. That equalization process will tend toward evolutionary change or further entrenchment into the stability-seeking habits of the machine's life.

It seems essence resides in the muscles, and psyche, the conditioned egocentric identity, takes over the nervous system. Given our mix of spirit and matter, healing modalities addressing imbalances will have varying occasion of usefulness, depending upon the nature of the disease at the moment. One might view illness as a point of access to the underlying causes of the imbalance. Flu symptoms will be addressed in their immediate form, but might also communicate to us the underlying immune system imbalance that created conditions for infection of the virus. What one will find is that it is all so interrelated we are wise to look from a holistic perspective, a platform, at the same time paying attention to the access point of the imbalance being provided symptomatically. This access point will determine the most effective healing modality to employ.

Long established pathways of negatively charged reactions that are automatic produce a negative force in the muscular system of the body.

There are different models of self-observation, and different platforms with their viewpoints will serve along one's journey. There have been times in my life when it was useful to "see" the chakras and to relate to balancing in terms of chakra energy. At other times the focus has been on the heart and its opening, my nearness or distance to the Beloved.

Sometimes I take my work temperature by noting the ability or disability in the non-manifestation of negative emotion. Then again, the reading might be found in my open countenance, the impartiality that allows for raw expression of the moment. Chemistry, psychology as it relates to evolution, physical posture, and breath — all of these represent potential means of accessing the pulse of our evolutionary movement. It seems the game is about balancing out what is imbalanced repeatedly in the constant flux that reflects the permanently changing state of the Primordial Being. And an expanding acceptance of what is at every step along the way will bring us closer to Center than will any fixed notion of what Center might be.

The move to stability has the best expression in our work in one area. The human biological machine will produce negative force as a matter of course in its functioning — in fact, its manifestations can be considered as carrying a negative charge while those of the essential self produce a positive charge. Long established pathways of negatively charged reactions that are automatic produce a negative force in the muscular system of the body. This force is produced willy nilly and deposits itself in masses at different points of the body. Lines of tension are produced between these points. These lines of tension can be stabilized, which is to our advantage. We will find pain and waste of energy when we do as is normal, build up these lines of tension, then through manifestation of negativity, dismantle them such that they have to re-establish themselves. It is this process of destruction and reconstruction that produces pain. When we do not express negativity, the lines of tension are maintained. The stabilization of these lines of tension will in turn provide conditions for the machine's awakening.

If we are asking the question how to get to Center, chances are we aren't at Center, chances are we are not experiencing the waking state of the machine.

In the practice of this, one will find Center to be a different experience, quite naturally. Center will not reflect a place of comfort as we might usually perceive of it. One of the first sacrifices we must make in this work is that of comfort.

This is further underscored by the very nature of the primordial being, which is in perpetual flux. We are after transformation, which of course implies change. So let's get used to riding the waves, gracefully willing to adapt our approach to the moment's necessity. If we are asking the question how to get to Center, chances are we aren't at Center, chances are we are not experiencing the waking state of the machine. If there is the presence of negative emotion, that pretty well seals it. Now that we have witnessed firsthand our machine's sleep, where do we sit relative to Center? If we sit in a place other than that which might be considered objectively scientific, our identification with the sleep of the machine has produced more sleep out of its sleep. If we sit in a place of informed objectivity without charge, we've used the machine's sleep to awaken. In any event the key will be found in the here and now.

One way to bring ourselves closer to the here and now is in *whole body awareness*. We help ourselves in conserving energy and handling it such that we maintain the above mentioned lines of tension. Unconscious muscular tension, on the other hand, is not useful, and we do well to relax our grip. Sensing the body, its places of tension, the posture — we might alter our state into deeper resonance with the moment by relaxing the places of greatest tension, thereby enabling a freer flow of air. When we relax our tensions we change our posture at least slightly and change of posture can effect mood change. Mood in turn is the rudder by which we steer ourselves in the Great Labyrinth. Gentle attention on the breath as it naturally flows will nourish us with prana, second and third-being food from the air and resulting impressions through gentle attention being placed on its intake. Sometimes just with a little bit of attention of this kind one is brought to a place where relative Center might be found.

Where do we sense our center of gravity to be? Often in this culture we reside in our heads, barely aware of the base of the spine. It might be useful to take a look at this. Another aspect of the human biological machine model is the presence of three brains that, such as they are, do not function as needed to serve transformation and work. These three brains have been linked to different parts of what we normally think of as the brain and spinal cord and are basically broken down into the intellect, the emotional and the moving instinctive. The reversal of the head and tail brain functions awakens the higher function of the heart and the possibility of real conscience which, in turn, will guide our actions.

Somewhere in all this we will find ourselves needing to address the tendencies that keep us from this process of reversal. When the human biological machine is operant as a transformational apparatus, the head brain is monitoring the movement of the body while the tail brain serves as the true "thinking" center. The Popcorn Exercise described by Gold has us following the movement of the body. One indication of this happening correctly, apart from the mood of adoration, is the cessation of the constant churning of thought. We can see how a machine part intended to function for the monitoring of movement when misapplied elsewhere could produce wasteful results. A little boat motor turned on when confined in one place will continue doing its work of propelling the water through, but to the end of churning its medium and creating bubbles rather than movement.

Muscular and intellectual tensions prevent energy from flowing. They hold us to the neurological network patterning that bind us to the three-dimensional tactile hallucination of consensus reality. Obviously during our transition away from accustomed patterns of intake of impressions, there will be experience of off-centeredness. We can learn to voluntarily move into the center of this off-centeredness. One way of freeing up these tensions is to intensify them voluntarily for a period of time. For example, recurring thoughts are like muscle spasms — we might do well with our deliberately placed concentrated attention on them, observing all that proceeds within while the attention is so placed. What we resist will persist and sometimes the strategic movement will be toward the direction of the storm, to its center. When we speak of riding the chronic defense mechanism, in a way we are doing just that, using the intensity and concentration of energy that also indicates the proximity of the waking state to get us to a platform from which we can dive into the moment's eternity.

One of the most profound and deeply surrendering experiences I have ever had was the culmination of many factors that included the movement in the direction of the storm. The set, setting and dosage of that experience cannot be described in their fullness no better than the mysticism that resulted. For the sake of brief notation here, I suffice it to say that I realized the space of growing a new heart at every moment to annihilate into the central sun over and again. The conditions that led to this included an intensity of sensation in the heart area — it was as though there was an invisible garden hoe scraping at the inside of my chest with an incredible heat that was unremitting. After many hours like this in which I fundamentally attempted to run away from the intensity, I finally went into my prayer cell and opened myself to the sensation as widely as possible, much like opening up in birthing. The energy produced by the psychological factors present created optimum conditions to launch me into the central sun, as it were.

What we resist will persist — sometimes the strategic movement will be toward the direction of the story, to its Center.

It is most useful to identify what is called the Chronic Defense Mechanism against the waking state, as well as Chief Feature, the electrical entity that is the astral embodiment of all habits and tendencies obstructing our awakening. These lead us away from the experience of True Center, while at the same time, cunningly, they give a sense of True Center through the establishment of a machine-based false stability. The chronic defense mechanism, if unknown, can be found by being awakened suddenly out of ordinary horizontal sleep. As for Chief Feature, that critter is a little more subtle to catch and name — it is best to have an expert observe, and even then the identification might not be put to use for some time.

That was my experience, anyway. I was given the name of my Chief Feature and at the time could do little more with the information than offer a vague gratitude — I could sense this was useful at the time, but *how* would take years to reveal itself. Now, with certain established habits of self-observation, this piece of information often gives me a sense of where I'm at. We can see the need for impartiality in this work of intense scrutiny. Every aspect of organic life can be potentially used for awakening and transformation, given the will and necessity for awakening. The choice is ours, though years of repeated habits unconsciously established will have us feeling helpless at first. Practical work on self, with the help and scrutiny of an Expert especially, will, in good time, yield results that replace helplessness with gratitude.

There are, of course, many different areas to look at when one senses disharmony in one's life that might be expressed as a longing for Center. Years of self-observation and accumulation of data have helped me to create a rough checklist to determine the nature of the dis-ease and the potential protocol to its cure.

But I have also developed an awareness of the fact that the movement of soul growth will not be limited to the range my intellect would keep it in. Bewilderment is a big part of the game, and so at times there will be effects that will baffle and confuse, with no accessible source of origin. The above mentioned experience of sensation and intensity that led to the mystical state of annihilation was not explainable in any ordinary terms. I call these episodes "quickenings" as that is what they tend to do to the evolutionary life, in effect. There are times when this checklist is simply rendered utterly useless, and the only thing to do is surrender to my inability to surrender.

This said, I might start by looking at the potential occult effects of dreams I had the previous night and any voyaging that may have taken place, to the best of my ability. Any data observed is merely noted and left buoyant — not grounded into conclusion. This I do with each level of information taken in.

I look at the physical chemistry of the HBM, (human biological machine), the balance or imbalance of hormones, the general health and vitality of the machine, the state of inflammation that can be sensed in my lungs and body stiffness. I have witnessed there to be something that is cyclical that could be called biorhythms, just as I have witnessed cyclical patterns that relate to the ongoing inner changes relative to the machine's awakening.

When viewing the overall functioning of the HBM, there are different platforms of approach. The Ayurvedic and Chinese Medicine models have served me well at various points when addressing healing of illness. Ayurveda was developed largely as a means of addressing the physical reality as it relates to the spiritual. Both speak in terms of energetic and elemental forces and this seems useful and copacetic with the school view of the HBM. The allopathic model has its time and place, but is limited in that it is symptomatic and disease is viewed in light of physical existence with little room for spirit.

Acceptance of all that we are frees us from the Chinese finger puzzle that has our grip and grips our having.

The waking state of the human biological machine is partly dependent upon balance between Serotonin and Melatonin. If we are making all kinds of efforts at awakening the HBM and meeting with no results, it could be we need to address this balance chemically first. Personal experience has taught me to have healthy respect for the power of those little hormonal secretions or lack thereof, and has also taught me to observe and work with the chemical states of the HBM. Amino acids can be used to balance with great effect. Certain dietary adjustments and changes in habits can also produce favorable results — it is up to us as responsible operators of a human biological machine transformational apparatus to educate ourselves so that we might operate our particular machine to the best work effect possible. The aim here is not to become a fanatic. Becoming too dependent upon any one approach denies the changes in the evolutionary process that will occur — all things with moderation.

When I pay gentle attention to the breath and work with intent to still the body, the presence of tension will lead me to exactly where energy is blocked. This requires the invocation of my concentrated attention and the will to apply it to the task at hand. With this we are reminded of the importance of developing our attention in this work. The stronger our attention, the more accumulated mass, in a sense, the greater the effect our attention can have.

Know thyself — knowing the state of the machine gives the opportunity to monitor responses to external stimuli accordingly. If the machine is in the way of the kind of right action flow that the waking state can offer, at least there is the possibility of not digging deeper into that path. If the machine is highly agitated, for example, and this has been observed impartially to be having an effect on my work with folks, I have enough experience to know fear and paranoia might be present in me. This fuels the move to give folks yet more benefit of the doubt as an adjustment, and not to make sudden moves based on the incomplete data being filtered through my state. As further adjustment, I might work to breathe deeper, to slow down in my movement and get into the body.

Thus the lead is gradually transformed into gold; bad habits of sleep can be transmuted into habits of awakening.

Years ago we were singing in the atrium of the main facility where E.J. works, and this singing was recorded. I remember I'd been in a particularly agitated state prior to that night's gathering, but I used the space to wake up, or so that's what it felt like as I sang and entered into a space of internal harmony and feeling of deep communion with the group. The next day E.J. made a point of letting me hear the recording. Now, you ought to be informed that I can sing in key; I sing publicly with the Flamenco troupe and have gotten positive feedback on my voice. However, on that recording, there was one voice that was consistently flat throughout the very song that I'd had that macro experience — that voice was mine. E.J. looked at me and said something to the effect of, sure would like to have gone where you were at the time! When he said this, I felt mortified that I was so very unaware of my surroundings, unable to hear the effect of my own voice. He said this to me once again on another occasion where we were filmed doing Afghani Rhythmics, and I was a hair's breadth slower in tempo than everyone else. Again, the machine had awakened somewhat from an agitated state. Unknowingly I'd ridden my chronic and with the help of E.J. and the conditions created that included obligation to the group's work of the moment, I was able to leap at the right time. Here again we see that Center is relative, and Center can from the outside look very off.

Attitude is everything in this Work.

I am reminded of yet another strong impression. There was a wonderful fellow by the name of Blair who died years ago. He passed from this plane at a relatively young age, and Patricia Elizabeth helped to coordinate his hospice help — folks from the community as well as E.J. visited Blair during his last days. I remember most vividly sitting in the space alone with him and the incredible intensity felt — he was clearly sitting between the two worlds of the phenomenal and the non-phenomenal, maintaining the cross between dimensions that his existence represented. It occurred to me that this is how we should be living . . . in a way, this is Center. It's intense, rather unpleasant, but unquestionably

Center-oriented.

Cautiously, I'll say here that one indication of nearness or distance to Center might be found in how alive one feels. Of course, here you need discernment, lest you be convinced by a false awakening like when the machine is adrenalized in sports. Aliveness that is not adrenal-based might describe what we are after. Scent will be a good helper in this regard — if you learn to identify the smell of your HBM when it is in an adrenalized state, you can immediately use this biofeedback to your advantage. It is quite humbling, and in that humility, balancing to note the odor of adrenaline emanating from the body in the midst of enjoying an activity and the feelings of pleasure center arousal. It sure puts things into perspective.

Because of the complexities of the mechanisms that keep us from the waking state, the more areas we have of obtaining objective data as to our place and state, the better. There is a whole realm of indication of one's state that is created within one's relationship to the school and from there the world. When my transactions with folks are jagged, it is not always necessarily indicative of my inner state, and I have developed ways in which to separate what may be other kinds of influences at play. Always there needs to be room left for expansion of my self-observation that will educate me as to the scope and effect of my personal emanations.

The way of this path is one that encompasses rather than excludes, from one perspective. We are encouraged not to live in isolation, but to embrace a life that is in the world but not of it. Our attention is best developed using the resistance of distraction in the world much as a body builder uses weights as resistance to strengthen muscle. We are always given the choice between using the life we are living for the purpose of awakening, work and transformation, or for the purposes generated by the life of the HBM itself.

Attitude is everything in this Work. If living a Work life, with awakening and transformation as possible and ongoing, we stand a better chance of making the efforts necessary to achieving this. When one finds oneself steeped in the primate, far from the pulse of one's work, remembering "this too shall pass," might help keep the attitude buoyant. Acceptance of all that we are frees us from the Chinese finger puzzle that has our grip and grips our having. We are part clay, part spirit. We have multiple dimensional existences that are sometimes not accessible. Whatever we are at this very moment, all and everything is being given to us that we need, if only we can learn to sit smack dab in it. Experience has taught me that we actually know a lot about how we are fooling ourselves into living outside of the present moment — it is a question of having the necessity and courage to learn how to look and see — and there is no time like the present.

The Difficulties of Being Human

...Don't keep repeatedly doing what your animal-soul wants to do. That's like deciding to be a strip of meat nailed and drying on a board in the sun. Your spirit needs to follow the changes happening in the spacious place it knows about.

There, the scene is always new, a clairvoyant river of picturing, more beautiful than any on earth. This is where the Sufis wash. Purify your eyes, and see the pure world. Your life will fill with radiant forms. It's a question of cleaning then developing spiritual senses! See beyond phenomena.

(Barks, *The Illuminated Rumi*, page 74)

A Moment Here Now
Grace Kelly Rivera, Mixed Media on Prepared Arches Paper, 30"x22"
© 2000 Grace Kelly Rivera

Fusing for Flight
Grace Kelly Rivera, acrylic on canvas, 4' x 3' © 2011 Grace Kelly Rivera

Topic Three

What Skills Best Prepare Me for Serving the Greater Good?

There are many different kinds of activities and tools for developing skills needed for Work that have been created by E.J. What are the skills that we need to develop?

"Work is available, a lot of work. You've had your fair warning. You'd better be able and willing to do what I'm willing to do — to actually do it. I'm here every day doing something: paintings, gardens, music . . . I am looking for coordinated and directed efforts; approaches with elan vital, verve, elegance." (Gold, *Learning to Do/Plasma At The Speed of Light*, page 8)

In addressing the question as written: what skills best prepare me for serving the greater good? A partial answer is implied in the question — one needs to have some relationship to the greater good in order to serve it. One is aligned in such a way that one can't help but respond to the moment's necessity with right action. We are accustomed to thinking in terms of the Evelyn Wood Speed Reading course, or any such course that is followed in order to gain a new skill. The more effective and shamanic way to learn a skill is by a process of alignment, a developing resonance which can involve using the technique of *as if*. *As if* is fundamentally employing our internal theater skills, adopting postures of what is known of the desired state, behaving *as if* our intention is actualized. We voyage through our lives *as if* voyaging in the great labyrinth because, in fact, we are, and eventually in this practice the reality of our situation will present itself.

When one becomes aware of voyaging spaces and has the flexibility to let go of self-concern enough to put the needs of a space above the personal, that behavior which falls in the realm of being a *malaprop* becomes clear. By definition a *malaprop* is someone who imposes his own needs and agenda upon a space of invocation. When this is occurring, how is it possible to see what is to the benefit of the whole? And while loud aggression might be an obvious *malaprop* trait, any manifestation stemming from an inability to shape-shift with the needs of the space can cause disruption. One useful skill is cultivating the ability to be actively passive in a space. In this all-centered posture of readiness one can allow what is and be available for whatever participation might be required.

How is one to learn to have genuine obligation and intention to a greater cause if not by plugging in to that kind of situation?

The work of this school on an invocational and at other levels requires cooperative group effort. When one fails to perform a function the effect is felt by the group. One learns to feel a sense of obligation that goes beyond the personal in a position like this, further knowing that this cooperation is affecting a much larger result that goes even beyond the group. This gives electrical mass and substance to the impressions taken in as one engages in this on-the-job training. How is one to learn to have genuine obligation and intention to a greater cause if not by plugging in to that kind of situation?

We are taught to become aware of spaces as the opportunity is provided in different ways that correspond to the needs of the Work addressed in the time, place and with the people present.

Our situation is such that we must move backward from physicality to the more rarefied in the process of awakening. The machine becomes passive as an electrical field, thus allowing the electrical field of the essential self to be exposed. Because of the conditions of our arising and many factors besides, electrical field anomalies related to the human biological machine as well as parasitic situations create barbs that keep us well-entangled in the outer world of phenomena and physicality. We are developing skills that help us in the process of awakening, which is essential for gaining the overview and alignment necessary to be of genuine service to the greater good. These skills involve developing a relationship with the human biological machine that serves us as essential selves. We will become adept at allowing the demolition work that must inevitably take place.

It's been likened to being imprisoned in wooden cages that the Master — or the Friend, as Rumi might put it — destroys by fire.

From **Wooden Cages**

Your faces are very beautiful, but they are wooden cages.
You had better run from me. My words are fire.
I have nothing to do with being famous, or making grand
judgments, or feeling full of shame. I borrow nothing. I
don't want anything from anybody.
I flow through human beings. Love is my only companion.
(Barks, *The Soul of Rumi*, page 102)

One of the communal practices that provided me with good opportunity for work on self was fire/night watch. The need for night watch arises periodically. When it happens, one or two folks stay up all night, keeping a fire going in winter, making certain that all is well so that the household and any invocational work that might be taking place can be well-protected. I was scheduled to do watch on this particular night and something had occurred that in ordinary terms would cause anyone to have a reaction of her particular chronic. At that time I was just about a full time involuntary slave to my anger. By this point I'd already had a few horrible episodes with E.J. relative to my anger, and learned to keep my mouth shut, which in itself was a big step, given my family background. I'd been conditioned to respond to unpleasantness with the famous Latino temperament. So I sat there in the dining room and seethed quietly, thinking I was doing well enough. E.J. did not let me remain to do night watch that night; he sent me home as even my quiet seething was disruptive to the space. The lesson and imprint was far-reaching. Not only did it speak to the depth of work necessary for the dismantling of my chronic defense, but it also inflamed my wish to serve, to do my duty. This was one of several key scenarios that showed me that performing duties in a school is a privilege, an opportunity. This opens out into realization that the opportunity to have a Work life is a precious thing, and in this way, I am released from the boundaries that selfishness and laziness will impost. Many strong impressions have helped in my movement toward freedom from such slavery.

Our emptying of self allows us to better align with a fundamental impulse of kindness and a wish to help that is part of pure Being.

The demolition process enriches our potential to deepen our experience of compassion. As we witness ourselves clarify, we might find ourselves more willing to undergo the clarification process which invariably involves death and absence. Absence here refers to the emptiness that follows the death of illusion with the equal opportunity for fresh spirit life to be awakened. In watching our own process unfold, in seeing a new world emerge from the ashes of the old, we wish for others goodness in their process. Our emptying of self allows us to better align with a fundamental impulse of kindness and a wish to help that is part of pure being.

So here we can see a couple of sets of skills that might be useful to look at developing. In knowing ourselves, we wish to develop skill in aligning such that we are put into situations that help us clarify. Getting ourselves into situations that will cause us to see where our need to clarify exists can help us gain the necessity actually to clarify. We gotta want it bad enough. Strong work wishing is called for. If we don't want it badly enough, we have to bring ourselves to the place where we do, and that means bringing ourselves into conditions where we can plug into higher will. The fact is we can't do it on our own will, we must borrow will from a higher source, and in this borrowing we must need discernment. If we don't see where the need to clarify is, there has to be necessity in finding this out. In the clarification and in the necessity we have for that clarification, there is an opening for experience of the quality of compassion that will bear effective relationship to the greater good.

We use our daily lives to establish our work habits, to change those habits that are not work conducive to habits of work. The tools we have available to us are really boiled down to our attention, presence, and will. In theory, every moment the choice is ours, how we are going to use the impressions, situations and opportunities we are being given, our habits will nail the three nails of presence, will and attention to a cross that will, in turn, define our reality. In practice, unless we put ourselves into the right set of circumstances, "the momentum of organic conditioning to the automatic continuum of life forces the attention to periodically wander in accordance with the same laws that govern the musical notations through the procession of the octaves, in seven definite steps, from one subject to another…"

(Gold, *Creation Story Verbatim* play, The Lord, Scene 5)

Due to inherent conditions of our arising on this planet, our will, presence and attention is likely not available to us without help and intentional development. We will find that our awakening, which gradually affects transformation, is cumulative of Moments of Freedom. Suggested here is the need for patience — the development of skills around patience will serve our work endeavors well. Patience gives us the ability to more readily be in the moment.

**What happens to us happens because we are
what we are.**

It serves us well to realize that the activity on one level does not matter. You will note that the skills mentioned thus far as suggestions for development are all of an internal quality. We are asked to develop our attention, will and presence in this work. We are also in the process of learning how to use the outer world, how to make passive the outer and activate the inner.

Again, referring to the model of *The Human Biological Machine as a Transformational Apparatus*, we as essential beings, seem to be *as if* traversing a tunnel of fixed tableaus. Applying strong attention to the whole gestalt of body in its set and setting can awaken the machine, inclusive of these fixed tableaus. What happens to us happens because we are what we are. We, as essential beings, have been drawn into the electrical field of the machine out affinity. In order to work, we must become something that can work. In transforming into a Work entity, we will experience the Work. To Work, certain conditions must come into play, including awakening the machine. We must wake up enough to at least be able to use our "fixed tableau" conditions for our Work. Eventually we develop the skill of intuitively finding our non-spatial home. Often a repeated discipline done with discernment will provide a key to that passage.

I am reminded of an experience I had during a morning practice. I was in my little sanctuary where I have some books that I will open to as Oracles. One of these is the *Angel's Healing Journey*, by E.J. Gold. I turned to it and was given the information such as the color cleansing radiation and meditation/prayer needed at this point in the journey. The cleansing radiation, which is brilliant, was red, and the color of the rebirth signaling lights that seem to offer refuge was a dull yellow. I went into a deep reverie as I worked with the candle lit before me. I'd had a strong session and felt quite diffused. One moment I am in a meditative state, and then without my knowing it, I derailed, locking onto the muscle spasms of the little brain, the "formatory apparatus," these brought me to a dullness that ended in a black out. Fortunately, there was enough presence to jolt me awake when I realized that the color radiation I seemed to be moving toward was in the direction of rebirth. My closed eyes revealed a light show comprised of mostly dull yellow color and this reminding factor was sufficiently in place to awaken me.

From this I once again gained an impression of how seamlessly waking activity can turn into sleeping activity. Further communicated to me was the fact that our work lives are comprised of moments. The activity, the outer form, is secondary to the use of attention, presence and will during these moments. There I was in the posture of practice in my prayer/meditation cell and I'd even had a particularly good session giving momentum to the space. In all of this, I am given gratitude growing grace. The reminding factors for our Work provided in a school and the opportunity to practice has brought me to a place of being able to use these tools effectively.

We start where we are. There are exercises and practices that are applicable in any situation, and these will give us leverage in our work to jump streams, so to speak, to move into a realm that has rendered the outer world passive. Let us remember though that the awakening experience has at times been described as "like this, only more so."

While I was experiencing what is called postpartum depression following the birth of my daughter, I despaired over much that I seemed to be missing because of having to do childcare with its share of mundane activity. This despair was well fueled by lack of rest — typically at that time I was up nursing five to ten times in the night. In the thick of it, E.J. phoned me. He let me know first that what was happening to me and my perspective was chemically based, that powerful hormonal changes were acting as drugs on me. He then let me know that the macrodimensional experience is available to me with a shift of attention and attitude. As he expressed it, there's Kelly by the stove cooking, but there is an ascent to other floors and chambers where this activity taking place is awakened and closer to the archetype.

One day I well recall — Sara had been going through a phase of teething that had her up much of the night and I was feeling particularly exhausted. At the same time, there was such a longing to actively participate in the activities of the school. I didn't want to nap, despite my exhaustion, but when I lay down beside Sara I was forced to surrender. I could not muster my body out of the invariable rest mode it would go into given the slightest chance. My efforts to shake myself awake seemed to only bring me into a hypnagogic state, a state of awareness between sleep and wakefulness that can proceed into out of body experience (oobe). Suddenly it was as though my consciousness was accelerated to an extraordinary rate where I no longer could recognize the quality of thought form that was proceeding. As if from a very great distance, with the sense of outer space, I had a vision of an intricate and incredibly beautiful grid with symbols that I could not even begin to describe, made of light, made of consciousness — this was superimposed over another grid of the same quality and it was seen that when these align, great Work comes about. For one moment, it all made Absolute sense.

Many factors inherent in my set, setting and dosage no doubt contributed to this little event. I cannot point to any particular skill or knowledge this bestowed upon me, yet I know it was a matter of spirit, affecting change indirectly. When I look at the skill involved to bring myself to this place, the view is simple. My attention was developed well enough and accustomed to following the thread of consciousness through the stages that lead to the body's sleep cycle. I also had some skill in allowing, in surrendering to what the moment brought me. There are definitely times for super efforts, but having a view of these as being a conquest with a lot of grunting and grinding is misleading. There is a balance we need to find that tempers good discipline with an open relationship to the time, the place and the people.

Our work will take place in the world but not of it. It is easy to lose sight of the inner when identified in the development of skill in the outer. For one, there is a posture of acquisition that seems to be counter to the way things are in transformational work. We are exposing that part of us that knows all as spirit by a process of removal of obstruction. In effect, we are curing a disease that is of the spirit really, which has fallen into an identification with and belief in phenomena. Sometimes this requires we engage in certain prescribed activity that will present opportunity for the appropriate dismantling of this identification and exposure as spirit. Sometimes as well, an activity will be a forum through which real work can come about. However, what is of consequence is not the activity itself, but the exposure of the diamond in the matrix that takes place within the activity.

One needs discernment. The first form of discernment we are asked to develop tells us whether we are immersed in the sleeping state of the machine or if the machine is awake. There is the skill in making effective efforts toward awakening the machine, which skill may change form in accordance with changing circumstances present in the relationship of the essential self and machine. When we speak of skill relative to awakening, let's remember that awakening is cumulative, not in the sense of acquisition of skill so much as the reduction of that which impedes awakening, and corresponding experience of exposure of the essential self.

Relative to artistic creation, the skill — once a certain mastery of technique has occurred — lies in the ability to get out of the way of the creative process so that pure creative energy can flow through unobstructed. It applies to awakening — we develop skill and agility in the art of seeing the opportunity to shed an impediment to the waking state, to replace love of ego satisfaction with yet greater self-knowledge and exposure and deeper wish for work. You gotta love it — "the throbbing vein will take you much farther than thinking," as Rumi puts it.

From **Body Intelligence**

The visible universe has many weathers and variations. But uncle, O uncle, the universe of the creation-word, the divine command to Be, that universe of qualities is beyond any pointing to.

More intelligent than intellect, and more spiritual than spirit. No being is unconnected to that reality, and that connection cannot be said. There, there's no separation and no return.

There are guides who can show you the way. Use them. But they will not satisfy your longing. Keep wanting that connection with all your pulsing energy. The throbbing vein will take you further than any thinking.

(Barks, *The Essential Rumi*, page 151)

In the *Creation Story Verbatim* play, after several scenes worth of build up, the Lord finally reveals her Divine message for humanity to Gabriel — *Be Who You Are and Do What You Do*. Gabriel, who has been waiting with bated breath for this grand announcement expresses disappointment at the apparent lack of burning bush energy to the message.

"Mankind has waited thousands of years, civilizations have risen and crumbled to dust, a million half crazed martyrs were crucified or reduced to mush in a lion's mouth and Western civilization was crushed under the iron heel of religious tyranny and for what, Lord? This is what you call a divine message? Be Who You Are And Do What You Do? And if they refuse, Lord?

"Use force if necessary," says the Lord.

(Gold, unpublished *Creation Story Verbatim* script)

There's a lot contained in these few lines. From one perspective, Gabriel represents the aspect of our being that strives toward perfection and is learning how to hang out with God. More specifically, hang out with God's suffering. To suffer here is meant in its meaning of "to bear," as in "to bear a cross."

To suffer is not to suffer. When one is bearing the weight, one suffers it, there is no suffering involved, there is simply bearing the burden.

When that burden is borne well, there's elegance.

There are many dichotomies that are to be transcended within the scope of this thoroughly modern mystic play — as an example, repeatedly we are told Angels can't evolve, but there is evidence given that they, in fact, do. And yet, when Gabriel feels closest to attaining his next gradation of reason, utterly convinced of the glory and ecstatic nearness to come, not to mention winning his extra points on his horns . . . his angelic bubble is soon burst. The Lord informs him there are no extra points on his horns, in fact. I can tell you that the Lord very much would love to see Gabriel evolve, from a certain perspective it indicates a spark of life in the sparkless creation to which she is strapped. But Gabriel does his own undoing by means of his focus, which is on his precious points at that moment.

We will refer to the human reality pump idea often in the course of working with these topics. Humanity functions, in effect, as a reality pump of sorts, taking finer matter that is received from the higher within and converting it into the gross, pushing it out to form the outer world. Eating and making shit, quite basically speaking, is what ordinarily happens. A person can, through an extraordinary set of circumstances, cross rivers, as they say, learn how to function in a different way. One can learn how to make passive the outer world, making active the inner world and in this way feed the higher, feed the body or bodies of spirit.

Special help is needed in this work of reversing the reality pump. There are factors with the strength of trillions of years of repetition behind them that have entrained us well into this habitual service of making real the outer. With help we might develop the skills needed to overcome the momentum of our state. As you might see from this model of pump reversal, given the fact of our unique arising onto the planet, with all our history in time and space and our unique configuration of traits, the crossing will be individual. We all have our own key anchor points that hold the illusion in place, just as we each have individual archetypal potential for functioning.

The conditioning and habits that keep our world view intact must be circumvented and therein lies a clue of skill needed.

Skills are needed for this work that are inner, spiritual in nature, yet a healthy ability to use the human biological machine as a transformational apparatus might render us more adept in our physicality. We are using what is available to us, what is for our Work. It is the machine that will bring us to a school where it may realize a level of functioning unavailable in the ordinary course of events. The conditioning and habits that keep our world view intact must be circumvented and therein lies a clue of skill needed. Skill is needed in recognizing, intuiting the way out of the prison of that conditioning toward the liberation of the waking state and evolutionary transformation. It is this quality of intuition that will enable us to discern times when super efforts can and should be made. Given the momentum of the ordinary reality consciousness and the habits that keep it in place, this subtle and highly specialized skill requires guidance in its development.

For the correct development of further skills, a fundamental ability we need to have is that of impartial self-observation. We can be given help in this by receiving objective feedback from different types of folks and especially from the Teacher. In any change of habit, which is what this entails on a large scale, one has to want the change badly enough. Our habits of sleep have to be seen as such, *"the terror of the situation"* revealed, and the only constructive way through the vision, the only place of true sanctuary is in our impartiality. School conditions can provide the perfect forum in which this can be impressed upon us. Sometimes we must be brought to the place where there is nowhere to go but to the present moment and the impartial place of witness. The intensity of experience provided by the force of the school, the Teacher's attention, the attention of our peers, all contribute to the creation of conditions where strong Work-worthy impressions can be made.

When we truly open up to Guidance, we will see what skills we need to develop and the means of doing so. At the same time, there will be an alignment process that naturally takes place as observation and transformational experience bring us more in resonance with the electrical entity I'll call the School or the Teaching — the Dharma.

We have been thoroughly entrained to think in terms defined by physical reality. Out of habit we might approach the question of what skills to develop thinking in terms of the outer world. In the doing of these skills, applying them to gratifying physical results, we might now work. And, indeed, we just might. But technique and mastery in art forms or gaming or any outer activity will not constitute work in and of themselves. These are but the rinds of the sweet fruit within. A forum is provided by which to access a different order of skill set that more directly affects our evolutionary needs, but which direct approach will not apprehend. This skill set we will be developing, yet still falls within the realm of attention, presence and will.

I see corollaries between the macro and the micro in the Universe that offer impressions of what I call Path Tendencies. My vision shifts to new juxtapositions and a different quality of patterning that is outside of the box, and I am coaxed into learning how to work with the tendencies in this universe instead of against them. One such tendency I see play out in various ways is that of indirection — there is an indirect aspect of the universe that reflects its illusory nature. It is a subtle quality that is not readily expressed. One example might be found in the natural world where plants are proliferated with the help of bees. Here's another illustration of a different kind — when shooting pool, sometimes one has to hit the cue ball to the side in order for it to hit the eight ball just so into the pocket. Another example — in order to receive nutrients from the food we eat, there is a lot of processing that must go on. So food does not directly nourish us, what we ingest is in fact the shell of food.

It has been said that only indirect methods can be applied in this work, and this indirection is reflected often in stories of Teachers and their methods with students. One illustration of this can be found in the film *The Karate Kid* where one of the main characters, a teenager, comes to train with a Master of the art. The method of the Teacher reflects true Mastery. The boy wishes to learn karate and goes to his lesson anticipating some kick-ass technique, only to be given the task of waxing the teacher's vintage car collection. Further, he must do so in a very specific way — wax on with one hand, wax off with the other hand, such that a sort of figure eight configuration is produced by the constant repetitive movement. He does this for hours, repeatedly, until the body has developed strong muscle memory. When he is given his first taste of a lesson in karate form, the boy finds he has developed a habit that serves him well.

So it is with all of the methods we have available to us within the framework of the school, they are but means to an end. This is what distinguishes our work with these mediums within the school — we do these things not for the pleasure or self-expression or development of artistic skill, but for the evolutionary potential these activities might hold for us.

Intelligence might tell us we can't really know the path except at the depth of the present moment. Yet we find ourselves asking questions and looking for answers that are based in a rather linear scientific method which fails to question the instrument of observation. Analyzing, we apply our scientific method to trying to understand the workings of our path, looking for answers in the physical, visual universe over the vast invisible. Yet we must accept ourselves as we are. We are steeped in the illusion of phenomena with time and space and physicality. So let us use that physicality wisely, if we are marked such that evolution is a necessity. Applying ourselves well, we give opportunity for three-centered activity. Out of this application we, hopefully, will grab hold of the reins of our voyaging attention and this will bring us to an occasional vision of what is needed.

In the practical application of these ideas, as they can be expressed through the changing outer forms in the school, eventually what stands out in some relief is a skill set that exists around learning. There is needed a fluidity of movement made possible when one has diminished oneself to a compact entity not dependent upon specific outer conditions for its existence. We need skill and knowledge in reductionism and shape-shifting, changing form according to the needs of the time and space. What is most important is the development of our latent faculties so that we can take on greater obligation in the Work. This development requires certain conditions that will be unique to each individual, but most often will entail the engagement in different activities that target different subtle areas of need. Applying ourselves to these different activities for the purpose of our work will actually give us leverage in adopting the fluid postures that make for good learning.

Given the fact that we are, from one point of view, a multiplicity, the development of an entity within that is able to observe without partiality or agenda will become critical in the process of cohesion that is part of this work. This entity is called "Impartial I." *Impartial I* will witness the machine's manifestations and with development can use the human biological machine for learning, mastering first the manifestations of the moving center such that the center becomes completely available to do as wanted. There needs to be enough presence available to have the will to do this, as well as the general functionality to take input and translate it into action. This skill is quite possible to develop — that is, being able to take input and translate it into action. One need only give up the negative and wasteful reactions to input. The inner posture is one of alertness and cooperation of the centers, unified and at the ready within. This indicates at least the temporary cessation of the mind-based emotions not proper to the true emotional body. There needs to be a break from identification with the dramas that keep these emotions in place.

Of course the glitter and glam of some of the skills we can learn, the rich pastry of physical expression of the spiritual tempts more than just us. That is to say, there are critters that we will come to know in our work lives with electrical existence and presence, powerful enough to rob us of the "moments of freedom" that move us in our evolutionary work. Namely, there is something called "Chief Feature," which is fundamentally an emotional body with an electrical identity that becomes attached to our being early on in our arising on the planet. The scope of this creature is too large to cover in this present topic and will be addressed in depth at a later point. However, we must mention Chief Feature as a way of defining what is meant by *moment of freedom*. *Moments of freedom* are those moments in which we are freed of this parasitic creature. For now, suffice it to say that much help and vigilance is needed to overcome the habit we have of inadvertently feeding the wrong aspect of our Being through our activities. But we can learn to feel these *moment of freedom*, which occur naturally every thirty seconds or so and use these moments for our work.

Until we have a better grasp of the situation, and even then, we simply have to carry on with ongoing remembrance of our spiritual schizophrenia. We are using opportunity for strengthening our work identity when able, at the same time honing skills and habits that render us less food source to the ever-feeding Chief Feature. The momentum is on the side of Chief Feature as our conditioning has been based largely on the care and feeding of this parasitic critter en masse. The ever-present reality of our spiritual origin is pointed to in part through Einstein's vision that *"The field is the sole governing agency of the particle. Energy is the sole governing agency of matter."* Fundamentally, all is spiritual in nature — the reality is that what we conceive of as reality, what we've been conditioned to believe as reality is, in fact, illusion. There is no reality outside of spirit, we just have fallen into the small sleepy hole of the illusion that there is. Now things are so thoroughly mixed up, we aren't going to get out of the illusion except by going through it.

There was given the recommendation of an exercise in which we experience our life *as if* remembering: one is at the place of source and these full blown three-dimensional tactile hallucinations being experienced are actually memory. This exercise, for me, produced at its height a state akin to what I've found myself experiencing when watching some of the Norton Street Videos, which, in turn, reflect a return to timelessness. We are at some level pretending not to know what's actually happening, or not happening, and the process is about exposing and removing the pretense, all the obstacle that is at some level self-imposed. There seems to be no getting around the deep universal being impulse to hide, to cover nakedness, and the equal longing to know no intermediary, to rend the veils. A shaman knows how to dance with this deep movement.

Let's return to the Lord's message: *"Be who you are, and do what you do."* What is essentially being asked of us is to be present and light up the tunnel of our HBM. One can see how this might somehow contribute to at least the development of habit toward cosmic maintenance. God needs help. That's part of how help can be given. As indicated, all that the Teacher wants of me or anyone is the Truth. We are given grace when we surrender our pretense. One has to be willing to die in the process of becoming that which will serve the greater good. There's no

way around it, the seed must die, so let us learn how to do so elegantly
— there's a skill right there. The ability to adopt periodically the
deathbed perspective and apply that within the course of daily life might
prove useful. Truly realizing that one is going to die helps to set priorities
straight.

In the process of transformation there is death. In the continual dying
and rebirthing and dying again, a formless something begins to present
itself as a new center of gravity that does not have the same quality of
stability once known, but seems deeper-rooted in permanence. Again I
see here Path Tendencies at play. The "Primordial Being" is described
in the *American Book of the Dead* by Gold as being in a state of perpetual
change. So it is with our transformational work. At the highest level of
development possible for embodied spirits on this planet, there is implied
even further potential for development and Work obligation. Throughout
it all, we voyage; there is change and yet through the change there is permanence. This is how I see the quality of the Primordial Being's state
poking through on the phenomenal side of the veil.

A shaman or sha-woman has the ability to shape-shift, and is thus
not so attached or identified with one form or identity. Some totem poles
depict the different morphological changes a voyager will have to undergo in order to reach the chamber at the top — these represent established pathways. We are advised in our voyaging to relax at the points
of transition, thereby going against the common reflex which is to tense
up. Developing a fluidity of movement out of one form and into another,
as we walk our path, seems readily practical within the scope of our daily
lives. We can learn to sense points of transition and see our patterns of
response in our day-to-day lives, and by impartial observation and
healthy experimentation, transform the ordinary into a practical exercise
in the extraordinary. With the development of Work will, we can begin
to change our habits in one realm and apply this to other realms.

I will offer a personal example here, only to give you a better sense
of where I'm coming from and thus, hope to offer better opportunity for
discernment. The calling to study Flamenco came through my life starting at a very young age, with a few strong but sparse impressions scattered throughout. It was not until I reached my forties that enough
necessity and corresponding opportunity presented itself. You must un-

derstand, when I say calling — it was not like I loved the art form per se — it was not a formulation like that but, rather a set of guided impressions, some of which fell under the category of mystical that led me to the place of developing skill in this arena. And this skill is but the husk of more subtle skills that have been developed. As one small example, the experience of non-adrenalized passion — Flamenco for me awakened this. Because it is an art form that includes movement, which initially is almost counter intuitive, yet with the deep pulse of more complex rhythm, it takes a lot of stamina to learn past the initial stages unless one has grown up with the rhythms. You can't hear them until you can hear them. Then you must learn how to do these movements completely faithfully to the rhythm as it is expressed in that moment — and in this, apply the profound skill of being right there with that moment, able to respond precisely on beat. The demand on different skills of attention is useful as this development is applicable to other aspects of one's life.

Other skills have included the ability to self-observe impartially under pressure, and further, the ability to adapt the correction needed in quick time. Fluidity and expanded range of movement and posture have been obvious benefits of my efforts. There is more confidence in the face of opposition, even in the form of what here is referred to as the *Antime* (anti-me), the part of one that is ruthlessly self-destructive. In addition, I have the ability to see where my attention falters, where my uncertainty and doubt block flow. There has been the development of whole body, split and voyager attention — the latter especially within the context of performance in group. It goes on, this list and Flamenco marked my transition from being a spiritual warfare near-casualty case, as it seemed at the time, to a working soldier once again.

Spirit dance, of course, more directly addresses many of the skills and energetic benefits I have derived from my Flamenco practice. But in my life, on my path, Flamenco has been and continues to be part of the way in which work-applicable skills develop. It was only after I started to study Flamenco in earnest that I found out my paternal grandfather came from Andalusia, the birthplace of Flamenco and my grandmother played Flamenco guitar. It was part of the DNA material, so it seems, and when seen in the light of the efficiency of the Work, how what is used is what is, it makes sense for my path.

Know thyself. Sit squarely in the center of that knowledge and from there see what you gravitate toward. Way back when I first met E.J., I'd just attended my first couple of workshops and by this point knew my days were quite numbered in my old life. I remember having the feeling of wishing to communicate about these incredible ideas that were opening me up like a bouquet — but quickly I learned how limited I was in my ability to communicate and discern to whom that communication should take place, and how. I knew that the wish to communicate these ideas effectively was something to hold, so I held that and it served as a beginning form of service for me, just holding the wish to faithfully pass on ideas that are useful. And here I find myself in a position of actual practice of that which I could at one time only hold as a wish. To wish is a very big thing, and this will become increasingly evident with the development of our attention and formulation of our Work Wishes.

What do we feel moved to do? When we get all still inside — and there's a skill in itself — what calls to us to be developed? What do we love and how do we love it? If we are bewildered, it's a good sign actually. Sometimes all we can do is ask for guidance. When we pray and ask for guidance that we might be helpful to the greater good rather than solely for our own glory, all the better, so it seems. It is useful, part of the sly man's way to give weight to a Work Wish by *wishing our efforts be used for the benefit of all beings everywhere.*

On the one hand, we have the drive, the longing, the calling and wish to Work, and at the same time, our striving can perpetuate the illusion of separation. It might help us to remember there is illusion in the experience that there is anything but spirit. The enlightened one has seen through the illusion and is not limited to the laws that govern matter simply because the recognition of all as spirit is a part of Being; it is the reality. In the state of spirit that is embodied, all is available to one, because there is a harmonious relationship with all. Navigation through and perception of the labyrinth in a non-phenomenal state is a different matter, so to speak, than what we have available, confined to ordinary human consciousness.

How this translates into action, where the pure force of love is put to good work effect will be unique to each of us as an individual. And it seems that this unique path of ours will present itself clearest when we are living a life that is focused on the fulfillment of duty to a greater good. Rumi says that the spirit self is a young child that comes out to play when engaged in selfless action.

You want to know what skills to develop for the greater good? Look deep within and connect with that longing to serve that is like a life-line to Source. Be moved from this place.

Aligning ourselves with knowledge of our possible function toward the greater good, the skills to be developed will present themselves readily. They will be given the force of greater necessity than what would occur in doing just for the self.

We Just Love Here
Grace Kelly Rivera, oil on canvas, 5' x 3' © 2011 Grace Kelly Rivera

Topic Four

What is the best strategy for accepting others' negative manifestations or manifestations that are unpleasant to be around?

"The least we are asked to be able to do as completed man is to suffer the unpleasant manifestations of others toward ourselves and others without resentment, to take no actions against wrongs done us and to have compassion for those whose nature is more powerful than their being." (Gold, *The Joy of Sacrifice*, page 99)

Fulfilling this least requirement for Completed Being calls for a perspective that only awakening can give. We must include awakening as part of the strategy for accepting others' negative manifestations. Learning to use the outer world to feed our awakening is a question of adopting new habits. The fundamental conditioning to feed and sustain outer reality will be altered only through our struggle with the habits that support this set of conditions. And this conditioning is nowhere more evident than in our relationships. Our dealings with others can provide the perfect forum for our work with reality pump reversal. We have great opportunity to learn to use negative manifestations coming from without or from within as fuel to launch us into awakening.

In the completed state, one has transcended individual typicality to a place where vision lends itself to archetype more readily. In this place of completion, one has realized the ability to adopt all possible postures for humankind, and with this ability, tolerance and fluidity is readily available. One has struggled against one's own tendencies to bring oneself to live life as an Essential Being. From this perspective, compassion is as natural as breathing. One can see others not in terms of their outer manifestations, but rather as Beings struggling with the reality of physical existence in a human biological machine. One is also aware of the whole in the part.

The height of our humanity can be expressed in compassion, in our ability to see ourselves in another and wish for them at least what we wish for ourselves. When there is no ability to know compassion toward a fellow human, we are sitting in the same state of illness as what we witness. I have a rather harsh example to offer from my own life that might serve to illuminate this a bit.

When I recovered memory of very early childhood abuse, the memory was from a perspective given by my morphology at the time, which was not confined to the physical body — the shock and pain had taken me out of body, and from this vantage point, I became all in that chamber — the walls, the characters, the ceiling and furniture — everything in the space. The state of Being was one of high indifference, all simply was. For healing to take place of these kinds of wounds, that are seeds for masses of electrical energy, anomalies to the electrical field of the machine, forgiveness is necessary. For me the perspective given from the out of body platform has helped in this forgiveness. As a separate character and victim, there are challenges to this forgiveness. There are psychological and karmic factors, complex considerations ranging from the ordinary to the metaphysical. But when I see the tableau, simply things aren't as jagged, because *all is one.*

In any event, we are looking into a mirror — it really is all done with mirrors. There are distorted mirrors, encrusted mirrors, and rarely, well-polished mirrors. When we do our cleansing heart work, we are polishing our mirror. While looking into distorted mirrors at the carnival usually leads to laughter and fun, the nature of the distorted mirrors we find in life situations with other humans tends not to provoke laughter as readily. It is a pity from one perspective, as laughing at one's own antics can show signs of lack of self-importance. When there is lack of self-importance, many things are possible, including the ability to laugh at oneself. What is meant by self-importance? It is actually a term that can be found in many writings and covers a wide expanse of meaning. For our purposes here, self-importance refers to impulses or directives that preserve the ego and its illusion of separation.

Self-importance is at the root of all conflict. To the degree we are awake, we eliminate the prison of our self-importance.

When looking at unpleasant behavior and reacting strongly, know that somewhere before us is a reflection of an inner condition of identification. Identifying that identification as it exists within us will be useful in paving the road to healthier transactions. This helps us in the development of our impartiality — we are viewing our lives as objective scientists. We are not feeding the drama or our sense of right and wrong. We don't have a lot of time to work and must stop wasting precious time and energy on the upkeep of our dramas. There are circumstances that call for righteous behavior, and there is a place for the development of warrior qualities of the highest order. At times, right action on a path might call for righteous response to injustice done to the innocent. But the perspective that would discern or intuit this kind of righteousness is not one of good and bad nature. If anything, the battle being fought is against the forces of both good and evil. The enlightened warrior feels the point of the arrow piercing at the same time that it penetrates his target, because he sees *all as one.*

We serve our work by limiting our self-importance, thereby expanding our capacity to experience *all as one.* Without help that takes place through very specialized conditions, it is difficult to get a good picture of the depth and range of our self-importance. But one can use one's own inner theater, as well as tap into deep memory, to produce the deathbed perspective. A mantra often used around here has been "dead is dead" — it is an effective tool for working with self-importance. It is useful to remember death in life in any event, but especially so for one that is evolving voluntarily. The movement is to die to the outer world to feed the development of the inner world bodies of spirit. Remembrance of death can pierce a hole in the bubble of our sleep. When dead of what meaning are someone's words or actions? A dead person no longer responds to outer stimuli. Yet I've heard it said around here that not even Death can take away your sense of humor. Humor's place on this path has been further impressed upon me by means of a couple of lucid experiences I'll relate here.

The first of these experiences occurred when the head of one of the Sufi orders held audience for Seekers that might be accepted to work with him in New York. Dr. Javad Nurbaksh was establishing a center for his order, the Naqshbandis. The first time I ever read the word Sufi the most delicious feeling came over me — a fine mix of wonder, elation, deep familiarity, reverence and love. All of these emotional tones were present on the day of audience, but overlaid with a whole lot more that rendered me quite nervous, albeit willing.

I sat in an ante chamber of sorts for quite some time waiting, noting a couple of women I could see preparing fruit evidently for the Master, discussing how he'd surprisingly taken melon the day previous and was asking for more. The relevance of this conversation escaped me at the time, only to come to light years later after meeting E.J. In the realm of voluntary evolution, what the alchemical factory is eating can offer insight into its workings. Without fanaticism, observation of what might ordinarily be called mundane can contribute to the study of the workings of the human biological machine and its functioning as a transformational apparatus.

Finally I was called into the main room, which was rather large, and asked to sit on a carpet in front of the Master. There were to my recollection only men present — if there were women they were not in my range of vision. I saw about a dozen students that stood behind where the sheik sat. His eyes were closed at first, then after a moment he opened them and stared at me quietly. I squirmed within not knowing whether to speak, sensing that I should stay quiet until told to speak. I was asked to present my reason for seeking the opportunity to work with him. What I said is not so lucid now, but I do have the clear memory of feeling terribly serious. We spoke through a translator. There was a long, very pregnant silence. Suddenly the silence was broken by the sound of that bearded, robed fellow before me laughing uproariously — just laughing and laughing.

I smiled wanly and after about a minute, which can be an incredibly long period of time when there's laughter going on that you don't understand, I looked at others around the room for a clue as to what this meant — all seemed as perplexed, though not too overtly. At some point the students started to laugh, but their confused brow signals to each other informed me they didn't have a clue as to why. Finally, one of them, the closest in proximity to the Master, said softly, "This is your answer" with a grin. The Master spoke — he would work with me, he said, and asked if I realized that to work with him, I would have to accept Islam. I told him I would have to think about it, thanked him and left. Think about it — I had to find out what in the heck Islam was at the time, because I was thoroughly clueless.

Years later, after meeting E.J. and moving out here, I had a lucid dream experience. In it I was with E.J. and others at a celebration and funeral for a great Sufi Master. It was outdoors in a beautiful park-like setting where there were several little stations set up, and one was to go to each of these and perform a ritual — the sense was that of honoring the deceased, but also of gaining blessings by virtue of the greatness of spirit of the departed. It was a very high and honorable event. I don't remember all the stations, but I do remember that at every one, when it came his turn to do the ritual, E.J. would do something quite outrageous and seemingly irreverent, as it was not according to custom. Yet his antics were completely accepted. At the one station, I do remember, one was to say a prayer and blessing while tying a ribbon onto some lattice work. When given the ribbon, E.J. took it and started flossing his teeth — need I say more?

The final place I found myself was somewhat separate from the other stations. There were two large and identical statues of that energetic configuration commonly known as Mary, or the Blessed Mother, or in her more esoteric aspect, Girlfriend of God. Rather confused, especially following E.J.'s irreverent behavior, I hesitatingly knelt and was about to pray before one of the statues, the one on the left, when I heard a rumbling sound coming from the second statue, and it started to quake until E.J. burst right through it, emerging out of the rubble. He looked at me and said, "In this school we do not use devotion, we use humor." With that I was awakened back in to consensus reality. I immediately flashed on the laughing Master from New York. And I was finally able to join him in delighted laughter of my own.

We see here a good example of how some impressions that collectively offer nourishment for our evolution might be impressed upon one over a long period of time. In hindsight, which is often 20/20 vision, one can see how experiences have been *as if* laid out in a particular order for ingestion and processing, building internal constructs that are useful for the containment of further data. These constructs may be temporary in nature, and it behooves us to be aware of the temporal nature of things manifest. When one sees the eventual blessed outcome of what might be some unpleasant experience involving others, it feeds patience. When it comes to soul growth, we are not going to grab it with anything we use to cognate. Let us be humble in this knowledge. A great sign of humility is the fluid ability to laugh.

Good humor begins at home. It is not laughing at someone at their expense, thus inflating one's self-importance. It is not the "dry barking laughter of humorless irony" that is described in the *ABD*. It is not sarcasm, emphatically not that. Laughter, good humor, these indicate the presence of pliability, of surrender. Laughter used to establish oneself as above a situation, or any humor born of ego-based self-protection will likely invite more unpleasantness. Genuine good humor can melt a sour face into at least a smile, give space to breathe, open one up to understanding and bridge gaps. To be able to laugh at one's own weaknesses sincerely when they are presented indicates some space, space that can only be bought at the cost of our self-importance.

We will transcend typicality and be able to deal with others' unpleasant manifestations in direct proportion to our ability to sacrifice self-importance.

We can consider it a good sign, indeed, when in the throes of anger or fear or whatever chronic defense against awakening, we are prompted to laugh by the absurdity of our own behavior. This seems like a clear indication of some work toward the disarming of the chronic defense mechanism against awakening. When we have disarmed the chronic defense mechanism, the physics are simply more advantageous for not perpetuating a negative state. We vibrate differently and there is a natural harmony that softens the sharp edges of the ego. One's energetic field doesn't stick out with anomalies that can invite resonant reactivity in others.

We can challenge the heaviness of self-importance with a healthy dose of humor.

In this way we release our addiction to self-image. Because it is only when we cease to be convinced and identified with our own dramas and their identified significance that we can gain distance enough for humor. With this quality of distance, of objectification, we may be given the overview needed to find a path of reconciliation and service. To really stop taking ourselves and our objectives so seriously means we have grown out beyond the limited playing field of ego-based satisfactions. At the same time, we temper our willingness to relinquish identification with a dedication to our work that helps us know when we must assume a different posture in its name.

In my learning about the use of good humor, I have lessons to cure my unconscious use of it as well. One strong lesson that was multifold in its effect occurred during a workshop that took place while I was living in the same school facility as E.J. I need to explain that part of the training we undergo while working in the school is that of invisibility; we do not advertise our school activities except to those within the Work Circle. The training helps one in creating conscious habits of transaction that protect the Work of the group.

We were outside where the group was gathered to receive instruction on an exercise. In the midst of his explanation, at what I thought was a good prompting moment, I led the group through a call and response of some kind — perhaps a couple of lines out of the film *The Adventures of Buckaroo Bonzai in the Eighth Dimension*. When I called out *"And what is the greatest joy?"* the group, comprised largely of visitors, readily said, *"The joy of duty!"* and laughed heartily. Everyone but E.J., that is, who very sternly admonished me for so carelessly and arrogantly jeopardizing the Work of the group by creating sound that could attract the attention of neighbors.

At the time I was going through a lot of difficulty in my work and it seemed that E.J. was always especially harsh on me. Giving others reason to laugh seemed like such a small indulgence but when he put it to me the way he did, something quite amazing happened within. I found myself genuinely wishing to change so that I would never jeopardize the

Work of the group again. I felt a profound remorse for potentially enangering the Work of the group and here caught glimpse of how much that really meant to me. After he said what he did, containing the fire that had been combusted in my chest, I looked at him and with all my being said, "I'm sorry. It won't happen again." He acknowledged me in such a way that I knew he was taking me seriously and this increased my wish for transformation even more. It was a moment that taught me much about virtue.

We have been given so many tools that can be applied to our practical work on self — like the invocation of presence. In the invocation of presence, we are applying our attention to the wish of feeding the invocation of the presence of our Presence into the present. The basic exercise is to create an internal altar upon which one sacrifices the moment's negative charged manifestation to feed the presence of one's Presence into the present. It is a clear magical act in the direction of reversing the reality pump. One is taking the outer-based reality and using it to feed the inner presence, thus rendering the outer world passive to the active inner. As this happens, one says, "I wish to use this to feed the invocation of the presence of my Presence into the present."

These are not words to be said casually and like prayer, an investment of energy is needed, an arousal of genuine mood as well as a concentration of attention for the wanted effect to take place. When we witness our failed attempts at work on self, these impressions can serve to add fuel to our wishing — to increase the longing. Using diffusion of vision is a good trick to help instigate a state of impartiality as we see the Patchwork Quilt where there is as is said in the *ABD*, "No one thing more than another." The vision is relaxed as is the part of the mind that wants to separate and categorize. All becomes as a quilt of different colors and forms, flat and extending to the farthest extent of our peripheral vision. This is a most effective technique for bringing oneself to a place of impartiality and remembrance out of the chaos of our identification.

When caught it is possible to simply realize our sleep and instead of using that realization to further incite our chronic to action, or beat us back to sleep through some misguided ego-based Work ethic, awaken compassion. Focus on the heart chakra and open it up to what is there. The heart chakra can reveal the truth to us if we can genuinely activate its intelligence. And, of course, our ongoing heart work is that of following, adoring our movement through space and time, applying the attention of the head brain to the task. When we reverse the functions of the head and tail brain — when we think with our tail brain and move with our head brain — we will have awakened the heart to its proper functioning, and thus the ability to radiate real emotion.

I once read in the Philokalia, ancient esoteric Christian writings, in the volume on Prayer of the Heart, that Anger can be transformed into benevolence through patience and mercy — mercy for those enemies that seem to come from without, patience toward those enemies from within — or was it the other way around? Both patience and mercy have their place. Anger is really a mask for fear, a fear reaction of humiliation over feeling fear. To see this one must be willing to get past anger, even if, and especially when, it seems justified. We must do away with our righteousness as it is applied to people, places and things of the outer world — we are in remembrance of what is essential, which is soul growth. At the same time, one stands in righteousness when willing to turn and face the monster. It's wise to go soft instead of rigid; in fact, soft implies strength over rigidity. As is indicated in the Tao te Ching, the soft will overcome the hard. One sheds the masks, surrenders the self-importance that makes monsters from without, recognizing all as one's own play of consciousness. To shed anger is to reveal fear. To shed fear is to be rid of the greatest of illusions, an illusion that goes right through to the top of the totem pole of existence. To truly be rid of fear offers the Creator and Creation a pure moment of freedom.

As we learn the more effective way of dealing with our weaknesses, which in part is to watch them impartially and not perpetuate habits any further through reaction, we begin to create enough space and distance within to disengage from the identification. With this space there is certainly more room for everyone and their manifestations and vivre le différence! One might begin to see folks as beings dealing with their particular HBM and all the influences we are subject to as part of the human condition. When you find out what some folks are dealing with, it's a small wonder they can get themselves moving in the morning — illness, auto intoxication due to impacted colons, crushing circumstances, traumas, past abuses, so much overlay. When we begin to unravel the coils of tension wrapped around our own traumas and see how coping mechanisms are created, there is naturally more tolerance and compassion.

How well we've followed our path of self-knowledge will be reflected in our treatment of others.

When someone is mean or unpleasant, somewhere they are in pain and they are in sleep, it's that simple. If we are cued to respond to someone in an unpleasant way, there is pain present within. We are not obliged to take on another's pain and if we find ourselves doing so, therein lies the opportunity to find out possibly where the barb is that keeps us getting hooked by that pain. Actually, there is a Buddhist exercise in which one does take on the pain of others intentionally, bringing it in to be transformed for the benefit of all beings everywhere. Given a well-developed attention, we can create the ritual of wishing someone well with the whole of our being, offering all we encounter this gift. Placing one's attention in such a way, radiating that quality, can have genuine impact when our attention has been developed. If we remember the game we are playing, which is the evolutionary game, then phenomena takes on a different meaning — no longer out to win an argument, our aim is to use tools of will, presence and attention for our work a little better each time an encounter gives us the opportunity for practice.

A Completed Being will have a different relationship to people, places and things than one who is incomplete. At some level, everything is alive and everything is made of light. When operating in the world without awareness and unconsciously handling objects without the care that comes from sensing that aliveness we are really mistreating ourselves. Because guess whose movie it is? It is said, "I had nothing but Myself with which to make the universe, out of Myself the universe was made." In this we are made in the mirror image of God. How we maneuver around spaces reflects our state of consciousness at the moment. I remember E.J. saying more than once how you eat, in the sense of the actual physical act of eating, is how you make love. And this in the context of knowing that what we call making love angels can call breathing.

Prayer does have its place here as well. I heard from someone that E.J. once told them he would sometimes sing *Amazing Grace* to himself while navigating through certain situations, and I have adopted this practice to good effect. We can pray within anytime. Another practice I've engaged in is the remembrance of the Lord's Prayer whenever I encountered someone with whom I had chronic problems. There are many beautiful prayers that are quite effective in establishing a particular kind of communication, contact and access. Prayer can be used to reprogram our salt water computers toward light from the dark. A prayer or mantra or focus of attention on the breath is quite useful in breaking away from the identification and adopting the habit of inviting consciousness in its stead.

Recently I received a translation of **The Lord's Prayer** from the Armaic that goes like this:

O Cosmic Birther, from whom the breath of life comes,
Who fills all realms of sound, light and vibration,
May Your light be experienced in the utmost holiest,
Your Heavenly Domain approaches.
Let Your Will come true in the universe (all that vibrates) just as on
earth (that is material and dense).
Give us wisdom (understanding, assistance) for our daily need,
Detach the fetters of faults that bind us, (karma) like we let go the
guilt of others.
Let us not be lost in superficial things (materialism, common temptations)
But let us be freed from that what keeps us off from our true purpose,
From You comes the all working will, the lively strength to act, the
song that beautifies all and renews itself from age to age
Sealed in trust, faith and truth (I confirm with my entire being)

Of particular interest here is the line: *"Detach the fetters of faults that bind us, like we let go the guilt of others."* To my view this is pure fact as well as a formula. When working with others there is given the opportunity to detach the fetters of karma and transcend typicality. We are given further hint as to how we can do this in the line —*"let us not be lost in superficial things, but let us be freed from that what keeps us off from our true purpose."* By focusing on our work purpose clearly, we can use the world of the material for our work and cut a path that frees us. Difficult encounters can eventually be seen as a blessing in this regard, providing the quality of energy that can make for good transformative experience. But this can't happen if lost in physicality and the agendas held there, titillated by all the primate intrigue that goes with it. Like the Fourth Way Folk Song goes — "What are you holding onto, what are you trying to defend, what is so important that you can't let go and blend?" Blend into what, you might ask? Oh, nothing much, just the *Face of God*.

On the other end of the stick, so to speak, you can bet caca is gonna happen. Being afraid of messy caca isn't going to help, at the same time we don't want to hang with it. Depending upon the situation, there will be different strategies employed to best effect. We want to use these situations to strengthen our voyaging skills. Whatever strategy employed, the one rooted in love and compassion, as opposed to fear, will be the most effective. I will qualify here and say love and compassion toward the work. And remember in the work, Attitude is everything.

Pushing for communication when it isn't really possible is rather silly, don't you think? It's smart to look at what actually is. If attempting to communicate with someone that is in the throes of their trip, and this is often evident to all but that person, we might find some way to communicate at another time when there is receptivity. Know yourself — we need to know our own state. If it's not possible to communicate at a later time, then we can be aware of the emotional tone of the person such that we match and slightly raise it, impartially, taking it to higher gradients as we successfully communicate. A person in a state is not apt to respond well to a bubbly enthusiasm. Wise voyaging would have us intuit a gentle approach that does not ripple and threaten.

Of course, this means we have to be free from identification with our own state. Our shape-shifting abilities are directly influenced by this freedom. Compassion for someone who is displaying unpleasant behavior is possible when there is recognition of what that Being is going through, and sight of how blinding it can be. If we are able to gradually bring someone to a place where their indicators have gone up, we have done a small part for world peace. It is useful to remember the fact of death and destruction on this planet — look at 9/11. It was something borne of a force that is intimately related to self-importance which has a vast range of manifestation. To the degree we engage in this sort of thing, we participate in those destructive forces.

What counts on this planet is growing a soul, nothing else.

It is useful to remember that folks will someday die — that everyone around us and we will someday die. Especially given the great advantage in this life to be exposed to ideas and tools that can help us live a work life, we are obliged to practice compassion. We are supposed to be among the folks who feel moved to be on the side of the solution, not the problem. Somewhere within we know the object of the game is not the manipulation of the phenomena we see around us, but rather, using the situation for what really counts. What counts on this planet is growing a soul, nothing else.

When we are feeling reactionary it can be useful to scan the body for places where tension is being held, watching, noting our physical postures and the places of tension. We can more readily access our moving center manifestations when in the throes of our states. We might see hint as to what we are holding onto or wanting or defending that is causing pain. If we have developed attention well, often the act of giving it impartially to that source of pain can begin the process of unraveling it. We are in identification at that moment — see if we can pinpoint the source of this identification, how it is held in place. Often, again with the correct placement of attention, the origins of a habit of identification will present itself and this can affect significant change.

Looking at the contents of our mind — is our want or fear or sense of injustice or whatever based on primate territorial directives with an emphasis on placement in the hierarchy? Rumi has a beautiful piece of advice — "_Never want what others have._" This reflects true self-knowledge, because, in fact, we are given everything we need to work. We have, at some level as a Being, chosen the path we've taken. We saw the possibility for soul growth in the path we chose. Even if all we have at the moment is misery, we can take that and feed our longing and wish for work.

I remember once at a group meeting complaining about someone's behavior that was disruptive and E.J. simply said, "_Just do your work._"

On another occasion when Robbert and I were doing *Creation Story Verbatim* at the Nevada Theater, I was just about to go into town where there was so much to be done — putting up posters, rehearsing, gathering props, memorizing lines, blocking. E.J. asked me, *"What is it you must be sure and do today — I mean, apart from all the play details, what is it that you must be sure to do?"* I ventured a guess — *"Invoke presence?"* *"No, not even that is necessary. The one thing you must do is function, not allow anyone to take your Work away from you, care about your Work enough to not let others' states derail you into dysfunction."*

Encountering difficulty, let us use it to full advantage — there is rocket fuel for our awakening work potentially available to us. The minute we gain mastery within, over our own animal, other animals are readily tamed. Most of us have been conditioned to avoid pain at all costs. We can see a problem here because we all know what we resist persists. The act of avoidance actually feeds the experience of pain. There is a fallacy in thinking there is such a thing as a painless life. I know that in some systems they speak of the pain body and it is only by virtue of it we experience pain, however, I have yet to meet someone that doesn't have a "pain body", so chances are good that on this planet, a state of painlessness is at best not likely. Unless, of course, we suffer the pain — to suffer here again is meant to bear. When we suffer the pain, we transcend it. Sometimes there is nothing to be done but just sit in the middle of it and experience it, feel it, give it our attention instead of running away.

So there we are, in the thick of it, as we have been so many times with that idiot whose very chemistry is an affront to the delicate nature of our Being. What to do? Go soft, fluid, invisible and diffuse the vision. Put attention on the whole body and where we are carrying tension. Breathe into the tension to release. If we can, see how this person is mirroring us at that very moment. Likely they are a gateway for us, in fact, gratitude is in order. Work to muster up the ability to radiate that gratitude. When we are able to turn an intense disliking to compassion, we have transcended our own typicality and moved into brand new territory. The air feels clearer, and there is a grand spaciousness. But we must first give up living in that tiny room where our attention remains fixated on a source of pain or fulfilling all the requirements of our typicality.

When we are off, we should have the bigness and objectivity to admit it, confess it and surrender. In the thick of indulging our negative manifestations, at least let us watch the show, not black out. Let's seek to move toward cleansing radiations rather than away from them.

We do well to activate remorse while shame is not useful to our work.

We can walk a path of communication with others that is extra cautious, knowing our weakness of the moment — giving folks the benefit of the doubt. If talking something out, it is useful to only refer to our own perspective, never to point outward. Speaking our truth as clearly and honorably as possible — we must also know that we won't get anywhere if we understand as our truth that the other fellow is an ass. They may well be behaving like some by-product of the posterior, but we don't have to go and wallow in it by further engaging.

Asking ourselves at the right moment "Do I want to be right, or do I want to work?" can be most useful.

E.J. has said his secret is he gives until it hurts and then he gives some more. If we find ourselves in a position of animosity with another that does not change over a long period of time, it likely does not bode well for our transformational process. Change in Being should affect change in relationship.

As part of ongoing work, it may help to do some form of recapitulation ritual that examines our encounters with an individual or situation and reclaims the energy that has been lost, energy needed for transformational work. To transmute a lead experience into gold requires energy. It is, in effect, through resonance that we invite the kind of radiant factors that produce corresponding chemical changes needed in our evolution. Recapitulation work helps to unleash bound up energy and unblock those places where the flow of energy is obstructed. In the process, if done with the right attitude, there is great insight to be gained. We can see our mistakes, how misunderstanding developed and the positions that were held in place contributing to the situation. But we examine from a platform that allows us impartiality. As a peaceful warrior, we must be willing to look within thoroughly and take responsibility for participation in a situation. If our finger is pointing to another in blame, we aren't there yet, where we need to be.

I've heard the advice *"Ignore adversity."* As sly folks in the work, we will take that a step further, making it work to our advantage. Remember, at every moment the choice is ours if we practice living where choice has room to exist. This quality of choice becomes ours more and more as we eliminate our barriers to present moment living. For example, this flawless, fabulous moment here, right now — will we spend it for the benefit of our work as an essential being or for the benefit of reinforcing the life of the machine? To find the strategies needed for dealing with the unpleasant manifestations of others, let us dive in deeper into Source, into the Zen of this moment here now. This moment here now spent as an essential being answers our necessity and gives us all the strategy we need.

The Immediacy of Movement
Grace Kelly Rivera, Oil on Canvas, 48"x30", © 1997 Grace Kelly Rivera

Still Beast with Life
Grace Kelly Rivera, mixed media on specially prepared Arches, 30" x 22"
© 2011 Grace Kelly Rivera

Topic Five

Chief Feature and Other Critters of Distinction

How do we work with the idea of Chief Feature?

I am struck by the angularity of language in expressing the cunningly subtle principles around the delicate topic of Chief Feature and other such occult entities encountered along the Work path. The fact that we are dealing with a form of occultism — meant here in the sense of being "hidden" — is tough enough, but add to that the conditioning that has come to us about such matters, and things get really complicated.

We may have a vague sense of our conditioning, but when we explore even just a little of the origin of some of the beliefs that have come down to us around the concept of evil and good, we catch view of the vast discrepancies that form their basis. Just to give an example, *Satan*. In the Jewish cosmology, descended from the Sumerian, there was a post that was named *Ha-Satan*, which means Holy Adversary, Holy Denying, and this post was held by different angels at different times. The task of this post was to prevent the return of the manufactured cosmos, or the Creation, and there were other functions as well. Lucifer is mentioned in the Old Testament. The origin of the whole Lucifer story was a Babylonian king who was overthrown, cast down for his arrogance, and thus became the poster boy for all the bad attributes. In ancient Sumerian magic, there was acknowledgement of electrical entities that might be called devils, but the whole concept of the devil as we know it in this culture is a medieval invention for the purposes of control. If you look at the social structure of chimpanzees and its hierarchy, much is explained about human history. What is claimed to be done in the name of the Maker is in fact often actually done in the name of the monkey.

The above is a completely different picture from the conglomerate of vague impressions that have formed my concept of Evil. Because of my vagary and reluctance to explore it earlier, there was a tendency created that conditioned me to respond to other dimensional phenomena with a stigma created by the threat of Evil. When I made the mistake only once of telling my mother about my astral projection, I was given the impression that this was a very bad thing, perhaps a mark of something evil that was upon me. The knee jerk reactions that are produced by this type of conditioning bear some occult influence. In my case, this influence served to impinge upon me fear of the waking state.

Whether we like it or not, despite our intelligence, the conditioning around evil and occultism is likely to have some effect upon our ability to work with an open awareness of the energetic barriers we may encounter along the subtle path. To look at the idea of Chief Feature in the eye, so to speak, one must have some ability to separate from and be impartial to the beliefs that have been passed on to us through many generations. I feel incredibly indebted to E.J., who has given us much information about energetic forms that exist, but not as we've been led to believe. It is especially useful to remember here that we are pointing at occult matters that have little relationship to the world of words. We are using models to attempt to grasp something we can work with.

Chief Feature is actually a term that is used for many things. One basic and working definition is that it is an entity comprised of the primary weaknesses, center of gravity and impulses that are counterproductive to Work. There are different classifications of Chief Feature, two of which we are interested in at the moment.

The first is Astral — the formation of an emotional body that is not completed, yet exists and must still feed. Ninety percent of supernatural phenomena are manifestations of this kind of electrical entity. It has survived death, but is not immortal, has some volition, but is a product of electrical accident. It has no real consciousness per se and is comparable in its mechanical nature to the HBM. Formed accidentally as a by-product of a shock or profound emotion, it has a duration that will be determined by its formation. For example, a monk spending many years developing a profound emotion might produce an emotional body that will have greater strength and duration than one produced by a murder victim, which will, in turn, have other dominant qualities created by the conditions of its arising. Actually, an electrical field of this nature can be produced in places of mass shock — and this can be considered a Chief Feature configuration of sorts.

There is another kind of Chief Feature type entity that will feed on negative force produced by the machine. It is a by-product of higher entities corrupted through contamination with bio matter. This form of Chief Feature seems to be distinct from other forms, providing perhaps a different and better set of possibilities through reciprocity. Regardless of source, we are given cause to reduce our feeding of negative force and to be aware that we will feed something, so it might as well be to our reciprocal advantage.

One intentional use of the emotional body phenomenon is in the creation of reading artifacts. A person, place or thing will be imbued with an objective, intentionally created emotion that can be extracted by someone who knows about psychometry and is able to read such artifacts. A strong and profound emotion producing an electrical field will be interwoven with the electrical field of an object, creating an anomaly out of the difference between the two fields. It is in this anomaly that the actual read occurs. In other words, the penetration and integration of the emotional body field with the electrical field of the object will produce a third entity of sorts, an anomaly in which the read takes place. This electrical field phenomenon perhaps offers fresh light on places of healing such as Lourdes. The visionary and transformative experiences of saints will produce a very strong electrical field that mixes with the electrical field of the space or objects surrounding and a reading anomaly is thus produced out of the difference between the fields.

In the model of the human biological machine as a transformational apparatus, the machine indicates the vehicle in which we seem to be passing time, but that vehicle includes the set, setting and dosage — the whole gestalt of these fixed tableaus that form the tunnel through which we as Essential Beings traverse. The object of the game is lighting up that tunnel through the awakening of the HBM.

The lower, rough vibratory wave creatures called Chief Features can feed on the negative energy that is produced naturally in the human biological machine. Negative emotions are tied to negative manifestation. There is no way to stop negative force from happening, by virtue of existence there is a positive and a negative and a reconciling of these all the way across the board. It is one of those "you can't change what is, but you can learn to like it" sorts of things.

Negative force is going to be created by the reflexive activity of the muscles in reaction to stimuli. The pattern for this reflexive activity in the muscles created very early on is marked by definite behavioral responses that are powered by the electrical energy of the muscles. The pattern created will be according to tendency. From the point when this is established, the same negative energy pattern will be produced time and again. We can't stop this from happening, but we have the possibility of stopping the manifestation of these reactions. We can learn to stop reacting outwardly. The inner can be in utter turmoil, but the outer remains calm.

In a Work community, lots of negative force will be produced. One advantage to this situation is that in a Work community we are given much education and a living model provided by the Teacher to help us get to a place of will to stop the manifestation of negative reaction. It seems the only way to get to a place of Will to affect change in habit is for it to mean enough to us. Here we are given force for this, we are given the necessity.

When we experience what we think of as a blow off of energy, when we manifest negative force, we are not actually doing anything with it, the only thing we have relieved is a particular kind of tension. As negative force builds, which it does inevitably, it is deposited in various locations in the body — remember, we are talking about something of substance here, electrical substance. These deposits of electrical energy in the electrical field of the machine will reflect some degree of individual tendency in terms of where they are deposited, but generally are the same for everyone. There are lines of tension that are produced between these deposits and what we want to do is maintain them. When we manifest negative emotion produced by negative force in the machine, we blow off the tension, but do nothing with the force itself, it continues to build. When we maintain the tension through non-manifestation and create equilibrium, we produce food that can feed the higher and, in this way, serve the Work.

Ordinary negativity, when expressed, comes back stronger than before. It can be said that the cause of our pain is our lack of intentional suffering. When we maintain our equilibrium of negative force tension, when we keep ourselves from manifesting negative emotion to the place where we are feeding the higher through this equilibrium of tension, we are suffering intentionally and in this intentional suffering, we are giving up our addiction to pain. Pain results from the release of tension that throws off the equilibrium, which in itself produces human biological machine conditions that are optimum for its awakening.

When muscles spasm and contract, they produce an irritant that irritates the membranes. Let's say you are bent in a position with lots of tension as one would be hunched over a desk working intently for hours. When one rises from that position, pain is felt from having held that posture for a long period of time, and the first instinct will be to go back to the position one held — there is where relief is found, in the habitual posture. It might be a posture of unnecessary suffering, but because it is habitual, it provides relief from the immediate pain that is found in the change.

This is how it is with our habitual blowing off of tension. We destroy and reassemble the lines of tension, and this is what causes pain. In not allowing ourselves to achieve the quality of equilibrium of tension of negative force deposits that can feed the higher and serve the Work, we remain in our state of pain. We have the comfort of familiar habit, yes, we avoid the pins and needles intensity of an awakening limb, yes, but we are stuck in the pain of our habitual posture. We are basically like addicts who can't get off the stuff, because we can't get past the pain of the downside of the trip and would rather stay high in our occlusion. When we somehow get the motivation to maintain these lines of tension to the point of lasting equilibrium, we will find the machine begin to awaken.

The human biological machine, if awake, with the equilibrium of negative tension, produces a living Teacher.

One set of impressions I have that taught me about the maintenance of the lines of tension and the possibility of entering the waking state again involves a butterfly. Many years ago I helped to run a shop called the Wildwood Boutique that was a conglomerate of the various Institute retail businesses — I was there with the Perfumerie. This was in an area called Lake Wildwood where there is a large gated community, and I lived in a group house there. I would walk to the shop as often as weather and time would permit — it was close to two miles and quite pleasant.

At this particular time things were incredibly intense at the group house as well as in my personal life. I was going through an ordeal that involved my heart and letting go of conditioned possessive feelings. The inner work around this was hard and there were times when I thought I would spontaneously combust from the amount of charge coursing through me without the release of manifestation. During these episodes that I call "ordeals," there is a lot of energy involved to transform what, to the ordinary eye, might seem like small and insignificant vignettes into grand theaters where surgery is being performed. With a voyager's attention, one has a sense of being tested. And so it was.

I'd passed a particularly difficult passage of this and found myself in such a state of raw aliveness, it seemed I had to will my body to stay together enough to perambulate home early that day from work. It was a beautiful day and in my tender state I worked to stay open and functioning, not allowing myself the break down that seemed to be looming. My attention was caught by a butterfly that seemed to be flying very near to me, at the level of my right shoulder. For quite some stretch it remained present, and at one moment, I turned to it with a very soft voice and gesture, I whispered a long Hiiii, while I made a gentle, rather lyrical movement toward it. It felt as though I kissed the air current of its flight. At the same moment, it came up to my face closer, with the same sweep of movement that mirrored that of my head — saying its hello, it *as if* kissed the air current of my movement.

It was astonishingly beautiful. The beauty and aliveness astonished me to a place where fear seemed to kick in a bit. I tested to make sure this wasn't my imagination by stopping three times to see what would happen — the butterfly would stop and hover with me each time, there was no mistake. By the third stop, my heart was racing. With this, the butterfly crossed in front of me and went on its way.

I took this as a good sign that there was strength in my inner work, enabling me to have some mastery of my own animal, while at the same time there remained work to be done with fear. I had maintained a set of tensions to the place where the machine was given the fuel to awaken. When one has mastery over one's own animal, barriers between species diminish.

Speaking of nature — the Tree of Life superimposed over the human biological machine can be seen as a model of these deposits of negative force and the lines of tension between them. Each of these lines or paths between the energy points is represented by a tarot card. This perhaps gives us a new way of viewing the tarot as a tool for our work.

Negative manifestation requires the functioning of the head and tail brain as they have been conditioned to function. Reversal of these functions awakens the heart and conscience. An awakened heart will not function in the same way and cannot, it's that simple. One will find oneself with more energy, similar to fasting in terms of one's ordinary food. The manifestation of our negative states takes up a lot of energy. When one gains a foothold here, the subtle lines of tension become clearly felt and impartial observation will identify the tricky trigger points where we habitually disrupt our lines of tension. When these trigger points are activated, thus disrupting the tension lines, we perpetuate the negative states associated with having to reassemble them. Witnessing this drama of build up and disruption over and over again, seeing this as cause for much of our suffering in sleep can be excellent incentive for our efforts.

When my daughter was first born, the onslaught of post partum chemistry and boiling hot school conditions rendered me quite powerless at times against the momentum of my negative habits of manifestation. Thankfully I was given a good deal of help from E.J. and many folks around me. Because my negative manifestation problem, under duress, was so pronounced, given my very rough Latino background, it was clear that non-manifestation needed to be a priority. I made the exercise of the non-expression of negative emotion a god and was working in this way when asked by E.J. to watch the brand new and beautiful Perfumerie built in a tiny window spot of the Fifth Avenue gallery in Nevada City around 1988. By this point, I had started to get a sense of riding on these lines of tension within, though I hadn't quite identified them as such. It simply felt like an accumulation of energy that was being maintained and was building.

On this particular day my ability to manage the increase in energy was intact. My state of surrender enabled acceptance of whatever came my way, with many more *moments of freedom*. Though I'd never worked with the Alchemical Gold Essential Oils to that point, I ended up making about two hundred bucks in sales just in the hour's time it took for E.J. and others to take their dinner break. It was easy because I was operating at a level where I'd accessed the school. There the knowledge was available to me via my intuition as to what simple blends to create when customers came by the shop. It was remarkable to watch these people reflecting my own inner open state — the energetic reality created by my accumulated force and easy Work Will of the moment was clearly dominant. It takes sustained accumulated energy to operate at a level that resonates with higher dimensional functioning. We have access to a lot of energy if we can learn to develop habits of conservation and shift our focus away from matter toward spirit. The movement involves diffusion and concentration as we navigate our way around multi-dimensional living. In Bardo terms there are distractions that can pull us off course into rebirth in a lower world. We learn to hang out in a quality of attention that addresses the particular and the whole at once.

In the context of a Work community, lines of tension can be produced between members that, when maintained in equilibrium, also enable the individuals maintenance of their own lines of tension within. It is this negative force transformed through stabilization of this nature that will produce food for the higher. Otherwise, negative energy ordinarily produced will simply feed Chief Feature and other such low vibratory scavengers.

It really seems to be all about feeding — feeding, eating — basic facts of reality. Negative force is going to be produced, and either it will feed the machine's own negative feeding system, or it will feed an emotional body like Chief Feature, or it can feed an emotional body of a higher order, one that serves the Work. Let us remember that we do not have the will needed to Work, we must borrow will from a higher source and we are wise to take care as to what that source is.

Whether we know it or not, we do receive a personal pay off in the situation of being fed upon. We like the sensation. It keeps us in the painful comfort of sleep. It is much like a cow that is being milked — it produces a relief of tension. But nothing of any benefit comes from this situation outside of avoidance of the discomfort of a change of state. It is the change of state from one to another in which we must break through a threshold. Learning to overcome the barrier to the waking state and then stabilizing there ultimately is better as one is freed from a permanent form of misery and sleep. When stabilized in the waking state, the human biological machine does not feel the pain of sleep.

Chief Feature can begin its descent upon us from its occult roots as early as conception, certainly by three months post conception. A definite set of events occur in the life of the child at birth, and various points until the age of five by which time it has completely clamped down. For example at two there will be an introduction of new behavior that is reflective of a firmer grip Chief Feature has on its host — the first growling of it as a permanent fixture. People tend in their ignorance to ascribe to this some organic or psychological-based origin, but, in fact, it is a manifestation of Chief Feature. Occult in nature. The terrible-twos are indeed so.

By the age of five it has become a permanent fixture in the life of the machine, completely taking it over through its ability to self-conjure. From that point on, under ordinary circumstances, all impressions — everything goes into the feeding of Chief Feature and, for all practical purposes, it becomes the basis for all desires, self-love, ideas of self, all impulses for relationship. All to create more ability to feed, it will provide moving center with moods, false feeling and the egoistic belief that these are our own.

Any emotion that produces sensation is by definition a moving center emotion. Higher emotion produces no emotion.

An interesting thing that I've heard is that the machine is rarely seen on its own. If it were to be seen without Chief Feature, it is a machine, but generally behaves with gentle, loving kindness. It is Chief Feature that is invigorated by negativity, negative force that is generated not only in the host machine, but through reaction in the surrounding machines. Once this force has been produced, Chief Feature descends and sucks it, eats it much like a vampire sucking on blood. If put into a situation somehow that it is unable to self-invoke, if it is prevented from conjuration, if moving center of the host is not provoked, it will seek those moving center moves and events that manifest mentations and organic states, which conjure it with greater frequency. Chief Feature avoids school conditions especially because they impose certain forms of obedience that make it difficult for its conjuration and feeding. In a school, because our manifestations are limited by obedience to certain laws, more or less, conjuring of Chief Feature takes place less often which, in turn, leaves us lost, confused, disoriented.

In school conditions there is the possibility of exposure to a different set of moods and radiations that can begin to carve out new neural network pathways of perception.

"Impartial I" has very little opportunity for development because it is robbed of it by Chief Feature. It is like an infant, unless developed, unless allowed to receive impressions with room to grow and learn. In a school, given the presence of a genuine magician, it is possible to produce conditions that enable "impartial I" to develop for longer. It is possible to delay the clamping down of Chief Feature until even the age of eight or ten. Make no mistake here, Chief Feature is an occult subject and must be dealt with accordingly.

Until the age of five, when the clamping down process takes place, there are certain possibilities that can occur. When speaking of the realm of Chief Feature, it must be in terms of conjuration — Chief Feature operations are magical operations. Only a skilled magician, a hierophant, can perform operations of banishing with Chief Feature, and this will not be a head on thing, rather, it will be a question of catching Chief Feature unaware and then making a substitution. Self-banishment of Chief Feature without help of a particular kind is impossible. However, under school conditions, the development of "impartial I" is possible through sufficient Work Will. After the age of five, only self-initiated efforts can be made, help from outside is no longer possible, it must include self-initiation. The good news is that self-initiated efforts move one along faster.

***We come to a school to gain strength to move this puppet
away from its puppetry and toward that which might
breathe real life.***

This brings us to a question raised — how do you identify Chief Feature? To my experience, one cannot identify one's own Chief Feature, unless by some extraordinary means there has been created already an impartial "I" identity with the wherewithal to point and say, hey — right there! We work with an Expert so that we may be given this kind of information under the best set of conditions for our intake to inspire practical efforts. We come to a school to gain the strength to move this puppet away from its puppetry and toward that which might breathe it to real life. Part of the process of gaining the strength is coming face-to-face with our weaknesses, and for this, there must be a catalyst, as there would be in chemistry, to give some distance between our being and our habits that keep us in Chief Feature's grip. We are going to need a lot of energy to produce the necessary effects.

Even if an Expert were given the opportunity to observe someone long enough to identify Chief Feature, its identification and description may not be of practical help until after certain transformations have taken effect. I was given description and identification of Chief Feature decades ago and yet, this information has become of real practical use mostly within the past five-year period. The ability to use this information seemed marked by the recovery of memory of childhood trauma that had been blacked out.

The outer circumstances were a sculpture workshop. E.J. seemed to perform what, to my experience, was akin to Brazilian psychic surgery that extracted embedded memory and subsequent unraveling of consciousness. Please understand I am describing something here that is as indescribable as childbirth labor — I've only heard of Brazilian psychic surgery, and this is what comes to mind when trying to explain the sensation and overall experience. In the moment it occurred, we both seemed to know something was happening, but did not know what. Teacher and Student seemed, from my perspective, at the time, under a very large and powerful influence.

I'd been working on a sculpture — my first — which was intended to be a Kwan Yin head. E.J. had allowed us to work on this without giving instruction initially, to see where we would go with it. As the piece I worked on developed, others seemed to like it. At one point he came over to me and asked if I minded feedback. Of course not, that was what I was there for. With that he took his sculpting tool and plunged it forcefully into the mouth of the sculpture — it was a bit shocking. Over the years I have grown quite accustomed to strong feedback like this in the forum of different art forms. But this was quite different.

Suddenly I was aware that I could feel the sculpting tool in my gut. He moved it with some force from side to side, explaining that the head needed a bigger jaw, opening the mouth cavity to produce this effect. I felt the eeriest sensation of the tool moving from side to side correspondingly. E.J. watched me quite intently, and the feeling I had was that he did not know or particularly enjoy what was going on, but he absolutely had to do what he was doing.

When he was done, I felt as though I'd been violated and at the same time there was a tremendous relief! How very strange, though theater training had awakened a latent tendency to experience multiple emotional tones at once. I somehow managed to get through the end of the workshop and was grateful when it was over — all I wanted to do was go home and lie down, which I did. I lied down and curled into a fetal position, with the strangest feeling that something had taken place that I couldn't put my finger on. It took my going into a hypnagogic state for me to get the vision — then it happened, I saw clearly from a morphology that included the room and characters in it, the abuse that had taken place with me as a very young child. This vision had come in dreams periodically, and I had dismissed it as being some bizarre twist of psyche, but in this hypnagogic state, following the "surgical procedure," this was revealed to me as the memory it was.

In hindsight, it was as though many years of preparation had led to this. Within the first year of my moving to California to work with E.J., he had indicated that there was once a blockage around the first and second chakra, as a note, but never referred to it again. The unraveling process that happens around memory recovery of this nature has translated into the removal of a chunk of obstruction and greater fluidity

within that is marked by such changes as the practical use of the identification of Chief Feature.

I tell you this to give you just a small taste of how my impressions
around the school, time, place and people have been formed. There are
countless examples to be given, some too subtle for rendering into words,
yet, with the overall effect of replacing old habits of sleep with new
habits toward liberation. Liberation can best be described here as victory
in the battle against the forces of both good and evil. Ultimately, the battle, of course, is fought within, and once the battle is won, no further bat-
tles need be fought. But the Teacher provides a very good example of
how to live walking a path of liberation. We need powerful necessity to
create mass enough to overwhelm the domination of Chief Feature. In a
school the Expert's own work forms some of the basis for the creation
of conditions that can give mass to one's necessity to evolve.

Everything in the universe has substance, no matter how
rarefied, like thought.

Think physics here more than philosophy. Everything in the universe
has substance, no matter how rarefied, like thought. The mass provided
by the group and the Work of the group can partner with one's own
smaller mass of evolutionary necessity, giving strength potent enough to
counteract the force and momentum of Chief Feature. To give an example of how this might play, if we are obliged to serve the Work of the
school through some job that must be done regularly, there is greater
chance for opportunity to make super efforts. The presence of the Hierophant who knows how to work effectively to disarm the power of
Chief Feature as needed, with cunning rather than force, is of the essence,
so to speak. Somehow, one needs to find a power source that can help
provide the force needed to break out of the prison of Chief Feature's
feeding.

Part of the conditions necessary for our effective transformations for
Work, of course, involve the heat, the alchemical fire that comes from
the conflict between what we thought we were, but are seeing we aren't.
We need the opportunity for scrutiny that causes our obstructions to the
waking state to stand out in high relief. Having a group witness these
and point them out, seeing our obstructions, first hand, as they reflect in

our relationship to the Expert in the energetic configuration that is the school, has a quickening effect. Rumi tells us that we live next to one another, each with a side opening that is unknown in ourselves, but that allows everyone to see clearly what's going on inside, even when we think we are hiding. That aspect of our Being that is part of the obstruction will curse this exposure being magnified and presented to us, and that aspect of us that wishes Work will bathe in the radiations present in the exposure. It is said we must know ourselves as others see us.

I was given a big opportunity to experience this shortly after arriving to live in the community. The circumstances arose around my having heard a partial conversation — half of a telephone conversation that was not my own, making an assumption about what I'd heard and coming to a conclusion that I passed on. Moreover, I passed it on, I thought, compassionately — it was passed on to be helpful. It turned out that my incomplete information caused a problem that escalated into an even bigger problem.

Sundays, at that time, were Karma Yoga days in which folks would go to the main school facility and work in the garden and property, cleaning, doing childcare, at times construction work or assemblage of written material in the days of snail mail. Strong physical labor was most often involved by those who could take it, and then there would be a large invocational dinner where incredible talks and spaces were offered for our nourishment — impressions, air and food — mingling to feed our Work.

In the middle of this particular Sunday the triangle bell was struck to call all the workers in earlier than usual for a special meeting. Just writing this now, the adrenaline starts to quicken, remembering the moment when I realized this was about me. Everyone was asked to gather, and I remember the configuration as being roughly circular.

I was on the "hot seat." E.J. spoke in a firm tone using words to convey the incident, the consequences of my actions and then the weaknesses in me that led to the unfortunate result. One big point he made that helped to really sock it to me was the fact that I'd given a bad first impression in an area of delicate difficulty, and once made, it is done. He then indicated that perhaps I had a tendency of having pride in knowing some information that another might not have, that this egoism was really at the root of what I mistook as a compassionate impulse. Then, to really hammer the nails to keep me bound for confronting this new vision of myself, despite my feeling of shock and ambush, he called upon folks around the room to give their impressions of my weaknesses, naturally calling upon those who would be the most critical due to typicality dynamics and other factors.

Each dealt his or her blows — that is, from my point of view at the moment. The body had its reaction of tears, but through these I witnessed something quite marvelous. The sum total of impressions served as rocket fuel that suddenly launched me into a different and more rarefied state of consciousness. In this state I saw that E.J. was radiating a profound love that I could feel, and moreover, it was *as if* he were winking, showing me how each type would respond to the particular set of circumstances. Though I was in the hot seat, it was the folks on the periphery who were on display before me. It is said that the Babylonians would produce reading artifacts that could only be read through the feeling center, and the key to opening up these artifacts was the feeling of humiliation. I would say that this experience was a firsthand taste of just how this phenomenon works.

The Expert's deft manner of using the moment's movement to the greatest possible effect pulls the group along like a dance between lover and beloved. One moment we are told that Chief Feature is the motivating factor in all our activities and we are powerless against it. Another moment we are told to realize that we are Bodhisattvas; we are given the instruction to go into horizontal rest that evening and wake up a Bodhisattva among other Bodhisattvas. Little by little we are wriggled out of our convention into a new way of seeing that does not have quite the angularity and opposition of our black and white linear modalities. Our voyager's vision is opened and with this an expanded ability to be with what is. It is a voyage, and each moment yields a fresh scene, yet no matter where we go, there we are.

The point of power is in this here now, the present moment. We have been advised to cease living *as if* we have a history and with that, history arrived at this moment. This habitual viewpoint keeps us locked in. When we've practiced our self-observation and developed our impartial witness to a point that thoughts can be caught unfolding, we will see that these mental, emotional and physical tensions revolve around past/future thinking. Further, they often reflect a disagreement that is going on between what is and what is desired. To get at the bottom of desire, fulfillment will only be experienced in the present moment, by sinking deep into it, opening and deepening like an inner cathedral. Much that we experience desire for isn't even our own, rather, is a product of conditioning. We are taught to experience lack and desire. Desire reflects lack and wish for something other than what is.

But we can use the very suggestibility that impressed upon us the state of lack and desire to our advantage. If we can remember under the right set of circumstances that we have all we need right at this very moment, infusing this with the power of our concentrated attention, we begin the process of changing habit.

Fulfilling desire, in a sense, feeds the impulse to repeat the "desire and seek" game. The real Lover is one who loves the longing as much as the fulfillment, perhaps more. Longing keeps one separate enough to behold the beauty while fulfillment annihilates the two to one. It is the difference between staying and coming, in a sense, talking Tantric sexuality. One is out to withhold from gratification, and maintain the tension present when ever so close to Union.

There is very good work strategic reason to live by the moment. It can be said that Chief Feature self-invokes every thirty seconds or so. By virtue of its existence, it also has a thirty-second period of black out, where a genuine "Moment of Freedom" can be experienced. We can learn to sense these moments and use them for the development of our Impartial Witness, our "Impartial I". There are tools and exercises found within the context of a school that help in the development of the quality of sensing and voyager attention needed to apprehend these moments for our Work.

The way out is through absorption.

However, there is another critter that complicates our potential Moments of Freedom and hence, our work with Chief Feature. It is something that has been named here the *Antime*. It is our chief rival, our competitor, and is a real thing, a body, a spirit — it lives. It is against us and exists to take us down. Everything we build, it destroys, everything we achieve, it will undo. Its origin of arising is the same as ours, it is a natural part of our existence, and we will not be rid of it. One manifestation that folks might have experienced of this creature, which is normally elusive, would be a split personality is found in the sensation of having the urge to jump when at a very high height.

We are bipolar creatures —
we suffer from spiritual bi-polarism.

We and the *Antime* normally have no communication. One definition for the word Yoga is yoke; one is strapping oneself onto something, taking on a yoke like an ox pulling a cart along a way. *Antime* Yoga is taking on the yoke of grinding down the *Antime*. One will not rid oneself of the *Antime* — rather one can only grind it down through its absorption, by fusion. The *Antime* and its polar opposite can fuse together to form a third kind of body we can call the *Uni-me*. Think *Star Trek* where Scottie and Captain Kirk fuse matter and antimatter together to produce warp nine. When opposites are fused, energy of a different kind is produced. The term "Meisnerize," when speaking of the fusion process, is in reference to a Science Fiction story by Damon Knight called *Four in One* in which four distinct central nervous systems are fused into one body, and the four identities must learn to work cooperatively. This gives a bit of a picture for our understanding.

The fusion is not going to neutralize as is often the case when looking at examples in science and medicine of two opposites combined. The *Antime* is not going to be neutralized; we can't think in terms of pushing it away, rather, it must be pulled in. With this process that corrects our spiritual bipolar disorder, we reduce and eventually eliminate the back and forth dynamic in which we are dominant for a time to do only to have the *Antime* become active and destroy what has been done. Do you see a possibility here for developing a humility that helps to protect against that great thief, spiritual pride?

I am prompted here to offer an example that demonstrates my practical understanding of this concept. I was getting ready for a business meeting at my house. Totally identified with the reality in front of me, my chemistry a wreck, I was multi-tasking. Of course, though there was a dull awareness of my state, it was not enough to pull me away from identification. At the height of my obsessive compulsion, while cleaning,

I found a daddy long legs and cupped it loosely in my hand with a paper towel to remove it out the sliding glass door. Our door is in an awful shape, with a bent track that is irreparable so that I'd been accustomed to slamming the door hard to get it over the roughly bent area. Well, incredibly stupidly, I had my left thumb at the wrong place, at the right time to really shatter it.

The first thing I did with registering the shock of pain was look down to see if my thumb had been severed. Then once I realized the hand was whole, with the increasing awareness of pain, there was a moment of intense anger that this should happen to me masking an urge to cry over the pain. By some grace at that precise moment, I saw clearly that I was in the presence of the *Antime*. Somehow, by instinct, I knew the thing to do was not be upset or fearful, but rather to demonstrate compassion. I cradled my thumb gently with my other hand and began nursing the body by getting Rescue Remedy then phoning for help to get me to the clinic. By the time I got there, despite the pain I was quite composed, to the point that folks seemed skeptical of my claim that it was broken. The x-rays showed it had broken in more than one place and the staff seemed quite impressed by my relative composure.

Since that time, to the best of my observation and feedback, it seems something changed in my relationship to my *Antime*. The accident was shocking and at the same time, so clearly a manifestation of the *Antime*, that it was *as if* caught in the act. Somehow I was able to initiate a response to this that applied what I will call the Force of Love, in such a way that a new relationship dynamic was created — dare I say it, a merging of sorts took place. Rather than react to the presence of my *Antime* with contempt when I was made aware of it, I had the presence to respond with loving kindness, and acceptance of all that had taken place. This has proven to have long-term effect on my relationship to the *Antime*.

It seems this movement of relaxing and absorption is going to play out in so many aspects of Work. Universes change by a process of absorption — the old universe is absorbed into the new. The Absolute reabsorbs creation back into itself, or so it is said. It makes sense that our Work movement will bear similarity to primordial movement. It is not going to play out in any way we think, this idea of absorption. When subject to school conditions, one has the opportunity to see clearly that no matter what we think, it *ain't* gonna play out that way. We are not going to figure our way out of the mess we might find ourselves in. And the quicker we get this and stop our attempt to find a nice neat and systematic way of handling things, the better.

Again, the point of power will be found in the present moment. In a moment one can change one's life radically, just by opening up to an expanded field of possibility inherent in it. Take the moment right here, right now — can we be in it to a place of completion? If not, identify the tension that holds back from this completion, and wherever it is, begin right there opening up to its existence, to include the tension in the gestalt of Being. Now where do we find ourselves with that? The tension might exist in beliefs around wanting to evolve. One can fail to be in the present moment because of repeated unconscious programming in the form of doing a particular exercise. If one can identify where one is withholding from the present moment by applying concentrated attention that taps into the power of the moment, real change is possible. It is amazing what happens when one has done this process of releasing a point of withholding so subtle it has been like a fact of the fabric of one's life. When this moment is enough, without anywhere to get to or anything to become, it is seen as the gift it is.

An enlightened being is a realized result of the absorption process. It doesn't mean the triumph of good over evil. It means the transcendence into another realm through the absorption of both good and evil. The aim presented in the *ABD* is liberation, and we are Voyagers because we voyage rather than remain in one state. Even the God world is a hindrance to true liberation. What would be liberation to a Buddha? Any form of attachment, even to awakening, keeps us from liberation.

So we voyage, accepting the moment and what is present without trying to maintain a hold on it. In developing the muscles that must be developed, to practice being with what is, we simultaneously weaken the barrier between ourselves and the *Antime*. We create space enough within to hold the two opposing forces simultaneously so that they may fuse into one unified entity. With the quality of space and gradual disintegration of our limited established personas, we might then be given the impartiality to witness our influences and their more occult origins more directly. We have all seen the unfortunate results of too much emphasis placed in one or another direction. Religious fanaticism leads one to profound and dangerous sleep, as does an occultism that is not well-tempered or a scientific approach that squeezes the life out of life. There are many elements that come to play in the changing perspectives of awakening consciousness, and fluidity is of the essence.

When we have accessed the inner school, there is a tremendous amount of energy and substantiality that vivifies our transformational efforts. The reality of Chief Feature progressively pales more and more by comparison, once we have been given enough momentum in operating at a resonant rate of vibration to that of the inner school. Achieving such resonance means increasing our energy and changing our focus. One way to increase our energy is to stop our negative manifestation. When I refer to *negative* here, I am referring to electrical charge as well as negativity. The HBM is considered to have a negative electrical charge to the positive of the Essential Self. So any manifestation that is machine driven, or Chief Feature driven, as it uses the machine, can be considered negative. The knowledge that negative manifestation serves Chief Feature can be put to good use, and our impartial observation of this playing out repeatedly in the venue of the machine's life might give us some impetus to act. Some advice from Rumi might serve here:

Guest House

This being human is a guest house. Every morning a new arrival.
A joy, a depression, a meanness, some momentary awareness comes
as an unexpected visitor.
Welcome and attend them all!
Even if they're a crowd of sorrows,
who violently sweep your house empty of its furniture, still,
treat each guest honorably.
He may be clearing you out for some new delight.
The dark thought, the shame, the malice,
meet them at the door laughing, and invite them in.
Be grateful for whoever comes,
because each has been sent as a guide from beyond.

(Barks, *The Essential Rumi*, page 109)

*Progress on the path is not necessarily made by any-
thing one does or becomes. The path is found through
surrender.*

Given the Will to Work, we gradually gain strength and ability at seeing and seizing our Moments of Freedom. It is like developing any muscle, skill, or habit — repetition is necessary. This repetition, combined
with the gradual removal of obstruction to the waking state, will show
exponential increase in resulting abilities. Growth can happen if given
enough space and time away from Chief Feature domination.

It is necessary to gain objective perspective of ourselves and see the
motive behind our actions. We are going to have to accept the fact that
we have Chief Feature domination problems, and like an alcoholic, our
only hope is in admitting to our weakness and inability to do on our own.
We need help in getting the ability to pull away from the influence that
keeps us bound. In the case of Chief Feature, when we are given enough
opportunity to pull away to see it from a place of spirit, it loses its power
after a while. In the world of spirit, Chief Feature is really a two-bit loser
of a thing, not much to it — a parasite — yet powerful in its domain.
Persistent, it is well-armed with the strong weapon of necessity to do
what it does for survival. Life of Chief Feature compared to that of Spirit
— or as close as we come to it, is shallow, dull and small. The vast spaciousness and grandeur of Spirit reveals the paltry nature of Chief Feature by comparison.

But in our state of forgetfulness, Chief Feature is very powerful, and
we are in its dominion. Knowing that by comparison we are very weak
initially, we do well to follow the guidance of one with discernment and
to stay in close proximity of conditions that limit Chief Feature feeding.
An alcoholic knows better, especially in the first few months of sobriety,
than to taunt himself by going to a bar with a friend, even with the intention to remain sober. It might serve to look at those activities we sus-
pect might be particularly Chief Feature-friendly.

I am reminded here, once again, of what is said in *The Joy of Sacrifice* about the least that is expected of us as enlightened Beings. We
should be able to tolerate the negative manifestations of others toward
ourselves, or others, without reaction or need to retaliate. It seems this

is applicable to our Chief Feature or *Antime*. Impartial observation gives us much information that enables us, if we can take the Moment of Freedom available to us, to circumvent, slyly, the destructive path of our nemesis. It also serves to undermine a big strategy of Chief Feature. We are led to be convinced of our false identity and when we self-berate over our falling from grace, we only serve that conviction. Impartial observation is based in present moment living. There is no future or past involved as when we are analyzing our actions. We simply are observing, yet in that act of observation, we subtly change the thing observed.

Impartial observation is our main strategy. There are others.

At a moment of confrontation, one way we make passive the outer world to our active inner world is by focusing gently on the natural breath, simultaneously releasing tension, thus encouraging a state of surrender. If we hang out close to our body, with an ongoing awareness of its tensions and postures by means of developing "Impartial I" observation, this sort of checking in on where tension is being held becomes second nature. Progress on the path is not necessarily made by anything one does or becomes. The path is found through surrender. That is when spirit is given the opportunity, the medium, for movement.

While it can be said that mentation is a key to mood, breath is a key to the moving center state. When one slows down the activity of the machine to watch the breath in its natural state, the moving center is affected such that unnecessary tension can be released. As was earlier said, we surrender. The unnecessary tension of the moving center feeds the Chief Feature reality that has us engaged and distracted. Moving center manifestations are one place we can start to surrender and find our way.

It is a question not only of learning how to conserve energy by not manifesting negativity, but also learning how to manage the inevitable tumbles we'll suffer in the learning. It is often not so much the actual events of our falling that are as harmful as our reactions to the situation. These entrain us further toward Chief Feature style momentum when we've given in to the temptation of dramatizing our disappointment in ourselves. This drama really is *Much Ado About Nothing* — in its most violent form.

When we gain experience in the realm of the spirit, we see the truth in the words "all is made of spirit, all phenomena is illusion". We have to get a first-hand experience of this that burns a sufficient hole in the Chief Feature reality bag we are trapped in. This will serve to make us uncomfortable in the security blanket of our Chief Feature routines. To quote a Parker Dixon Sufi folk song, "Comfort and security just makes them tense." Think about it: Chief Feature has used sight, sound, taste, touch and hearing for its ritual of self-invocation — robbing us of many opportunities. Just realizing this can fuel our wish to take advantage of every possible moment to use sight, sound, taste, touch and hearing for our transformational work.

As for our *Antime*, we cannot fight it; we must join it to form a *Uni-me* which is able to tolerate the waking state. With the development of the *Uni-me*, when we have produced the stabilized waking state, we can enter the Kingdom of Heaven. There's no room for Chief Feature in the Kingdom of Heaven. Substitute "Waking State" for the "Kingdom of Heaven" in the Bible, and think in terms of instruction that Jesus was giving about the waking state, and we find a useful perspective. This potential of the waking state exists for us at any time. We invite the possibility of stabilization, which doesn't mean awake always, as nothing, not even God can remain always awake, but in stabilization we learn to tolerate greater and greater levels of awakening. As a matter of fact, one definition of the Great Work is the tolerance of the waking state.

> *We are a combination of good and evil, light*
> *and dark — we must accept this to get to the*
> *place beyond both.*

When this quality of fusion occurs, there will be no victory for either side in the battle for our soul that starts when we take life form. We are a combination of good and evil, light and dark — we must accept this to get to the place beyond both. And the way *there* is through assimilation and acceptance — a working with rather than working against. It is not a coming together so much as an absorbing of each other, a full inter-polarity.

This state of bipolarity is a good snapshot of God — God is a giant Bipolar Disorder of the Absolute and the Relative. The suffering of the Absolute can be pointed to by the experience "I want to be alone," and then a panic over the intense loneliness. In correcting this within ourselves, we produce a third entity, the *Uni-me*. At this stage the real misery begins, in terms of taking on greater obligation and transformation for tolerance of the waking state to serve the Great Work. In its development, the *Uni-me* will need to further develop the way of going limp, of not fighting, of relaxing as it absorbs a new half of something it, in turn, is part of.

One gets a wisp of endlessness in the possibility of greater degrees of awakening — it staggers the mind, as does Love. For the Lover, the misery brought on by the Beloved is readily borne because all the Lover wants is nearness, service to the Beloved. The move to tolerate greater degrees of awakening cannot be instigated through ordinary Will. One will come under the influence of a higher Will, and here, knowledge of where one borrows Will from is well-advised. This knowledge combined with inner school conditions are strong allies that give us the strength to liberate ourselves from Chief Feature dominance and create a new functioning whole that will better serve the needs of the Work.

Welcome difficulty.

Learn the alchemy True Human Beings know;
the moment you accept what troubles you've been given, the door opens.

Welcome difficulty as a familiar comrade. Joke with torment brought by the Friend.

Sorrows are the rags of old clothes and jackets that serve to cover, and then are taken off.

That undressing, and the beautiful naked body underneath, is the sweetness that comes after grief.

(Barks, *The Illuminated Rumi*, page 77)

Illuminating Sphere
Grace Kelly Rivera
Mixed Media on Prepared Arches Paper, 30"x11"
© 1998 Grace Kelly Rivera

Flight Through the Elements
Grace Kelly Rivera, acrylic on canvas, 50" x 40" © 2011 Grace Kelly Rivera

Topic Six

Handling the Fear of the Waking State

Fear plays a big role in our fixation with the organic, keeping us well-bound to habits of consciousness that support sleep. How do we learn how to handle our fear of the waking state?

" The Feeling of Danger and Fear of Permanent entrapment — being stuck in a macro-reality for what feels like forever — is ever present."
(Gold, *Life in the Labyrinth*, page 171)

It seems there are two emotional tones that can sound in the realm of Essential Being — in the realm of Angelic Being as well. One of these is the longing to help. The other is Fear. When our impulse to help overpowers our fear, we produce good soul-making substance.

Regards the longing to help, there is documented experimentation that was conducted with toddlers — still at an age where conditioning hadn't encrusted Being. A scientist staged situations in which he demonstrated needing help — such as dropping a book. Consistently, toddlers would help him no matter how many times an action took place, so long as the need for help was clear. However, when he would do something to demonstrate that he was asking for help, but didn't really need it — for example, if he threw the book across the room, toddlers would not respond. It seems to me this demonstrates a quality of soul intelligence that is present in all. In the light of such intelligence, we can see that how we are with the world, so it is with us.

When you consider the situation of our Creator, such as we have come to understand it within this school that acknowledges God's suffering, it makes sense that the move to help would exist as part of soul intelligence. Clearly, it points to a quality of the Force of Love. And of course, Angels are all about helping the Lord, though, evidently, they are not without their brand of vanity and other human-like attributes that actually render them readily invoked under the right conditions.

The Man on the Cross, which symbol was around prior to the time of Jesus, can be seen as representing a human being bearing the cross of time and space. From an awakened point of view, that cross is always borne, whether we are conscious of it or not. When one is awakened to the experience of Man on the Cross, one is realizing the "made in God's image" aspect of our human state, and is, in this capacity, able to serve as a lightning rod of sorts enabling God to be momentarily invoked into creation. This, in turn, alleviates a situation of suffering that is a consequence of creation.

The Endless Creator is strapped endlessly to an unconscious creation. With this we come to the other fundamental emotional experience of multidimensions — fear. Only under certain extraordinary conditions are we able to know the experience of being helplessly strapped to an unconscious creation. In this knowing, one feels moved to help at all costs and this help constitutes a part of the great Work. The fundamental move to help is thwarted by the equally pervasive experience of fear.

Fear is with us as the strongest of illusions, moving right up the Jacob's Ladder of existence. The very fact of our experience with physicality, this three-dimensional tactile hallucination, testifies to our willingness to be fooled and distracted away from Reality — fear rides on that willingness and feeds well the illusion of separate identity. Of course, without identification, even just a little, nothing would happen. Our identification with physical reality plays a significant part in offering us the possibility of evolving. Given the theater of manifestation created by identification with physical form, we can identify with the Voyager aspect of our Being, the Angelic, or the strictly human organic. At any level in our development, it seems we are likely to encounter something that at least relates to fear.

I am moved to mention here again the massive idea of Chief Feature. The concept of Chief Feature is present in Fourth Way writings and has more than one meaning. As indicated, to my understanding it is present in all humans starting at a very young age. It is basically an emotional body, bearing some electrical existence, but as completely mechanical in behavior as the human biological machine. It is parasitic and uses the life of the machine for its feeding, like a vampire. It feeds on substances that might otherwise be used for our evolution. The mutual reciprocal initiation process that is possible between the human biological machine and the essential self is disrupted by means of Chief Feature, in that Chief Feature will take over the life of the machine and thus, prevent the essential self from experiencing that life for its development. Chief Feature feeds on our higher being blood and will lead us in our unconsciousness to situations that will increase its food.

A look at a lot of entertainment reveals it is fear-based, playing on the fascination with what frightens as a means of captivating the attention. Look at the amount of energetic disturbance that comes about at a football game. The feeling of all that adrenaline being rushed is sickeningly palpable. That feeling that is called excitement by many rides on a quality of fear. All of those glandular secretions gathered together in one place create a feeding frenzy for Chief Feature.

When humans started gathering together for the purpose of competition, this replaced what might have been gatherings for the purpose of Dear Oobe. Feeding lions replaced worship. Something is invoked in mass gatherings like football games, and that something does not produce radiations or substances useful to work, quite the contrary. That is about all to be said at this point about the wide scope of Chief Feature's influence. We do well to be aware that a repeated unconscious fear reaction might be just the triggering mechanism for the circumstances that lead to feeding Chief Feature. This should add incentive to our work with fear.

Fear-based constructs can be seen within the communication system set up among primates, particularly chimpanzees, where there are a number of reactions that are accepted behavior toward those within their society considered alpha. Bowing the head, extended arms and certain smiles and grimaces are used to display subordination while attempts are made to please the alpha chimp. In this light it is most illuminating to watch one's own facial mask and body postures when dealing with others. On the other end of the spectrum, we will encounter fear reactions to Bardo situations and training for these situations is imperative to one who wishes to maintain the thread of consciousness in transit.

How do we know that we are afraid? We experience sensations triggered by the "flight or fight" mechanisms of the body, long established by the species as well as those conditioned in our lifetimes. We come to identify these clusters of sensations as fear. The experience of anxious expectation eventually can crescendo into full-blown terror. Remove desire for anything and anxious expectation ceases to exist. Cease to have an agenda of your own, including that of separate existence, what is left to fear? In fact, the heart can reach a place of wishing to grow a new life with every breath to annihilate into the Central Sun again and again. These are not just words, they point to an eternal event. All this by way of saying that it seems fear is relative.

One of the habits we are developing in this Work is that of voluntary attention. What is meant by this is the ability to place and keep one's attention on any subject or object at Will without interruption. Working with the fears that are not of the genuine "fight or flight" variety can offer good opportunity at the same time to develop one's voluntary attention. To overcome a fear requires the attention be intentionally placed at least to the degree it takes to be open to a new relationship with the object of fear. Success in part depends upon the ability to override fear reactions with one's will of presence.

When struck by fear without the immediate need for "fight or flight", we can readily take an internal photograph. If one has been working on self and successfully shedding some of the encrustation that impedes waking state living, the attention moves with more facility and potency. Depending upon the quality and actual mass of attention, its intentional placement and focus may be sufficient to act as an effective catalyst for transformation right at that moment of increased tension.

We want to use every possible moment toward our Work, and with practice, have our chronic defenses springboard us into the waking state. Attention placed on those areas in which one finds oneself frightened without the threat of death can yield valuable information to help in our work of releasing these anchors that keep the sleeping state in place. At a bottom line we are always dealing with the fear of death in our trans-formative work because any change implies the death of the old. An ex-perienced voyager will learn how to shape-shift smoothly with minimal resistance.

A fundamental fear of the waking state is that of being stuck in an eternal chamber without such comforts as time passing and company that support the machine's life. Once the HBM is intentionally awakened and then brought back to its comfort zone repeatedly, the machine gets the communication that it will not remain stuck in the awakened state. The chronic defense mechanism against the waking state is thereby dis-charged, being no longer necessary. The machine eventually begins to get the idea that fulfillment is made possible by means of its transfor-mational relationship with the essential self and the new whole this mu-tual reciprocal initiatory process is creating. Fear of the waking state will change with experience. Repeated experience of the waking state even-tually disarms the chronic defenses against it and begins a process of transformation that leads to higher degrees of awakening.

Fear requires some level of identification for its existence. No matter what the kind of chronic defense mechanism, there is present a fear of the waking state. It is useful to observe how this fundamental fear plays out in our lives. To find out what your chronic defense is you need only have someone wake you up suddenly from a deep rest — your very first reaction upon awakening will be the chronic. Most of us are well-aware of our reaction patterns that of course hint at the presence of the chronic. It is useful to see these patterns in the light of fear of the waking state. Perhaps in self-observation we might see our negative states in this light and gain valuable insight.

When we find ourselves agitated by something someone says, we might first note the sensations purely. Repeated observation can eventu-ally expose core beliefs and habits we adopted in response to trauma or strong impression. These beliefs and habits are what hook us into our identification. Somehow we must be brought to the point of wanting to expose these over and above the moment's glittery phenomenal offering. The information to be gleaned is far more important than the situation

— to work at reversing the reality pump, we use what is before us for what counts. What counts is what feeds soul growth. When we pursue the course resolution of the phenomenal for the sake of our ego, it is as though we have chosen to throw away the fruit and eat only its shell. When we find ourselves bereft of soul nutrients, how can there be any wonder?

Obviously, first one must be on a track of wanting waking state living over the win of an argument or situation. One runs this track by habit, habit borne of a deep necessity. Habits require the first step be taken with intent that is renewed with each practice of that habit. The choice is always ours from one perspective — are we going to use this moment here now toward evolution or away from it? But even if we have lost the round and fallen into the muck, if we can even just look back momentarily at what possible threat experienced, how that moment threatened to bring us to a waking state, we might catch a glimpse under the glitter of the drama. At the root of all drama is the play of much ado about nothing.

At the root of all drama is the play of much ado about nothing.

In my own practice, I see that when I follow the sensations of fear down, often they are to be found in the area of the solar plexus and/or heart energy centers. Placement of the right quality of attention and its focus will often reveal the energy blockage producing the sensations of fear. It was, after all, my relentless confrontation of fear that led to the state of Dear Oobe. As Rumi indicates, we all have ego wounds that draw the flies of our self-protective feelings to it — a Teacher will wave away those flies. We are asked to keep looking at the wound, because eventually that is where the light will come through.

I remember in the film *Strictly Ballroom*, the male lead is being shown something about flamenco dance, where the rhythm must be felt is here, says the grandmother showing him, placing the hand on the solar plexus area. She says, "Don't be afraid." Years after seeing this film I was performing flamenco and suddenly had the experience of feeling the rhythm right there with a rush of energy, but more, feeling something essential to my own Being at the same time — it propelled me in space with a jolt of electrical energy. I got a picture of the contrasting way I normally operate, within a small range that is kept in place by the sensation of fear. Fear in this regard is like attempting to disallow God from being the individualized expression I am.

I followed E.J. up to Canada from New York and participated in some earth-shattering workshops. I never made it back to work after the first weekend, having called in dead ironically, to my job at Windows on the World on top of the World Trade Tower 2. I was asked to create a poster for a workshop — the key phrase written on the poster was *Pas de Panic* . . . don't panic. It's okay to have fear; what gets us into trouble is reacting to it, panicking with a sudden move. This is a good little piece — the reality of the illusion of fear is definitely going to be there, at least for awhile, but we are given the grace of knowing we can let it exist without reacting to it.

It reminds me a bit of the approach offered when I asked about something relative to Prayer of the Heart, and I mentioned in passing the obstacle of head brain chatter. E.J. asked why I would want to stop it. It's just like a muscle spasm — the thing to do is increase the attention, learn to grow the attention and place it on the heart, for example. At one point he asked, "How about the breath?" indicating that attention could be simply focused on the natural breath as a means of moving around the head brain muscle spasm.

Attention must be trained and developed voluntarily to be effective in our evolutionary Work. We want to develop Work habits that replace those habits that keep us bound to our fixation with organic life — this will require the power of our voyager attention to accomplish. Fear plays a big role in our fixation with the organic, keeping us well-bound to habits of consciousness that support sleep. It seems the best attention training for between-lives voyaging happens precisely in the conditions which appear chaotic and counter to those that support meditative, contemplative life. We do want to know that place of stillness and silence within, but let the path be found while in the maelstrom so that we are well-trained. As has been said around here — make friends with resisting force — that resistance is a great strengthening agent.

In spiritual warfare a lot of courage is needed because we are repeatedly confronting fear. There are different types of fear to be found at different levels of Being, as has been indicated. On the flip side, however, fear has the potential of bringing us to the interior altar where Dear Oobe is performed, if we follow its thread. This is actually employed in one method of Dear Oobe. An activity one might do is to allow the fertile imagination that exists in all of us to work on behalf of our Work. Bring up a small fear, then with all the power of one's inner theater, conjure up that thing vividly in the mind's eye, taking it to its fearful conclusion, confronting it all the way through to the other side, from the dark to light. I would advise one proceed with caution as this technique can be incredibly effective and life-altering. This fundamentally is what happens in certain so-called primitive cultures within their rites of passage — the voyager is caused to confront a situation of fear, the passing of which endows one with a fresh power that fundamentally has to do with Attention and Presence and Will.

With the confrontation or absorption of fear, we gain the energy that has been used in sustaining the illusion. That energy which is really our consciousness brings us closer to energetic resonance that might bring about awakening. I am brought here to another big and useful idea.

The human biological machine as an electrical entity will produce negative force just as a consequence of its existence. This negative force accumulates at different points of the machine's electrical field as it is regularly produced. Between the places of accumulation of negative force are created lines of tension, in keeping with their electrical nature. If we were able to maintain these tensions to a place of equilibrium, we could be given force to bring the machine into the waking state. But typically, what occurs is that we blow the energy at a certain point. Our pain comes about because we must then rebuild these lines of tension again, as the negative force will continue to be created by the machine and accumulate in various parts of its electrical field. To break this cycle we must find a way of getting past our boiling point, because just on the other side of our false barrier is the waking state. The waking state offers us sanctuary from the pain of building and destroying these lines of tension over and again.

Everyone will have his or her own formulation of it, but one of the fundamental things we are avoiding through our fear reactions is the knowledge, the deep inner knowledge, that all phenomena really is illusion and that at some level, at the God level, "I had nothing but myself with which to make the world, out of myself the world was made." All we are confronting is our own play of consciousness, which play is sometimes hide and sometimes seek. When we hide, we cover ourselves with as much phenomena as possible, including the sensation of fear, so that the secret is kept. But with this we invite a corresponding longing to expose, to rend the veils and know the secret. Longing is good when it spurs us to obliterate our fear with passion for freedom.

All we are confronting is our own play of consciousness,
which play is sometimes hide and sometimes seek.

We must get to know fear in the many forms it can take. Another little life story seems appropriate here. When I was a kid the skateboard first came out and the early ones were rather crude, no more than steel roller skating wheels on boards. We lived within walking distance of my elementary school in a huge apartment project, and the playground there was a place where kids would gather after school. There was a hill made of asphalt where cars would drive between the back upper parking lot and through the nicely tarred play area. The hill was quite steep and that's where kids would take their skateboards which would go really fast, but with lots of room to slow down once you hit the relatively smooth play area. I wanted to learn to do that, and I was really afraid. So I started first at the bottom of the hill, and every day after school I would apply myself to inching my way up a little bit more, until finally the day came when I was riding my skateboard all the way down from the very top.

But one day I went down from the top, made it all the way to the bottom fine and was cruising along, when I saw in front of me a bottle cap that I knew was going to trip me — my consciousness was altered; it must have accelerated, thereby causing everything to go into slow motion. From that accelerated consciousness and the objectified perspective, there was plenty of room for movement off the collision course, yet it seemed I was destined to hit that bottle cap and could not break from this path, despite the seeming room to move. Interestingly, in that state there was no fear involved and I watched the whole thing with a sense of wonder and a high indifference. It seems the intentional aspect of this activity, the fact that I had deliberately, slowly faced my fear, opened my consciousness up to such a state of impartiality. Another possible thing to have been demonstrated here was the lack of development of my Will of Attention as an essential self at that time. As an Essential Being, I was present, attentive and impartial but without the will over the machine to control the action.

Steady steps, even if baby at first, are wanted in our work with fear. It seems to me one reason the school has provided so many different avenues and tools for work is to offer as many different types of folks as possible an opportunity to overcome obstacles to work that invariably will involve fear. If one can get over fear of blowing the Zen flute, and all the considerations and blockages found within, then those same skills can be applied to working with the waking state — because, in fact, one is working one's way to a waking state in the practice.

When we hit the place of fear, we do well merely to see it for what it is, which will require impartial observation. Anger is a mask that fear will wear readily — it is intended to keep us from experiencing the humiliation felt over having fear. We need to experience fear in its raw form, that is, as the set of sensations it is. We want to establish a habit of impartial self-observation, which resonates with the natural state of the essential self. It is possible to train oneself to react to a frightening situation with peace and lucidity. In dreams, when one finally confronts the monster, the calm clarity of the aftermath is delicious. I recall E.J. giving a psychologist advice about doing art therapy with children that had witnessed a traumatic event. He said not to be surprised to find some of the children painting pictures of themselves smiling when asked to draw what they saw — they may have been propelled by the shock into an out of body state, and/or a state of profound calm and peace.

Our most accessible point from which to begin this process of observation is with our moving center manifestations. We have the ability to focus our attention on the sensations of fear, to isolate and experience them as sensations. The beauty is that when these masses are unraveled, they release energy that can be applied to waking consciousness.

There is a wonderful exercise given as part of the mask workshop E.J. created years ago. We were given a lump of clay that was hard and needed to be softened and warmed to the place of pliability. To gather the energy needed to "warm the soul", as was indicated, we were led through a meditation that had us gathering our scattered energy deposited in past experiences, like a trail of toys a child has left behind. This clearly demonstrated to me the fact that attention has substance and can increase in potency, in mass. In fact, that is often what is difficult for folks to deal with — the amount of energy that can course through when there is release of a blockage and a reclamation of attention. One has to learn how to deal with this level of energy, how to manage it.

In birthing, the mother experiences an intense amount of energy and sensation. Given the distance from natural process that our society has conditioned in us, an expectant mother does well to train, if possible. The attention is thus trained to open up to that intensity, allow the work of the contractions to do what is intended, which is to push the baby out. It is good training in learning how to open up when the impulse might be to recoil. And one is given a tremendous feeling of the sanctity and responsibility of providing an open portal through which the Being can make entry into the world. Here it is clear to see how obligation to something outside of oneself, bigger than oneself can help us overcome our limitations.

At one point, while working with an intense contraction in my daughter's birthing, I visualized myself as the Lord birthing creation and just this little exercise revealed something to me that no other set of circumstances could have revealed. Point is, those times of heightened intensity in our lives can be used to work effect if one has the presence and work habit to do so. One practices daily for readiness to use such moments. The evolutionary play is going to take place in the theater of one's own life provided one's life has met the conditions necessary for evolution.

The little seemingly insignificant habits we have are actually quite important to look at because they hold the postural keys that keep us bound to our organic fixations. In some cases, we might even catch glimpse of their relevance to Chief Feature. When working with even one small habit, we begin a process of creating space from which to observe our character. By starting with our small fear-based habits, we build our strength of Will toward confronting the bigger fears we might have. We might see our fears represented in their more diluted form and perhaps expressed as anger or confusion at first. Bringing what consciousness we can muster into these patterns repeatedly, eventually can lead us to their points of origin.

If one is able to do so, periodically spending time late at night quietly in front of a candle with no agenda, but presence can be quite valuable. I have found that the veils seem a bit more flimsy in this kind of situation and as a consequence, one might see barriers to the waking state present themselves more clearly. If we can keep our gaze steady on our fear obstacle rather than react to it, merely hanging with it, looking at it, we might gradually strengthen our Will to Work through to the other side. This relates to the aforementioned lines of tension. Invoking presence is also called for here — we can offer the energetic intensity that might arise as a sacrifice in exchange for the presence of our presence with the radiation to dissolve the impediment. One thing about being here now — there's just "is-ness". Problems require past and future to occur. In invoking the presence of one's presence into the present, one is utilizing a particular and fundamental attribute of the Absolute relative to change. It is indicated that a universe changes by way of absorption — the old is absorbed into the new, and one universe is replaced by another.

> *When we invoke presence successfully any*
> *significance of sleep is absorbed, replaced*
> *by presence.*

One replaces one habit with another — that is how change of habit comes about. The habits that keep us bound to organic life and its fixations can potentially be replaced with habits that support our awakening and work. But before we can find our way out, we must see our way through. Whole body attention will give us information about where our tensions are held, and impartial observation of these tensions especially at key moments of intensity will produce change. To change the automatic habitual reaction to even just one recurring event can give us the space to breathe a slightly different atmosphere we eventually learn to prefer. At some point we might begin to see our habitual investments of energy for the diversions that they actually are.

We learn to adopt deliberate voluntary habits of attention. Conservation of precious energy needed for our work is reason enough to change the habit of allowing ourselves to identify with and lend energy to the negative dramas that are played out in the mind. These are often fear-based, and we can see this for ourselves, if we can catch and follow down the thread of their origin. There is a simple thing we are asked to do — that is *to be present in the moment*. The more we can remember this and all it encompasses, the better off we will be. To produce or be seduced by the mechanical, negative scenarios played out by the mind is a foolish waste of energy.

When we carry around unnecessary tension, using more force than necessary for simple physical maneuvers, we feed our unconscious habits of posture, often adopted originally as a fear reaction. By practicing conservation of energy, keeping in mind the energy we need for our work, we shift the center of gravity away from unconscious habit. Whole body attention and a growing cooperative relationship with the moving center that enables us to relax tension will serve as good replacement habits to our unconsciousness.

As has been indicated in Fourth Way writings — we would conserve a lot of energy by eliminating what is unnecessary, which in the realm of emotions can be called worry or anxiety. These are given expression through moving instinctive tension and unnecessary movement. In the intellect, waste of energy takes the form of unproductive thinking and commentary that we, in our identification, confuse with reality. One good question to ask ourselves when lost in speculation about potential disaster especially: Is it true? This question might help us adopt new habits of verification.

We are well-advised to learn new postures of response to our fear, postures that feed awakening, Often this means tactfully moving into the storm. To be able to make efforts of this kind, we need some support, some substantiation which is to be gained through experience in the waking state. When we learn how to take good advantage of the Moments of Freedom, the moments of opportunity that give us awakening experience, this will gives us a place from which to push off into new directions of response to fear triggers. In some cases, awakening experience will render these triggers no longer operational.

I would like to emphasize here that much support is needed in this kind of work. But that support is not necessarily going to be given in the way that one might perceive. The knowledge of how to create conditions that will engage the voluntary attention of the essential self, that discourage the wrong kind of feeding, is exact and at the same time it is an art.

Especially when dealing with matters around fear, which can get to very core areas of our Being, we must take care to put ourselves into situations that genuinely support our Work. We must educate ourselves and find our way to the place where the Will and support we need is available. This means: *Know thyself* — and as often is the case, know thyself can translate into know what one is not. Fear can point this out in high relief and if used well, will cut a path to our awakening beyond the boundaries it creates.

Luna Del Sueno
Grace Kelly Rivera
Mixed Media on Prepared Arches Paper, 30"x11"
© 1998 Grace Kelly Rivera

Tree Shadow
Grace Kelly Rivera, oil on canvas, 48" x 48" © 2011 Grace Kelly Rivera

Topic Seven

Repaying One's Debt to Nature

How (by what action) does one repay one's debt to nature prior to taking back one's substance to use for inner transformation?

"We must pay to Work."
                    (*The Pump, The Physical Body*: A talk by E.J. Gold)

One of the many advantages to this work of producing material for the Oobe show has been the exposure to Work ideas proven timely and most nourishing to my own evolutionary process. In particular, the idea of the physical body as a pump has offered a perspective that I return to again and again.

The body can be viewed as a pump in its ordinary function of making real the outside world by taking the inner-sourced finer matter and pumping it to the outer. This is as nature intended — humankind functions as a cosmic apparatus, a membrane of sorts, for the process of making the outer world more real. Quite basically, humans take food and make shit, in the objective sense, as they convert the finer to the gross. Crossing rivers in terms of one's evolution involves the reversal of this process — taking dense matter and processing it such that it makes food for the higher. Everything is material. Our Work is to take everything back from the world we gave it and send it back up in the direction of the higher. In this way we experience the truth of the mantra "There is no reality but God. God is the only Reality."

As we redirect our attention inward, under the appropriate alchemical conditions, bodies of different rates of vibration are produced. The different Being bodies — the astral, mental and causal grow such that each functions as a shell within which the respectively rarefied bodies are created. The astral body is created within the shell of the physical body while the mental is within the shell/encasement of the astral and so on, each body requiring the pushing or denying force accumulated and made cohesive in the process of making the outer inner, the inner outer, the two one. The outer active must be made passive, the inner passive must be made active, and these results combined create denying force for the subsequent body. Each body is of more rarefied material, slightly decreased in size than the shell or encasement in and out of which it is produced.

Basically, humans like the situation of receiving energy and converting it to the gross. In this condition the would-be astral body serves as denying force for the Physical Body. It is denying force rather than active that serves as the pushing force in the process of pump reversal, pushing the energy back in to be sent up. The evolution of the astral body has the possibility of occurring when the outer world has become the denying force. The outer becoming passive gives this pushing force, the inner becoming active attracts denying/pushing force to it, then the two become one, unified as denying force for the mental body.

Let's remember we are looking at a model describing a phenomenon that can only be pointed at with language. A Completed Being will have developed certain characteristics, such as Higher Being Bodies, and there is a set of cumulative conditions that can be made sequential in description, but we do well to keep ourselves at a distance from linear interpretation of this process.

Just as we exist multi-dimensionally and in parallel worlds, the ongoing developments described will not necessarily follow a pattern our time-line thinking would have us conceive. It has been indicated in the past relative to the *Brother Judas* ceremonies which mark seven definite stages of development of Divine Being, that they are ongoing, recurring in the divine life every "year", yet describing the process of completion. The same holds true for the Sacrifices in *The Joy of Sacrifice**, so it seems that "completion" does not necessarily mean permanence as we might understand it.

The development of the Being Bodies will bear a similar ongoing quality, not sequential in the same sense that we experience moving through grade school from grade one to twelve. We may have experience of the astral body prior to our realizing the steady ability to make the outer world passive. At the same time, it seems when we are brought to the place of humility and emptiness of anything, save the wish swiftly to know the Great Return, the Beloved gives as much as we can possibly receive. Profound changes can seem to take place within the confines of short-lived experiences. Transmission tends to be silent. I say this to help us take away some of the grandiosity that might be implied — these ideas become alive in a profound and subtle way that is easily covered over by the ordinary circumstances that form their context.

The means of doing, taking the results of the outer to feed the inner, reclaiming the energy given to solidity and form and sending it back up to feed the higher, is not to be found in outer change. Outer change might become a necessity to enable expanding manifestations for Completed Being, but one starts exactly as one is, within the structure of one's life.

If misery is what we have, we use that misery as fuel for disengagement from the reality structure upon which that misery is based. In effect, this is what happened to me when I came upon Prayer Absolute prior to meeting E.J. in New York. The circumstances that led to the energetic launch into the waking state that night were quite ordinary — I had just gotten home from waitressing and was doing some drawing at my drawing table when I became aware of, once again, the fear that seemed to be in every frame of the movie of my life. And I got sick of it — sick to the death of it. This state of Being, completely fed up with my fear, launched me into my contemplation about fear, and moving into the storm, I discovered the path of Prayer Absolute. This brought me to a place that required I make further change in order to fulfill the evolutionary obligation such an experience bestows upon one. That change was to move out to California and live in school conditions. But it all started within the circumstances of my life just as it was.

To back track a bit here, in speaking of expanding manifestations, I am referring to an idea that the total possible manifestations required for Completed Being are symbolized in the Tarot. These are found in the physical (wands), emotional (cups), mental (swords), and in essence (pentacles). It is indicated that as a Completed Being, one has the capacity for all manifestations represented in the Tarot archetypes. Our fluidity of movement through postures — whether they be of physical, emotional, or mental nature, or lack thereof, can give us a good gauge and handle. Moving toward archetype helps disengage from the particulars into the realm of the whole.

We might be given good indication of where we are relative to a basic requirement for Divine Being — to endure the unpleasant manifestations of others toward oneself and others — by our increasing or decreasing ability to voluntarily adopt all possible postures. This skill set will be made clear in our ability to communicate and interact with many different types. Effective communication requires one sit with another, wherever he or she may be, bringing that person from this place to the vision one is communicating. When we are steeped in identification with our own typicality and its agenda, we will invariably find ourselves at odds with other typicalities around us, resisting those manifestations we find unpleasant to be around, but which, nevertheless, might comprise some of the possible postures that contribute to Completed Being. Evolutionary change can, to some degree, be indicated in one's ability to communicate with people of different typicalities.

There are a couple of things going on here. First, there is chemistry — we simply have chemical reactions to other types. Overcoming habitual reactions that are based upon identification with our own typicality can pry us loose from its grip. We want the fluidity suggested here because it is essential to work in the macrodimensions.

Secondly, we are going into the partial space of judgment, disabling the quality of consciousness that sees and functions in archetype. So when we are in identification with and resistant to any of these possible archetypal manifestations, there is indication for work, the opportunity for transcendence of our own type. Gaining impartiality precisely at those times when another's manifestations are at the most unpleasant can give one significant momentum in their work toward freedom from the boundaries of typicality. This perspective may at times help in grabbing hold of the ability to establish conditions of pump reversal, which indicates a process of dying before we die.

In reversing the pump, we lose our identification with the world and the desires of the body for the things of that world. There is detachment without disgust. Rather, there is interest in what is happening in the moment, one is interested highly, but not highly interested. We are describing here a symptom of the results that occur when the body loses desire, which in itself also happens symptomatically of other action and conditional factors.

We can use the description of these symptoms to *as if.* There is the cessation of urgency, but not activity. This is key — the cessation of urgency — even the urgency to lose our urgency. Sensing our urgency will inform us of the Work we have to do — we can be led to what helps animate the outer world, the tensions that maintain the hypnosis of separate identity. We awaken to the fundamental creative act that lies behind this urgency by dying to the urgency, identification and importance. In this dying a good deal of energy is released, just as at death.

In reversing the pump, we lose our identification with the world and the desires of the body for the things of that world.

Thus, we make the outer form passive for the astral. The correct alchemy requires the inner to be in total upheaval while the outer remains passive. The turmoil has to be about something important, not ordinary, something like a Center of Gravity question. A Center of Gravity question is a temporary intentional god, of sorts, that one has established for oneself, and all of one's life serves in relationship to this question. One can hold six or seven Center of Gravity questions at once, each producing the alchemical catalyst needed to begin to develop real "I," addressing transformational needs of our mental, emotional and moving /instinctive centers.

The original question is: "How (by what action) does one repay one's debt to nature prior to taking back one's substance to use for inner transformation?" In order to take everything back, that is, EVERYTHING back that we have given the world, we must substitute our death in payment to nature. At death there is a tremendous release of energy and this energy has to be accounted for — we must somehow pay to be free to die in a different way. It seems the solution lies somewhere in the vicinity, if not right smack dab in the center of dying before we die. Dying before we die, we voluntarily pay our debt to great Nature and give up our place and significance prior to death at our own rate of passage.

Speaking practically, this means we have adopted and are daily substantiating the posture of pump reversal and thus, use experience in such a way that enacts our dying before we die. There are skills and certain impulses required for this to be done effectively. Given the power of present moment living, and the right attitude, with knowledge, we will find Moments of Freedom when big movement can take place in seemingly small and ordinary ways. For example, we find that we have gotten into an argument with someone, waking up just enough to see that we've allowed identification to bring us to this level of transaction. At that moment we can die, just die and go utterly limp, no longer participating in the resistance or identification that is needed to argue. This may also translate into making choices that go against the grain of mechanical life, for example, giving up wealth and position in order that one might spend more focused time on the development of more subtle faculties.

Around here there has been an expression used — eat shit and die. In light of the reversal of the pump, it makes perfect sense. Our lower centers are conditioned to make the outer world active. Our unconscious responses are often the result of trauma that is based on this fundamental arrangement of active outer to passive inner. In bringing some of these unconscious responses to consciousness without identification, we have the hope of reclaiming the choice point and reprogramming ourselves to respond consciously toward the higher. If we have the Work Will to make passive the outer, and further, to observe the resulting inner reactions, we might gain in our ability to process and refine.

If we haven't the Work Will necessary to engage this process effectively, we must borrow it. A school is a place in which the Work Will can be borrowed. One is given conditions that are ripe for evolution, which include factors of a radiological nature, the correct kind of stress to produce the alchemical effects required of the transformational apparatus, and a strong necessity that counters normally weak intention. Conditions of necessity, peer pressure, Teacher scrutiny and other such factors produce a splint of sorts that will keep us responding straight when we might otherwise go crooked. In this way we open up correspondingly new neural network pathways.

We want to facilitate expedient use of our outer lives as food for our Higher Being Bodies. Electrical anomalies and crystallized postures may be in place that block or impact this process. Typically, we develop a certain limited number of manifestations or postures within any given center. In an ideal situation a child is exposed to every possible range of typicality and manifestation in order that she might learn through mimicry, and thus have the fluidity this suggests. Generally in our culture we learn from parents and caretakers certain postures and remain with these alone unless we intentionally seek development.

A person may have a wide palette of feeling tones; however, that feeling may be solely produced by the emotional part of the intellectual center, the emotional center being completely undeveloped. It may take repeated impressions or shocks of a particular kind to get through, to break the habitual postures and begin to communicate to the actual center new information. Without the special kind of help that a school can provide, what often happens or passes for development is simply a new configuration of the same limited number of postures held in the various centers. We need discernment to know what we are feeding just as we need discernment to know whether or not we are awake.

To die before we die indicates sacrificing identity and dealing a little at a time with the resulting rawness of our Primordial Being, which is profoundly alive, in a state of perpetual change. To become aware of and develop our ability to manifest postures as an objective actor potentially helps us in the sacrificing of identity, breaking us free from the confines of our limited repertoire of posture and manifestation. This ability to be fluid in our postures also gives us a form of feedback as to how close we are to the pointless mark of freedom.

Our adopted postures will often be inclined toward one center or another and a life lived in this manner of taking in impressions through the filters of these postures can create a situation of basically burning out a center, using the energetic potential up by imbalanced overuse of one center. One excellent exercise given for helping to repair this situation is the recapitulation of salient points of one's day at its end. These scenes are passed through three times, as seen through the moving instinctive, emotional and intellectual centers. In this way we reclaim consciousness and encourage balanced functioning of the centers.

To break through, actually to know transformation, requires the clay become soft, malleable. We make friends with denying force, which is really our ally enabling us to realize our evolution. Initially, we work to observe impartially, so that with data and help, this process of reprogramming becomes possible. By means of conditions produced by the Expert and group, I have been delivered compassionate shocks where needed to break down walls established by habit, thereby enabling new impressions to come through. In school conditions, with the example of the Teaching and the sense of work purpose that the Teacher can give, help is given in making Work choices at times of stress. These choices repeatedly made become habit, work habit that gradually replaces habits of sleep. We build a Work life.

Dead is dead. When we are working with this idea of dying before we die, we can ask ourselves if our activity reflects dying to the outer. We are given a good hint of our position by the presence or absence of urgency. When one is dead, there is no urgency, obviously. Urgency is a quality that will be present in relationship to our outer lives, dependent upon future and past living as opposed to present moment living. If we can maintain a sensing awareness of our HBM, paying particular attention to places of tension that might indicate the presence of urgency, we are given good ground for transformational practice.

Now, I have watched E.J. outwardly manifest with what someone might interpret as urgency, but given even a bit of discernment one will experience that in fact his manifestations are clean without the quality of reverberation that the same manifestations *involuntarily* made can produce.

I was once given what seemed like good insight. We were putting together a little chocolate gift for a friend of mine who seems to be open to some ideas. There was a specific tissue paper he wanted that was supposed to be located where a lot of other things are stored. There was a lot of intensity as we searched in the storage area, and a persistence that I alone would likely not have ordinarily mustered for the occasion. At one point he indicated that we wanted to find the tissue paper and complete the gift wrapping right away rather than postpone it, in order not to lose the momentum of the action. What he said was informative, yes, but there was something about his presence when he said it that seemed to take me to another place energetically — a new light went on. To one who is dead to the world, helping others in their achievement of this pump reversal, the motivation for activity will be differently sourced. In that moment I saw force and energy, and his manifestations were clearly a product of that energetic perspective, he was sculpting energy. In this light I was able to see him handling the force, aligning with the favorable work momentum created through my friend's state of receptivity.

We need energy for our work, and awareness of our energetic exchanges helps us in enlivening the inner over the outer. Long-established habits can serve situations of energy leakage and it behooves us to repair these leaks as expediently as possible. It is advised to begin by observing moving center manifestations. Invocational work is largely moving center-based. Posture will lead to mood in acting. An awakened Human Biological Machine is in effect invisible, passive to whatever being bodies present, whatever gradation of reason. At a biological level, it requires a particular balance between serotonin and melatonin for awakening. We are advised to eat physical food that is highly nutritious to our particular body while requiring the minimal amount of energy for conversion to nutrients, yielding the maximum amount of energy for work.

Impactions in either processing or elimination of by-products of nutritional elements will of course affect the chemistry balance. If our body is taking in dense food that is difficult to process, this will reflect in our chemistry and ability to awaken. We do well to know ourselves from this viewpoint. Impaction and the resulting density will keep us strapped to lower center habits. Much valuable energy for work can be gained by giving this issue impartial attention, just as you would examine a machine of any kind that wasn't working right to see if you might get it to work properly again. When we can find the energy leaks, much of the battle is won because often it is simply in acknowledging their existence that the mending takes place, and we learn how to die to the identity that has those energetic leaks as part of its makeup in the process.

We awaken by removing obstacles to the waking state rather than imposing Will in the ordinary sense of the word.

Again, it behooves us to know ourselves from the point of view of our postures. An individual might not have but two possible postures accepted and present in the moving center, and it might take the prescription of repeated hard labor in the garden before finally that person is open to receiving fresh impressions in that center. An Expert can observe much about an individual's condition, with instincts toward work that are razor sharp. We need scrutiny, direct observation by someone with genuine knowledge, who can determine what the best healing route might be for us. If we are looking for exotic remedies, this will likely not be the place to get them, but if we take the remedies given, they will prove effective.

The question was raised about the risk of one center dying before the others, thereby creating a situation where work is not possible. First, there likely is an answer or more than one answer to the question of how one knows when one center has died — with genuine necessity, one can find this out. What I want to indicate here is that there are some school ideas that seem to be presented as a means of offering an expanded view of what's possible, in this case, perhaps serving to put a small fire under our tail brains. In this culture of consumerism there is a tendency to take for granted accessibility to resources — and we are not given much reason to consider our body/mind/spirit complex as a valuable resource and commodity. To have our attention pointed to what we have as something worthy of careful consideration is most appropriate.

Hope does not seem to be the thing to inspire as it suggests future, and with that we are brought out of the present moment. Inspiration is to be found in this here now. To the degree that the question: "How do we know when a center has died?" betters the ability to be here now, the question serves. We must allow our deepest necessity to guide us. We start exactly where we are, and enter with presence into our outer life willingly, at the same time rendering, through our Work Will, that life passive to the active inner. Dying before we die is not a grim thing. In fact, it is a process that opens us up to a greater capacity for life force.

The Mystery of Renunciation

*Some clouds do not obscure the moon, and there are mornings when
drops of rain descend from an open sky.*
A saint is a cloud that's here, but with its cloud nature erased.
*Something in us wants no intermediary, no nurse, just to be the wide
blue merged with the mother's breast, sublime emptiness.*
*There is a way of leaving the world that nourishes the world. Don't
do anything for applause. Khidr scuttled the fisherman's boat, but that
demolishing was kindness.*
*What you are is a soul that is both food and hunger, longing and what
the longing is for.*
Remember that, and try then to experience renunciation.
(Barks, The Soul of Rumi, page 243)

The *Invocation of Presence* exercise offers a perfect formula for the
process of dying to our identity. I wish to use this to feed the invocation
of the Presence of my Presence into the Present — in this elegant formula
we create an altar upon which to sacrifice the machine reality of the moment for the reality of the presence of our presence in the present moment. We exchange one life for another through detachment from the
phenomenal thus freeing what belongs to Nature and using our creative
free will toward our return to Source.

Given the perspective of expanding our ability to assume postures,
one can see the necessity to at times stop the world as we usually know
it and try something that dissolves postures enough to allow fresh impressions to be taken in. Starting with moving center work is recommended and to that end there are a number of possible paths — not least
of which is Spirit Dance.

Spirit Dance is a practice developed by E.J. in which one allows the
body to move freely to loops of music of his composition, using the beat
as a point of focus and working to move without falling into habitual
postures of social dancing one may have developed. Such phrases as
"riding the wave" and "dancing between air pockets" are used to point

to the flavor of the inner space one wants to get to where eventually one is one with the "beat." Spirit Dance helps in the development of so many factors including the quality of sensing that can help us to work with the idea of conservation of energy more effectively. By means of Spirit Dance, there can be made a connection with those electrical anomalies that may block our ability to reverse the pump. As a practice it also serves as a way in which energy can be reclaimed that has been lost through misaligned associations. We have plenty of energy available to us if we can learn to conserve and accumulate it to meet the needs of our work.

There is an ebb and flow to all of this and we each have our own rate of passage.

There are so many factors to keep us earthbound, dense, away from a more objective quality of perspective, at the mercy of our machine attention. Of late I have been refining the ability to surrender to the state of non-surrender. I was once told, in response to my question about surrender, that there is no such thing as a wrong way to do so. Either one is surrendered or not, but there will be degrees, stages of surrender. It seems sometimes the secret needs to keep itself so that it can be revealed to our best advantage in due course. There is also such a thing as periodicity, one is given the opportunity to plant Grief Seeds so that we can know the experience of being human and transform it.

How Will You Know the Difficulties of Being Human?

How will you know the difficulties of being human if you're always flying off to blue perfection?
Where will you plant your grief-seeds?
We need ground to scrape and hoe, not the sky of unspecified desire.
(Barks, *The Illuminated Rumi*, page 75)

In one of the *Brother Judas* ceremonies for the manufacture of Divine Being is stated — "I see Death, I know Death, I am Death — take Death and make it life as you would take evil and make it good." When we reflect on our changing understanding of an idea or practice, we can see that we have lived lives and died deaths, turned over the refuse and made blossoms. The sacrifices described in *The Joy of Sacrifice* are a means of consciously changing the habits that bind the psyche to habits appropriate to Completed Being. Sacrifice has much to do with voluntary "death".

The Crystal Quartz Radio Technology (CQR Technology) is useful in our work to die before we die. With the cumulative effects of gathering our parallel universe personas, clarification and the corresponding expansion of experience in a wider range of possibility, it becomes easier to create space between ourselves and what we once perceived of as our identity. With this comes the possibility of aligning ourselves to paths of elegant death and rebirth cycles. There is readier acceptance of living as a work in progress.

When one undergoes frequent voluntary death cycles, there is less impulse to solidify identity and a new identity that is flexible emerges. The flexibility can be tricky when one is working to have a foot in both worlds. Until one gets one's sea legs, so to speak, the trip can prove stunningly rocky. At times it seems other things want to take up the space of emptiness, fill the void readily, and one needs enough strength of presence to be vigilant. But this vigilance is not military. There is another quality of consciousness, that again, is more fluid and open, which is wanted.

In my own experience with Parallel World Personas, it seems things happen indirectly. I have had numerous experiences in parallel universes. The guidance I've been given in response to and as a product of these experiences prescribes a subtle form of discipline. This discipline calls more for non-action than action — maintaining as best I can a state of active receptivity. It has been said that the Work is like a woman, that God is best described in terms of embodiment by woman, and I believe it is the ideal principle of active receptivity that is being invoked by this chosen symbol. When you look at birthing, a woman does well to be with her breath and take advantage of the contractions to help, opening and allowing the intensity to wash on through, waiting and relaxing as best as possible in between the contractions. To me it describes an excellent way to live and work.

One universe changes by dissolution into a new universe. Dissolution of one form into another suggests an approach to our voluntary work. Nothing is possible without discipline, but our approach to discipline might warrant examination. We want to have the quality of self-observation available to us that will give us the intimacy and discernment needed to know when and how to apply ourselves. First, we build discipline in a number of ways — by maintaining practices and simultaneously obligating ourselves to the needs of the Work, and by gaining enough vision and experience to inspire our effort. With the development of real "*I*" we will find ourselves losing the control we imagined ourselves to have, but at the same time there will be the developing presence of absence enough to respond to the Work calling, bringing us where needed when necessary.

Dissolution of one form into another suggests an approach to our voluntary work.

It is easy for a human to develop pride or other form of attachment to a practice or discipline, and this can mask itself as our dearest foothold on our work. The development of conscience constrains us in a particular direction. It becomes essential to develop our voyager attention and discernment to recognize the signs of attachment. Somehow we want to get to the place of disengaging that attachment and dissolving into a new identity that is freed of that attachment.

We can see just in this aspect of the process of dying before we die, how it is that the guidance of an Expert becomes quite necessary. We can develop attachment to a form of service as well as fall into the deadly trap of pride of service. Rumi says, "We should always pray for discipline." Just as we can develop a range of awareness that gives us a pseudo impression of wakefulness, we can fool ourselves in the line of duty. Let us take care to look for some scrutiny of our work. This is a Tavern where you hand the Tavern Keeper a gun and ask him to hold it to your head to make you drink what quenches soul thirst.

We will learn something new in place of willfulness in dying before we die. As Rumi says, "One closes the mouth here to open up with a shout of joy in another realm" — if we can remember this, perhaps we can shimmy our way into higher functionality.

Learning to die before we die is learning to surrender.

Offering service in terminal midwifery can be valuable in this process for the obvious reason that we will find guidance relative to death and rebirth and navigating through the Bardos. With this study supplementing our work with the process of dying before we die might learn to recognize and voluntarily bathe in the cleansing radiations needed to remove our obstructions. To those with the eyes to see, radiations can be found in everyday life. Learning to die before we die is learning to surrender — we are surrendering what we borrowed of the outer life, leaving us naked and completely open to the pain of life in form so that "the uncreated can be one with the created," as indicated in the *Brother Judas* ceremonies. There is love — and death comes as a lover. There is the beauty of the sweet emptiness our essence longs for.

Emptiness

Essence is emptiness.Everything else accidental.
Emptiness brings peace to your loving. Everything else, disease.
In this world of trickery, emptiness is what your soul wants.
(Barks, *The Soul of Rumi*, page 31)

And there are all the stages in between as we reverse our pump, cutting our path to the Heart of the Maker.

Mujer
Grace Kelly Rivera, acrylic on canvas, 72" x 36"
© 2011 Grace Kelly Rivera

Topic Eight

The Sacrifice of Comfort

In track 6 of Disc 2 of the CD titled Habits, *E.J. mentions that the 18 sacrifices he "outlined" in the book* The Joy of Sacrifice *are a system for creating new habits. Is there any additional material detail that can elucidate the first sacrifice, The Sacrifice of Comfort, which you can add or find in his work?*

From **Mamas Don't Let Your Babies Grow Up to Be Sufis**

A Sufi is sorta like ice cream with ketchup and hot sauce
He doesn't make sense, he seems kinda dense,
Comfort and security just make him tense . . .
(IDHHB, *Holy Hobo Handbook*, lyrics by Parker Dickson, page 67)

I am going to address the question within the framework of the larger subject of "Sacrifice". Remembering the cyclical and non-linear aspect of these Sacrifices outlined in *The Joy of Sacrifice*, we can see that the Sacrifice of Comfort will actually play out repeatedly in different forms along our journey of transformation. The transition from one gradation of b\Being to another will, to some degree, entail the sacrifice of what one is, for that which is coming into Being. In effect, there will be produced labor pains in birthing new Being, contractions designed to open us up. Of course, once the habit to sacrifice comfort is in place, it makes for readier ease of movement.

There exists an inertia we must overcome, and the exertion of effort to this end will result in some form of discomfort. To do anything, to move out of our particular status quo hurts, in a way that might be described by a limb that has fallen asleep, then had blood course back through the veins again. There is a tingling, electrical sensation of vitality that is rather painful at first, until we are acclimated and the blood is fully flowing.

Work entails operating through an invisible machine, a machine that is passive to the essential self active. While angelic entities were made to do as they do in their support of the Throne, the wise use of our having been made in the image of God for the assumption of the Cross enables momentary alleviation of suffering on a much greater scale. That this happens voluntarily presents an unutterable joy to that which would bear witness. The Cross and its assumption will be of different flavor dependent upon the individual while simultaneously when one ascends to the place where all is One, all is indeed One and the same.

In this we are sacrificing all kinds of constructs that keep our perception safely anchored to our three-dimensional tactile hallucinations. Stop and think about that for a moment. One of the things we are asked to do is be willing to hang out where there might not be any platform, where the mind's constructs begin to fail and there is only left something that might be called a burgeoning faith to replace what we know as an identity.

The Sacrifice of Comfort is begun just in hearing these ideas, because to genuinely hear these ideas disrupts one's peace of mind. One reaction to having that deep chord struck can be an intensified move toward comfort, toward oblivion. Hearing these ideas, the spirit is nourished and quenched, but there are habits and conditioning in place, forming a static identity and false sense of security that is threatened and not readily relinquished. The raw aliveness of spirit, its immediacy, is covered over by the comfortable layers of our beliefs about the nature of reality and the conditioning that supports these beliefs. When these ideas reach us, there is an exposure that can, if we are fortunate enough, facilitate more Moments of Freedom in the direction of adopting new perceptual habits. But if we have highly reactive habits in place, the reverberations of our reactions to awakening can drown out these Moments of Freedom where evolutionary movement can be made.

Essentially speaking, as a voyager, we are a body of habits or tendencies. Repeated exposure to human experience has left its electrical imprint with results that present, in effect, like a path well-worn through repeated treading. Breaking these pathways with their neurological/psychological/physiological and other kinds of logistical manifestations is no easy feat. There are many factors to consider, and that is in part why there is great need of help. Discernment is needed in exposing and rightfully cutting our diamond in the rough. It takes an expert's skill to remove matrix from the diamond without damage to the diamond itself. And the appropriate habits to replace those of sleep must be known, because that is how habits are changed, by replacement with other habits.

There are habits that will support greater gradations of Being, and gradually adapt us to functioning with the minimum identity configuration necessary. This reduction of identity will facilitate voyaging and work in the macrodimensions, as well as maintenance of the thread of consciousness throughout passage in transit. The adoption of habits that contribute to the reduction of identity as opposed to its enhancement will, of course, influence our progress. But progress is actually in reduction, in simplification.

There is a demolition of one reality structure for the revelation of another, and in this one might be given a glimpse of the minimal identity configuration beneath the elaboration of personality.

Sacrifice can be seen as a form of making voluntary the inevitable surrender of all that we think we have, including our own identities, including that which we may currently consider as being of spiritual origin. But sacrifice can be a tricky thing as it is possible to make useless sacrifice that produces no results other than to enhance a false sense of spirituality or morality. Our business is reversing the pump, giving back to the higher what would normally be spent making real the outer world. If we can remember this, having also tasted the possibility of this process genuinely, we can help ourselves stay aligned. There is a demolition of one reality structure for the revelation of another, and in this one might be given a glimpse of the minimal identity configuration beneath the elaboration of personality. It is this configuration that can possibly serve Work on a higher scale of Being.

To sacrifice comfort, in a way, is to embrace death, to learn how to face death as a lover. It is the exposed rawness left after coverings are removed that we run from, but in running from death this way, we run from life. In death lies the secret of life. When we begin to cease running from this rawness, eventually the warmth of the sun that does not set can be felt.

Habitual reactions of personality and its constructs will be seen for the phantoms they are during our voyage. We might find that our misery has in fact been a source of comfort, cloaking us in long-held beliefs and convictions about the nature of reality. But sacrificing these core reality structures to some unknown that feels uncontrollable can seem impossible without help of a special kind. It takes one Being completely out of one's mind to really sign the dotted line according to a conversation I once heard between Lee Lozowick and E.J. on the subject of the Great Rapture. One must be completely, maddeningly in Love, in fact.

I am reminded by the language and tone of the ideas as presented in *The Joy of Sacrifice* of the time, place and people factor. While the timeless aspect of the material is ever present, there is certain emphasis and choice in verbiage that to my ear rings as being a direct reflection of the moment's necessity. Given the technological advances and the Teacher's ready embrace of these for the application to Work, how this sacrifice of comfort plays out within today's environment is apt to be different. And all you have to do is take a quick look at the Laws of Seven and the Laws of Three and their interplay that produces the complexities of the phenomenal world to see how individual the unraveling of these constructs will be. On the road to the place where all is pure spirit, there are many layers to unravel and they will fall away in the reversed sequence in which they were formed.

Our octaves and their interplay with the triad of primordial forces affirming, denying and reconciling have culminated into this moment's reality. Each of us has issues to be dealt with in order to be able to maintain a center of gravity at a higher gradation of Being. Sure, it is possible to induce temporary states, but these, without the foundational work that prepares one for the challenges of that gradation of Being, are limited in their scope. Our sticking points, our issues will be individual. At some point and at some level of Being, we saw something that terrified us into hiding out in the phenomenal world. We wouldn't have existence on the planet if it weren't for the fact that we have issues to work through.

The correct sacrifices under the right conditions can produce in us the results of adopting the basic habits needed for Completed Being. Thus, sacrifice is seen as a tool, a necessary tool, for our voluntary evolution. Sacrifice of a devotional nature is different than what I have found in this school where so much is about diminishment of belief and tendency. Devotion requires an activation of strong belief in something while here verification over belief is the order of the day.

The force and needs of the Great Work seem to be fathomless until one is outside of one's mind, completely taken up, enraptured by that grand necessity. We are swept up for an eternal moment into both the need and the healing of that need, sacrificed, annihilated quite willingly. Growing a new heart every moment to throw into the flames — this is the Joy of Sacrifice at its supreme. I am speaking here of a movement of utter surrender that pushes one to fling oneself into the fire of the solar absolute to be burned and consumed time and again. This is a deeply real impulse. The path to the place of this altar within invariably leads to the heart, where the treasure of the sun is buried.

What is this evolution we feel moved to volunteer about anyway? We make the sacrifices, including that of comfort for the sake of facilitating the conditions of our voluntary evolution. When we begin to be taken up by a mighty hand moving us along, it becomes obvious that voluntary evolution does not mean control. One may find oneself better able to fulfill obligations to self and others, but this reflects discipline, and the quality of humility that discipline can bestow.

We volunteer ourselves to undergo evolutionary transformations through our activities, intentions and exposure to school conditions that are designed to help in the removal of impediment to the waking state. In a way, it is a question of our location, and that can be partly described by vibrational frequency. We are looking for lightning to strike and produce the transformational conditions that will bring us to the place of lightning striking again.

The wish to help is a fundamental property of Being.

On another level, Chief Feature, our guaranteed opposition to awakening, is a creature that opposes our Work self. It is said to be self-invoked into our electrical field every thirty seconds. The existence of this invocation creates an equal and opposite condition of a thirty second Moment of Freedom from this invocation. We can learn to be aware of and utilize these Moments of Freedom to our work advantage. Every action has an equal and opposite reaction. But there is a way of doing that is not doing. And it seems that this is a way of getting things done along the Way. For these non-doings we will look for Moments of Freedom.

My training and experience informs me that evolution is for the service of something bigger than our own personal enhancement. One function I have learned about relative to our evolution has to do with the alleviation of a particular kind of suffering that is the result of an involuntary creation. Through the suffering or bearing of greater and greater degrees of consciousness, we participate in cosmic maintenance.

Practically speaking, this means clarifying through various processes and creating the chemical, biological and radiological circumstances for transformation that will enable us to function multi-dimensionally. Angelic Invocation and corresponding cosmic maintenance work serve this transformational process in its radiological effects as well as the chemical and biological factors that result in consequence. With on-the-job training, an alignment of sorts takes place. The possibility of being recruited for more Work is enhanced.

Yes, this Work is all about service. The wish to help is a fundamental property of Being. From one point of view, everything, all of creation, at some level, knows its origin and everything yields to that knowledge in its own way. We are not separate from everything, so in a way, service is even a pointless concept, except to demonstrate a particular orientation.

Looking a little at the Angelic model, we will see each energetic configuration has its range of function and characteristics that work together, yet maintain their integrity in cosmic maintenance. Seeing that there is good evidence in many writings and visions to support the idea that such a thing as cosmic maintenance and service exist, it might be wise to look at our position from the point of view of what we are serving at the moment. Are we serving what we want to serve? Assessing where our alignment is in this respect will yield much more than just looking at our individual characteristics alone. With the concept of service, we pull in a greater mass of necessity, a form of energy that can often give us clearer pointing to true north. From here we might be given insight as to what the Sacrifice of Comfort might mean to us at this moment.

This stuff is uncomfortable. We are inviting more electrical input for transformation into our circuitry. Think about it. Have you ever received an electric shock? The machine will feel the effects of what are real electrical experiences, if not during an invocation, certainly after. When on the job, for example in an Angelic Invocation, one is inexorably bound to the situation of posture, light, sound, mood and particular sensation throughout its duration. One will serve the needs of the space selflessly, despite any discomfort that machine reverberations might produce. The object of the game is finding skill in rendering ourselves useful in this way. We are opening ourselves up to the Divine and turning away from the realm of egoistic identity. We have to be out of our minds to be seeking this out, literally.

In a way, alignment happens by a process of seeking out the best means of alleviating the pressure there is to evolve, which often translates into removing impediment. In a school, the presence of the Teacher helps to quicken and create conditions where impediment might be removed more readily, at the point of brinksmanship that makes for the smoothest possible transition, while yielding the maximum benefit to one's evolution. It is all self-initiatory, but with guidance and the opportunity to borrow a higher Will. We evolve because it hurts too much not to evolve. Remember, pain is a product of the illusion of separation and sleep. When we awaken, we realize all as spirit and there is no relative pain in this condition. But in death there is the unraveling of illusions we cocooned ourselves in, and in this process there will likely be pain felt.

While we might have a trace of the angelic character that is "driven onward by a passionate, painful ecstasy of hopeless yearning for fulfillment" (quote from the Lord in *Creation Story Verbatim*), we also can blow the energy away readily when the lines of tension reach a certain threshold. We don't hold the post of an angel yet, and thus, do not realize the level of obligation and necessity they were made to know. Alignment in the Work brings us to a place where we might realize obligation and a level of necessity to evolve in order to meet this obligation.

There is a story of a Zen monk cook who demonstrates his perfect Zen by skillfully using his old, trusty, and immaculate blade, used over many years, to butcher some meat. His Zen was seen in the marvelous use of what is present to accomplish the task impeccably and at the service of the moment's necessity. The blade glides through the meat because of its sharpness. It was kept sharp through skillful use — he would only apply it at the places of greatest weakness in the carrion, striking his quick blow with the blade such that little force was needed. He lived his Zen as a cook, and quite clearly, in all aspects of his life.

Likewise, as we are clarified, less becomes more, quite clearly. Clarification will also lead to speedier karmic feedback that shows us that, indeed, for "every reaction there is an equal and opposite action" (ref.: the *Creation Story Verbatim* play). The greater the force we apply to the banishment of something, the greater potential energy we offer the thing to be banished. As is said, "all things in moderation," but I will include moderation as part of this. There is a time for great ferocity of purpose that is manifested in the application of will and intent over any outward show of force or might.

Now I will offer a couple of impressions that are related to the method of the Zen monk and illustrate an approach to this work. My typicality and my background contribute to a ready appreciation of the formulations made clear in the *Book of Sacrifices* and *My Brother Judas*, which describe specific steps for the assembly of Divine Being. Indeed, I have returned to these texts many times. For the latter of these — *My Brother Judas* — initially I followed the cycles sequentially working with an intensity and concentration, committing it to memory. Then this stopped, working with it no longer seemed appropriate. What subsequently happened was that I found myself periodically in a set of conditions that were confounding and yet familiar. Without intending and through guidance, I have found myself engaged in the Ceremonies in a deeper way, immersed in the state without the mind having created the intent for this. The evolutionary theater space for the enactment of these ceremonies is to be found in my life. There is an experience of brinksmanship that is beyond my ordinary intelligence, with the profoundly intimate precision that only jugular vein proximity could produce.

It is so subtle how these impressions are made, yet in the realm of the subtle, they are seen as precise, for lack of a better term — intimately relevant. The subtlety of these evolutionary theater plays render them difficult to describe — regardless, I will make a small attempt. The Sacrifices described in *The Joy of Sacrifice* seem to avoid spiritual pigeon holds. I found myself loving the text, much like I loved Rumi when I first encountered him, but my understanding was quite limited — it took repetition over a long period of time to be able to feel the deeper pulse of the Teaching in his poetry. Similarly, I have read *The Joy of Sacrifice* many times and with the repetition, I have come to a new quality of seeing and understanding. The information seems to have cut a new path of neural network experience by means of repetition and intentional efforts at understanding. Efforts at direct understanding and linear pursuit have been only good insofar as they have engaged me. However, the happy result of this engagement has been indirect. This new perceptual experience seems to register, note and acknowledge deep repeating cycles of experience that relate to the sacrifices in a way that is not available to ego constructs.

I can offer a glimpse of how this seems to have played out for me relative to one of the Sacrifices — that of Control. It seemed to me at the time I was pregnant that circumstances conspired to keep me at a distance from the activities of the community. My limited view of what it is to Work caused me great suffering, as it seemed that with motherhood I would be engaged in activities that were not "Work related," steeped in the mundane. Simultaneously, the hormonal bombardment and changes to this body really shook me loose from any feeling of control. I found myself incredibly diffused at times, and it took a lot of attention to keep myself functioning.

This quality of lack of control was given a fresh perspective with E.J.'s help. Many impressions had, by this point, been formed around the experience of no longer being my own person — it seemed to be a theme. At that time E.J. would eat food from a local eatery and on this occasion there was a small group of us sitting at a booth in the wine cellar section of this delightful restaurant. David — Sara's dad — and I were sitting together across from E.J. and others. I was feeling particularly diffused, forgetting the simplest things, and at times I felt myself riding the waves of this new Being's transit experience. In fact, just as an aside, it was in the midst of one of these transit episodes, during my third trimester, when I found myself in an old archetypal bookstore in Los Angeles that suddenly transformed into a distinct transit station. In that space I looked for guidance as the intensity of experience was disconcerting. There, at that precise moment, I saw before me an old hardbound copy of *Sacrifices*.

But let's get back to the restaurant with E.J. Pregnancy had brought about such aversions and cravings that when the waitress came to take our order, I found myself slightly panicked — I couldn't remember what I liked! I turned to David and asked him if I liked mushrooms anymore because I couldn't remember, and with this E.J. seemed quite delighted — his emotional tone combined with the quality of attention he gave me sounded a bell for me.

Several months later, now a new mom, and well-experiencing that my life was not my own, I happened to be present for a talk he gave. I don't recall the context, but he, at one point, mentioned intentional shocks that are administered at specific intervals to further a person's Work octave. He indicated that shocks were not always abrasive in nature; in some cases a shock might come in the form of complete idleness.

With this, the inner bell was sounded again. I was given reason to look at my present circumstances from the point of view that perhaps they were guided and that in fact all taking place within the context of the school had Work-related potential. I was further guided to re-examine the Sacrifices and when I came upon the Sacrifice of Comfort, where "one allows all one's actions to be directed by another who is responsible for one during this stage . . . Even one's toilet must be guided to some degree by another . . . One allows another to guide one in everything until the desire for control dies away." It dawned on me that motherhood was a good theater space in which to enact this sacrifice intentionally. Doing this within the context of the school, with the presence of the Teacher who has the Work force available to enliven our efforts can produce self-initiatory results.

But these results are not going to be experienced the linear way our limited language would suggest. Initiation and transmission are subtle, and to my experience, often have a quality like a silent avalanche. There is an all-at-once-ness to this that defies our language, which is so steeped in the world of linear sequence.

This Battered Saucepan

Whatever you feel is yours the Friend pulls you away from. That one does not heal your wounds or torment you more. Neither sure, nor uncertain, that one keeps you moving.

Decisions made at night seem strange the next day. Where are you when you sleep? A trickster curls on the headboard. Restless in the valley, you go to the ocean. Then turning toward the light, you fall in the fire. Who jiggles this battered saucepan?

The sky puts a yoke on you to help with turning around a pole. Teachers get dizzy like students. The lion that killed you now wonders whether to drag you off or tear you to pieces here. There's a shredding that's really a healing, that makes you more alive!

A lion holds you in his arms. Fingers rake the fretbridge for music. A compass revolves around the metal foot point. Some grow fond of battle armor; some, satin clothing. Others, like me, love the word bunches called poetry.

(Barks, *The Soul of Rumi,* page 174)

Sometimes we are *as if* being led astray only to find ourselves in the perfect position, at the greatest extreme of our weakness, most willing to strike a swift blow of the sacrificial blade. With this non-linear vision in my mind's eye, I once asked E.J. to offer me guidance as to what Sacrifice was most up for me in that moment, and he indicated that I did not need to concern myself with that; I was on the Path of Sacrifices and the quality of specificity I was stuck in was not useful. What he actually said was, "Don't worry about it, you're making them — you're here, aren't you?"

It wasn't the words said; rather they were the shell of a deeper communication which was immediate, complete and unmistakable. And that deeper communication broke open to something even deeper, an invisible building block for my inner temple. There was a further substantiation to the aforementioned quality of attention which registers and acknowledges the deep inner cycles of the Sacrifices.

The One Thing You Must Do

There is one thing in this world you must never forget to do. If you forget everything else and not this, there's nothing to worry about, but if you remember everything else and forget this, then you will have done nothing in your life.

It's as if a king has sent you to some country to do a task, and you perform a hundred other services, but not the one he sent you to do. So human beings come to this world to do particular work. That work is the purpose, and each is specific to the person. If you don't do it, it's as though a priceless Indian sword were used to slice rotten meat. It's a golden bowl being used to cook turnips, when one filing from the bowl could buy a hundred suitable pots. It's like a knife of the finest tempering nailed into a wall to hang things on.

You say, "But look, I'm using the dagger. It's not lying idle." Do you hear how ludicrous that sounds? For a penny an iron nail could be bought to serve for that. You say, "But I spend my energies on lofty enterprises, I study jurisprudence and philosophy and logic and astronomy and medicine and the rest." But consider why you do those things. They are branches of yourself.

Remember the deep root of your being, the presence of your lord. Give yourself to the one who already owns your breath and your moments. If you don't, you will be like the man who takes a precious dagger and hammers it into his kitchen wall for a peg to hold his dipper gourd. You'll be wasting valuable keenness and forgetting your dignity and purpose.

(Barks, *The Soul of Rumi*, page 150)

It is useful to remember how adaptable the body can be. We can easily become accustomed to the quality of austerity indicated in these sacred texts, enamored to the point of mistaking the manifestations of this austerity for the end result wanted and not applying discipline as it should be for real change of Being. There are times when we will need to adjust manifestation to allow practical application of another sacrifice. At the same time, there is a natural process of preference and accumulation of tendencies that will occur in our evolution — there will come a point during which the density of our physical body will be felt as a weight, a burden, as experienced from the perspective of our more rarefied Being bodies. We might sometimes confuse the difficulty of our ordinary lives as the burden we bear. The quality of burden we are speaking of here has nothing to do with any specificity within the range of phenomena, rather, it is the fact of phenomena, the gestalt of making concrete the outer world that is implied in this suffering.

There are so many traps related to the concept of Sacrifice — we merely have to look at what is happening now in the Catholic Church to see Sacrifice done incorrectly can produce results that possibly bring one to a worse condition than the original. I think it is an important idea to remember that we are out to diminish the impulse to make real the outer world, or perhaps rather, to use this impulse to a conscious effect of reversing our reality pump. Against the backdrop of this perspective, if we find that our work with sacrifices has the effect of solidifying and entangling us in the phenomenal world, it seems wise to take another look at our practice.

In speaking of sacrifice of comfort or any sacrifice, I need to address a little here the relationship of the student and Teacher, because this will reflect my experience. The sacrifices to my view are enlivened and made possible by the example provided by the Teacher, as well as the force of his or her work.

The relationship of student and Teacher is, like many aspects of this work, both simple and complex. On the one hand, it encompasses and embodies all relationships — sister, brother, father, mother, daughter son, lover, Friend. On the other it is simply a reflection in a mirror. By virtue of this wide stage in which the theater of one's evolution can be enacted, our efforts at sacrifice can be enlivened, vivified and given momentum.

The Teacher will play the part of resisting force and we are advised to make friends with resisting force. In this process of making friends, we learn much about the Sacrifice of Comfort. Our comfort level and the habits of sleep that keep us bound there will stand out in high relief. This tends to happen within a short while of being around a genuine Teacher.

The dynamics of the courtship with resisting force will change as we progress on our journey. The sacrifice of one form of comfort will then reveal fresh sacrifice to be made. We will invariably come up against resistance to what seems a good work move, for example within the scope of a work project about which we may feel impassioned. In my experience the Teacher has offered all kinds of disruption of projects my sleepy eyes have seen as Work worthy and bound toward success. Repeated experience eventually teaches a new level of discernment. The eye unclouds, one is given the light to see what one was reaching for in the dark, and a new level of trust is revealed. There is no Teacher/Student relationship without love in this Work. It's impossible, because in fact the relationship one has with the Teacher is the same one has with the force of Love, with the Friend.

Betrayal plays a part in this whole thing. Without betrayal there can be no resurrection — some aspect of a reality must betray its creator somehow in order to invite the creator to resurrect in a new creation. It seems written into the script. When we fall in love with our Teacher, we do so in sleep. We may have been awakened by his or her presence more than momentarily, but our Love has not been awakened to its fullness yet, it is what will undergo transformations in this process of betrayal and resurrection.

From **The Hoopoe's Talent**

When school and mosque and minaret get torn down, then dervishes can begin their community. Not until faithfulness turns to betrayal and betrayal to trust can any human being become part of the truth.
                            (Barks, *The Soul of Rumi*, page 93)

So invariably, that initial first Love, the phenomenal side of it any-

way, will undergo change and part of that may be experienced as betrayal. The process of diminishment is like diamond cutting — just the
right amount of pressure and method is needed to expose the brilliance
of the diamond from beneath its matrix. It takes great skill to remove the
matrix without damaging the diamond. The process is delicate, but can
be experienced as rather harsh, dependent upon our degree of attachment.

In the course of my work with E.J. on the *Creation Story* play there
has been a lot of wind and water that sometimes become storms out at
sea. I was once left in a state that I can hardly describe except to say
that all of my consciousness was needed to perambulate away from a
park where we were filming parts of the play using a traveling carnival
as backdrop. There had been a lot of preparation as I see it in hindsight
— my emotional state was ripe for the blow that knocked off a huge
chunk of matrix such that everything was in swift need of reconfiguration. I found myself unable to speak, think or move with any automatic-
ity, rather everything had to be volitional. Something died and the
reintegration of what remained had not yet created scar tissue over the
fresh wound. It was a moment of super effort when, after being severely
reprimanded for protesting what seemed like absurd behavior on my
Teacher's part, I nonetheless formed my mouth into the words, "Are we
done for the night or do you need me further?"

Chickpea to Cook

A chickpea leaps almost over the rim of the pot where it's being
boiled.
"Why are you doing this to me?"
The cook knocks him down with the ladle.
"Don't you try to jump out. You think I'm torturing you. I'm giving
you flavor, so you can mix with spices and rice and be the lovely vitality
of a human being. Remember when you drank rain in the garden? That
was for this."
Grace first, sexual pleasure. Then a boiling new life begins, and the
Friend has something good to eat.
Eventually the chickpea will say to the cook, "Boil me some more.

Hit me with the skimming spoon. I can't do this by myself. I'm like an elephant that dreams of gardens back in Hindustan and doesn't pay attention to his driver. You're my cook, my driver, my way into existence. I love your cooking."

The Cook says, "I was once like fresh from the ground. Then I boiled in time, and boiled in the body, two fierce boiling. My animal soul grew powerful. I controlled it with practices, and boiled some more, and boiled once beyond that, and became your teacher."

(Barks, *The Essential Rumi*, page 132)

A Teacher/Student relationship is documented in moments. Our work with sacrifice is documented in moments. These moments are precious beyond anything words can say. I can't help but point in the direction of yet another moment....

Years ago I used to live at the main facility with E.J. It was much different then, a lot smaller and not as grand a place as it is now — the barn was not yet in existence, things were configured much differently. I used to have my little corner with a drafting table under which I slept and on top of which I created illustrations for publications like the *Talk of the Month*. At this time I was working on an illustration of an archer shooting an arrow that, at the same time, was pointed within. Those days I did a lot of childcare for other community children, as well as fire watch duties, and often missed out on talks and dinner invocations and the like. Something happened on this particular occasion where I had been promised relief of childcare duties, but was left to complete another person's duty time as well when that person did not show up, and from there went on to do night watch alone. By early morning I was completely broken down, worn to the thread and sat at my desk weeping.

Folks came into the kitchen, happily chatting about the event I'd missed, and this intensified the spiritual battle raging within. Through teary eyes I looked out the sliding glass door that was there at the time and watched how the light played on the beautiful surrounding nature. And then suddenly, miraculously, I saw something very clearly. I saw that the Shekinah turns herself inside out in utter, utter, utter Love for the Beloved, and out of this movement of "utterness", the creation comes into Being. I gasped a small gasp and at that moment, softly, warmly, a hand came to rest on my left shoulder. It was my Teacher's. I didn't turn to look and there was nothing to speak — what is to be said when there are no boundaries to separate? We just were there for a moment, breathing together. In that moment I saw clearly as well, that he felt everything I was going through and his wish for my freedom is profound.

Look to the Zen Monk Cook's way and get a hint as to how sacrifice can be made. Find the places of most and least resistance, keeping the sacrificial blade sharp and good by using it well, to the greatest effect. There is love for one's practice, well-nurtured, which allows for the aliveness of change and the vast space of permanence within that change. This underlying Love for the Work will lead us to awaken the heart and conscience and further us down the path, so let us nurture it. When love is truly guiding, what to sacrifice and how is given the light to be seen.

Meditation
Grace Kelly Rivera, mixed media on specially prepared Arches, 28" x 22"
© 2011 Grace Kelly Rivera

Topic Nine

Alchemical Oils,
Atmospheres of Transformation

How do I use Alchemical Oils in my work?

Everything, including thought, is material. We wish to develop tools that enable perception of more subtle forms of material that have direct and indirect influence on our inner work. With this quality of perception adjustments and fresh juxtapositions lead to a knowledge of correspondences that can be used to good effect. Working with essential oils is a way in which one can begin to train the attention in these subtle realms. They are the product of successful alchemy that beautifully demonstrates the idea of reducing identity to a form that will survive death. The plants that produce the essential oils die, but their essence, when extracted, lives on to become mixed with other components to produce new accords, as they are called, similar to musical chords that blend well, harmonizing to become a new whole. The whole becomes greater than the sum of its parts.

One theory of alchemy wraps around the thought that all is on its way to being gold, at different stages and with different rates of passage. To one with knowledge of the process by which this transformation occurs, the possibility exists of making gold from lead by intentionally quickening that process.

Alchemical perfume composition will have an intent that is
spiritual in nature as opposed to self-enhancement.

In Essential Perfumery the perfumer, or Guide, is in a process of unfolding while learning how to participate in the unfolding of another's
true perfume. As the layers fall away in the alchemy of the perfumer's
life, the chemistry changes which affects one's own natural scent and
sense of smell, in fact, all senses. Like incense on fire, the heat of our
lives and what is being evaporated by means of that heat, produces a fragrant offering. A life consciously lived will use radiations and other factors to remove veils and one learns the art of balancing the changing
structure of identity with elegant rebirth patterning.

There is more than one way to classify the different Alchemical
stages. Here is one classification that I have found useful:

Calcination (Roasting, reducing)
Dissolution (Dissolving, breaking down)
Separating (Sifting, filtering, cutting)
Conjunction (Re-uniting, fixing)
Fermentation (Putrefying, digesting, congealing)
Distillation (Making potent, multiplying)
Coagulation (Fusing, projecting)

Added to these alchemical ideas can be the universal principles of
As Above So Below and Solve Et Coagula — dissolve and recombine.
Each of the seven stages described will undergo deconstruction followed
by reconfiguration. Alchemical perfume composition will have an intent
that is spiritual in nature as opposed to self-enhancement. In the synthesis
of the many into the whole, experienced as chord structures that evaporate off at different rates, there are repeating patterns of the whole. It is
reminiscent of something I once heard about Tibetan Buddhists and their
knowledge of the dying process and the between-lives states. He noted
that life patterns will reflect death patterns and vice versa, implying that
this knowledge can be used to create intentional cycles that include elegant rebirth patterning.

Each of the alchemical stages indicated have their own set of scents
associated with them. For example, the process of calcination or roasting,
which reduces things down to a particular quality of concentration,

would be expressed as a biting, perhaps a rather sulfuric scent and dissolution would be acrid in nature to reflect dissolving, breaking down and so on. Another classification of scent is the Elements — here viewed as the four elements of earth, fire, water and air. In the Alchemical Gold oils work, I was given the following assignations — for Earth, Patchouli; Fire was given Jasmine Orange; Water, Frankincense and Air; White Musk. Each of the oils will fall under those four categories, and it is through the development of our intuition, careful listening to our gut feeling that these will be discovered and used to good effect. Our ability to respond to this gut feeling will reflect our purification. We must bear in mind that relationships between oils might alter their elemental assignations and fluid flexibility to the changes before us will prove most advantageous.

Ayurvedic and other holistic systems allude to states of health and cleanliness that are so high, the human organism no longer produces any foul smell. I have witnessed a lot within the scope of my own gradual chemical transitions that gives evidence to this potential. Of course, pristine health is not our focus in the Work, while at the same time, we need to care for the machinery so that it functions effectively.

An experiment took place in which the Teacher worked with a student's attention such that the student achieved a very high state of Essential Being. At the beginning of the experiment we were asked to smell the skin of the student which we did at the pulse points of the wrists. There was a pronounced, rather unpleasant food odor with lots of garlic present in the emanations — she obviously had not been following the recommended diet. A series of guided instructions helped to bring about a state of Essential Being, and this was given the tremendous boost of the powerful attention energy that the Teacher can provide. There was a definite change of atmosphere. We were asked to smell the student's skin once again. It smelled like the most exquisite sandalwood incense you could imagine!

It was explained that the awakened heart produces a radiation that dissolves the layers from within, radiating outward. Eventually the fragrance of the Essential Self is exposed. Considering scent as a part of the structure of an ambient space, this idea is especially intriguing. Scent can trigger the effect of time travel. The physiology of the sense of scent is such that pure sensory signals bypass the cerebral cortex and are received directly by an exposed part of the brain, sometimes called the old olfactory brain. We can, therefore, respond intuitively to a scent before we can think about it. A scent can instantly summon up all of the different tactile, auditory, visual and other elements that were present at another time and place. As a powerful bridge, it can be used to great advantage. This aspect of fragrance makes possible the practice of using one's own personal oil blend as a reminding factor for remembering the invocation one is pursuing.

The experiment also left me with a strong impression of the power of attention and its function in the awakening of one's life. It was by means of the attention combined with the orchestration of the correct mood that the voyage to a chamber of Essential Being was made. In a way, you live where your attention is. The conscious development and use of attention presents the foundational basis for our voluntary evolutionary work. It is the attention of the essential self on the machine that slowly, over time, grinds the matrix down to the diamond. Like wind and water action that eventually wears the strongest of geological formations down to dust, strong attention work will dissolve away the matrix of ego. The development of our attention is of vital importance to this dissolution process.

I have another life story that could serve to reflect what changing internal atmosphere can do to one's experience of life. As indicated before, in New York City one of my flexible jobs for pursuit of art was at Windows on the World, the restaurant and lounge complex atop one of the World Trade Towers.

My favorite busboy was Hugh, who also happened to be my hairdresser. We worked well as a team and I was happy to have him as my partner anytime, but especially on this night. I told him we needed to really do well in tips as I'd been out of my favorite perfume for some time due to finances, and I intuited that not having my fragrance, Fidgi by Guy Laroche, was in itself detrimental to my prosperity. I'd long had a sense that with the right perfume, one's personal magic was enhanced in potential.

Despite all our positive thinking, Hugh and I did dismally in tips that night — in fact, it was one of the worst ever nights in waitressing history!

I was completely bummed out — more than that, I was confounded by the mockery that life could sometimes be. I'd noted what eventually was identified as a fundamental law, the more I wanted something, the greater the force of opposite reaction to that desire. For every action there is an equal and opposite reaction. There are other laws to be sited in the world of manifestation and in conjunction with the laws of attraction. But for me personally, I have found impartiality — a freedom from preference of result to be the more effective inner posture.

Descending the 106 or so floors down the elevator, by now I had adjusted to the changes that the body goes through in that rapid descent, so my mind was thoroughly occupied with the injustice of it all. My way of rebellion was to play forward what had happened to me instead of sublimating it. So I determined that I would not give the cabby a 20% tip, which is my custom for service folks. I feel for them from lots of experience. But that night, at that moment, my compassion was obscured by the cloud of misery and a wish to shake my fist at the Creator.

When I walked out — it was around two a.m. — the air was balmy, very pleasant. Surprisingly, a beautifully clean and new cab was waiting for me — the cabby, a good looking Middle Eastern fellow who spoke flawless English. He was standing outside of his cab enjoying the night air and so opened the door for me as I climbed in with all my bags. I had cleaned out my locker at work and was especially laden with extra baggage.

I remained stoic despite the marked goodness with the mantra of no 20% tip as we made our way uptown to 96th Street and Madison Ave, where I lived at the time. He asked me if it would be all right to play music, and I gratefully said yes, happy that this would not be a chatty cabby so that I could sit back and steep well in my angst.

The music was delightful — a fusion of world music and Jazz and before I knew it, with the lights of that remarkable city tickling my eyes, I found myself uplifted despite all intentions to the contrary. Naturally my thoughts reflected this uplifting. It was remarkable the perspective shift that occurred actually. I remember precisely the feeling of surrendering the former posture of injustice and in exchange experiencing gratitude for the moment, the comfort of that clean cab, the polite driver, the music, the fact that I was alive and living in that fabulous city, the balmy air lightly hitting my face. Of course this kind cabby had to be given a 20% tip.

By the time he pulled up in front of my apartment building I'd experienced quite an epiphany — I felt incredibly free within and told myself that tonight's act of giving the cabby the large tip was one of faith, faith that all would be well despite my financial struggle of the moment. I paid and thanked him and rather awkwardly got myself out of the cab, collecting my bags. I noticed a small clean brown paper bag with something in it — though I didn't remember it as mine, at the same time I had enough self-doubt about my memory to feel okay to grab it from the floor of the cab as I stepped out. The cab took off and I opened the bag to look inside. To my utter amazement, there I found a brand new unopened bottle of Fidgi Cologne.

The mystery and profound wonder of that moment I cannot begin to describe, and yet it was but a foretaste of the wonderment that continues to unfold.

There is a relationship between one's internal state and external reality. That relationship can be used well, ignored or abused. Impartial self-observation will reveal this relationship well over time. When we are on a path of refinement of our functioning, things clarify to the place of being able to sense and see what may normally be out of our range of detection. The quality of space and its effect on one will be made clearer. Aromatics can become important tools for clarifying a space that is now sensed to be dense with unwanted energy, as well as in the creation of a space of elevation of the general and personal ambient atmosphere. In this we tap into ancient practice.

The knowledge of the use of aromatics for clarification, purification, elevation of atmosphere, ritual and invocation has existed in most cultures throughout the ancient world. The highly developed use of aromatics in Ancient Egypt is well-documented. The priests lived a disciplined life in order that they might produce fragrances used for sacred ritual, mummifying, and for the regular anointing of the royalty as the living embodiment of the deities worshiped. The creation of atmosphere was an important aspect of everyday living.

Perfume translated from its Latin roots means "through smoke." The ethereal nature of essential oils has rendered them apt messengers to and from the unseen world as a medium enabling communication and appeasement of the reigning deities. As was said in Egypt, the gods love fragrance. Worship was central to the ancient Egyptian cultures and the Pharaoh was viewed as an embodiment of the ruling deity. It was the job of the priests to help in the invocation of these deities upon the Pharaoh in order that he could maintain the atmosphere of magical power that kept him or her on the throne. The High Priests were also involved with the maceration of essential oils and the creation of the special oils and unguents that were used in the magical preparations as well as in the everyday life. Incenses were burned ritually for worship and for healing purposes.

Evidently there have been some scientific experiments made that have shown sound will carry better in a room where Frankincense resin is burning. The scientific explanation behind essential oils is as elusive as fragrance, though one common function seems to be protective. There are present in their make-up chemical constituents that hold tremendous healing power about which volumes have been written. Our area of special concern is the *Science of the Alteration of Atmospheres*, which cuts a path into the very nature of our personal reality.

Essential oils are not oils actually, but one of their properties — being soluble in alcohol, but not water — characterizes them as of an oily nature. In fact, to describe them a little more precisely — they possess a volatile oily nature. A pure essence has the characteristic of evaporating — that's how you can tell if something being sold as a pure essential oil is free of any extending product such as a fixed oil like jojoba or a glycol — if you place a drop of the essential oil on a tissue and it leaves a stain after many hours, likely it has been extended.

But fixation of the perfume is not so much the aim in the alteration of atmospheres as that of producing atmospheres which invite the participation of the essential self, and the lasting transformative effects of its relationship to the HBM, serving the work of pump reversal, easing the transitions between life/death cycles experienced in the process of refinement.

They call perfumery the art of evaporation as one is composing a pleasing fragrant experience that will unfold into new tonics as the different components evaporate, each at its own rate of volatility. The first notes to hit the nose will be high tones mostly comprised of some floral constituents and citrus or mint. These will evaporate off to reveal the heart tones, and gradually in time down to the base notes like Sandalwood, Labdanum, Oak Moss and Vetiver. The thick extraction from Benzoin gum has long been used as a fixative. In modern perfumery, fixation of the perfume is of prime importance, and to that end, chemicals have been produced to give lasting power to the volatile essential oils, but those can be harsh to the body.

In natural perfumery, we use essential oils, or secondary products of natural sources to produce fixation. But fixation of the perfume is not so much the aim in the alteration of atmospheres as that of producing atmospheres which invite the participation of the essential self, and the lasting transformative effects of its relationship to the HBM, serving the work of pump reversal, easing the transitions between life/death cycles experienced in the process of refinement.

Since we are now talking about the oils themselves, I'll add some information. I am working with the understanding that they are ultimately but a medium that provides a vehicle for work-worthy possibilities to be realized, and this is just one example of such a vehicle in its finer details. The Alchemical Gold oils that form the foundation of our practice in custom blending are still based on formulas E.J. created with the help of a chemist friend. These fragrance oils are comprised of pure essential oils and naturally sourced aromatic chemical constituents that are combined to produce a bouquet which the perfumer further combines into her complex creations. They are made of essential oils, isolates and in our case, naturally derived chemical constituents. Some aromatic sources like gardenia, for example, contain such volatile components that they elude the distillation process and one is left with the natural essence of gardenia lacking the full body of the glorious bouquet the flower will produce. It takes the process of synthesizing — that is, recombining chemical constituents, adding them to the essence of gardenia to produce the closest possible approximation to the flower. To this end it becomes important to work with high-quality fragrance products compounded from natural sources, and this describes the Alchemical Gold Oils.

To be alive is to know change — to be aware of and make use of change goes into the realm of alchemy. We are not the same person we were a year ago. When we can change intentionally, with consciousness, we are working with our lives instead of against them. Essential oils can be potent carriers of intent that have the ability to bridge gaps and bring us to the realm where we might affect subtle adjustments in the alchemy of our life.

A primary intent in our work lives is that of clarification or the removal of impediment to the Work. This, of course, includes the disarming of the chronic defense mechanism against the waking state. Just as every essential oil each has its own properties and way of being extracted, we too, bear our own unique way to unfold from within, with our own Essential Being properties. It takes a skilled distiller of spirits to be able to coax essence out from its matrix, just as it takes skill to compound these essences into an aromatic synergy that produces favorable work effects.

With clarification will come a natural repugnance felt toward old habits that were counter to work and then, of course, further clarification will bring one to impartiality over repugnance.

Learning how to work with Alchemical Gold oils places one in a position of necessity for seeing the principles behind these skills which can be said to relate to alchemy. Being in a position of service, offering a school tool that serves essential self-dominance, helps to enable awareness of atmospheres. Before taking in the atmosphere of the Voyager/Customer, the Guide has to be sure his/her internal atmosphere is clear. Diet, school impressions and practices — such as wishing that the work be used for the benefit of all beings everywhere — while applying oils on people, help to nourish and develop certain subtle muscles. In the process, we are training the attention away from distraction that could lead to the collapse of a work atmosphere. This work is about instinct and intuition — there is much about essential oils and correspondences that can be learned, of course, but at a bottom line, one needs the ability to respond well, with knowledge. Clarification will give us readier access to our intuition as will the development of good work habits, and with time and experience, we develop our discernment.

It is important to remember that we are always invoking something at some level. The sum total of our personal atmosphere will invite corresponding energetic possibility. Different presences will dominate a space dependent upon its atmospherics. Some atmospheres feed our sleep and others are conducive to presence. With clarification will come a natural repugnance felt toward old habits that were counter to work and then, of course, further clarification will bring one to impartiality over repugnance.

I mentioned Contamination earlier and this is a topic of great importance to our work with essential oils. It is easy to understand the idea of contamination and how it applies in a research laboratory. The need for control of conditions in which an experiment is being conducted is obvious. In order to get accurate results, contaminating factors with potential influence over outcome must be controlled or eliminated. In a chemical lab, precautionary measures must be taken not to mix two substances with adverse chemical reactions — even in the household you'll find an example of the need for caution when using bleach and ammonia, since their combined fumes can cause illness.

When a perfumer works with essential oils, care is taken not to contaminate them with any foreign substances. This has an effect of requiring the attention focused while one does simple things like pouring or placing items like droppers and caps. These activities and precautions can, however, become mechanical with time and repetition. A modern day perfumer receiving extensive training in chemistry in pristine outer conditions is unlikely to consider seriously the contaminants that may exist within the mind and be expressed through thought energy. These chemists may be vaguely aware of personal atmosphere, of atmospheres in general, but it is the rare person who compassionately considers one's own effect on the atmosphere.

The responsibilities and aims of the ordinary perfumer and the person studying the alteration of atmospheres are very different. Correspondingly, some of the practices take on completely different meaning. In the area of contamination, you are considering a wider field of potential that ranges from macro to micro. Cells can potentially store memory that remains active even outside of the body. Evolutionary alchemists are forced to protect themselves by means of intentionally developed habits against contamination brought about through the accidental introduction of enough cells containing recordings, memories, that are counter to the evolutionary effort. Conversely, contamination can be used intentionally as a means of gaining access to information as well as factors of a radiological nature that are necessary to one's evolution.

There are several ways to look at this that all together might give a little sketch of a very big and easily misunderstood idea. One is basically looking to increase the electrical conductivity of the vessel. This happens in gradual states and is approached in a number of ways simultaneously within the context of evolutionary school conditions. We have spoken about the clearing of one's palate through diet and the radiation therapy that comes about through the exposure of the essential self attention on the machine. Further, one will seek transformational radiations that come through group and individual invocations of presences that provide radiations and data that benefits our work.

Resonance is a key means by which this kind of work becomes possible. One who is operating at a low density of vibration is not apt to attract higher density of vibration experiences, and if by some chance there is exposure to the higher, there is likelihood of lower vibration reverberation dominance. We are not likely to run into the Archangelic presence of Gabriel while engaged in the postures, atmospheric conditions and activities of a pizza party. Nothing wrong with a pizza party, but the corresponding density of vibration, the mood and aromatic atmosphere, as well as the haphazard, unintentional ambience, simply does not offer the correct conditions for a landing of an Angel any more than an average driveway could accommodate a jetliner.

Someone evolving out of the drunkenness of a sleeping machine has to stay away from certain events and experiences in the earliest stages of cleansing. The activities will be different for different folks, but one general movement will be away from that which stimulates a lot of adrenalin production, which can be counterproductive to evolutionary work. Pumping up the machine full of adrenalin through competitive sports, for example, can produce effects that simulate Machine Awakening, while, in fact, the activity creates density and substance that is useful only to the substantiation of the organic life. However, given the subtleties that must be taken into account when considering all aspects of an individual's evolutionary path, no one rule can apply to every person.

In time it becomes more a matter of natural inclination — one simply has no business or desire to be in certain spaces and situations. As the occlusion is lifted, the senses will seem magnified, but in reality we are just *as if* seeing, touching, hearing, tasting and smelling for the first time. An awakened machine is just that, awakened, and all its functions become activated to their fullest capacity as more electrical energy is allowed to come through due to the removal of barriers to the waking state. This translates to a lot of input and diminishing buffers to that input. One becomes sensitive to other energy fields as a result of purification, and contaminants accidentally ingested can have a detrimental effect on the delicate balance of one's evolutionary alchemy. Someone going through certain stages of the transformational process is going to be wide open, vulnerable and subject to influence — much like a newborn baby. These states require conditions that nurture their unfolding.

Here is another way in which aromatics can be put to good use and have been throughout history. It is possible to use fragrance as a way of creating a form of protection around oneself. One way is by keeping the ambient atmosphere elevated such that the corresponding elevated states of consciousness are more readily supported and triggered. The invocation of presence is more readily done in a good aromatic atmosphere and with this invocation, one forms protection, filling space that might otherwise be filled by something unwanted.

It is also possible to cleanse away vibrational debris. "Know thyself" has many shades of meaning. At a subtle level we will want to know our own atmosphere and presence to be able to identify influences that may have a negative contaminating effect.

At a biological level, when we put food in our mouth using hands that have not been thoroughly cleaned, we run the risks of bacteria, yes, but also of ingesting eggs of some form of parasite that will gladly use the warmth of our inner bodies as a home and nesting place. This condition robs us of energy that can be utilized for the purpose of evolution. It also can lead to serious complications and illness in the body. Anti-contamination practices teach much related to attention, and the ability to keep oneself on course. We are learning to function in such a way as not to take in unwanted contaminants or make Bardo moves that take us away from our Work path. The impulse just to pick up food and eat without washing the hands and even spraying them with hydrogen peroxide must be changed in the evolutionary alchemist; the effort to change requires discipline of attention.

In time, one develops internal signals that give a little jolt to the attention when one has fallen asleep and done something contaminating. The practice of impartial self-observation might develop out of the pressure of having to know where your hands are all of the time. The effort to develop a new habit is also useful in learning about the mechanics of the HBM and its existing habits, including habits of learning. The habits one adopts around the area of contamination are among the most important and far reaching.

It stands to reason that when applying the oils onto someone's skin, one is also contaminating, in a sense, the recipient, or Voyager, with an evolutionary work contaminant. While the various essential oils will bear different properties, they all have the quality of being receptive to intent as well as the vibration of those handling them. Just in this alone one can see the need to take care in one's handling. The oils penetrate the skin, but then evaporate off after having mingled with skin oils. The heat of the body gets the whole thing going and this action provides a window of sorts to better enable the essential self to invoke its presence into the life of the machine by means of the alteration of the personal atmosphere. It is very important that the oils remain uncontaminated by the skin oils of either the perfumer or the perfumed. For this reason, special ph balanced papers are used to apply the oils blends onto the skin when testing. Apart from this, the perfumer has the responsibility of not bringing personal issues into the space. The space of the perfumer and customer or guide and voyager is sacred. To guide is actually more a receptive activity, one is active in the passive, or actively passive.

The work with Alchemical Gold oils is both introductory and advanced, spanning a wide range of potential use in our evolutionary efforts. One of the ways it is introductory is that it can provide an intentional form of a special work contamination, a vehicle that offers a subtle atmospheric nudge to the essential being/human biological machine relationship. This is also advanced because the guide, or perfumer, that would engage in providing these vehicles, takes on an obligation to be a clear messenger. The concept of contamination and all it entails is introductory and advanced — introductory in the sense that the practices around it are attention training devices, advanced in the transformational effect ongoing practice will produce over time.

There are many things I feel gratitude and a sense of indebtedness about in my relationship with E.J., quite naturally. His tolerance of what must have been my dreadful, impacted, adrenal smell and atmosphere when I first started working with him was most gracious. Through the refinement of my olfactory — in fact, all my senses and the corresponding sensitivity to atmosphere, I am given hindsight, so to speak.

I arrived, or more precisely, was found in New York in a fairly encrusted state. My habits both reflected and supported occlusion that came into brilliant light upon encountering the school. To clarify the encrustation away so that the Alchemical Factory might begin to function as it should was essential. By moving out to California, changing my habits and the quality of impressions ingested, being given a steady diet of the school's radiations, living with the ideas in a setting where friction gave heat with which to cook, gradually the process of clarification was revealed.

I was given the task of performing the *Creation Story Verbatim* play, playing the part of the Lord prior to my involvement with the Alchemical Gold oils business. It made sense — I'd trained as an actress and God had been a fundamental issue for me starting from the time I was a very young child — I recall being afraid to go to sleep because of dreams such as a huge hand lifting me out of my body while hearing the words "God wants you" at around five years of age, and an even earlier recollection of my first encounter with Mary. I could not fathom when I first started working with the oils that this work would bear significant relationship to my invocational work with the play. But in time the relationship was clear.

How incredibly ingenious and subtle is the art of brinksmanship a master knows. Some data is emotional in nature, requiring the awakening of the real emotional center. E.J.'s brilliance as a creator of subtle conditions through which evolutionary movement can be vivified is clearly seen in *Creation Story Verbatim*. This modern mystical play contains a lot of data and the potential of invoking conditions with benefits that are radiological in nature, for the production of transformational substances useful to our evolution. In this we learn about the use of mood as a rudder through which to steer our way through the Great Labyrinth, as "the model of the thing becomes the thing itself." With this, I have come to an understanding of the clear relationship between the art of the Alteration of Atmospheres and Theater. The theater space can provide a potent forum in which to observe changing atmospheres as well as learn how to intentionally change atmosphere for the purposes of the higher objective of invocation.

My work with fellow actor, Robbert, and the *Creation Story Verbatim* play evolved out of the Bunraku Puppetry. We used to tour with the puppets as the North American Bunraku Puppet Theater. A few times we had the great opportunity of performing in trade for a booth space at a festival where E.J. would sell jewelry and oils. At some point two significant things happened that deepened the cleansing process already begun. First, most of the troupe members smoked cigarettes and we were told to quit smoking, as our Teacher didn't see how he could work with someone who was so enslaved.

Then, a while later, we eliminated garlic and onions from the diet, and followed Dr. Marstellar's cleansing diet. The Marstellar cleansing diet (later referred to as "the diet") change and discipline, but without the sexy radical quality of some other cleansing diets, and thereby, is well aligned with the wind and water way of the school. Dr. Marstellar created the cleansing diet to bring the body to a place where it could be determined what best feeds it. An indirect and perhaps even more work-pertinent effect of this clarification was the corresponding clearing of personal atmosphere.

My body was once used as an example of an important point having to do with diet. Because of my natural background — I was born in Puerto Rico — there was something about my body's workings that did well with the ingestion of a bit of coffee, in moderation. The way I have come to understand this is that there are conditions created in the blood influenced by type and other factors that will predispose one to requiring certain foods over others. It is not necessarily a question of having grown up accustomed to eating in a particular way, though this, no doubt, is a factor in the equation. There are many other factors that come into consideration that will be unique to each individual. At this present point, my chemistry and clarification process is such that coffee is not tolerated any longer by the body — the chemistry has changed.

Eventually we learn to work in partnership with the body, feeding it the food that actually nourishes it, yielding the maximum energy with the least amount of expenditure of energy to process that food. This becomes quite a practical matter the more aware we become of our energetic selves as we clarify. As indicated, alchemy is like a map of change, and change is the one constant we can count on.

When you are working to sustain a high platform for invocational work, such quick triggers to the organic can prove disruptive and destructive of delicate labyrinthine chambers.

Another near-constant is the fact that in our culture garlic and onions are used extensively in cooking. We were given no option but to stop ingesting them if we wished to work with E.J. on a daily basis. It was necessary — the sensitivity of the invocational work he was doing, the delicate conditions were such that the emanations of someone who eats garlic and onions could be disruptive of the intentional atmosphere being produced. The effects of invocational work can create a set of uncomfortable symptoms that are referred to as radiation sickness. Part of these symptoms is raw sensitivity and an exposed quality, with a sense of being hollowed out, a partial result of managing an incredible amount of electrical energy that comes coursing through. "Lightning handlers crackle" as is said. There is a lot of rapid exposure to cleansing and other kinds of radiations and when the invocation is done, or in between invocational sessions that may be required for a working to be complete, participants will find themselves highly sensitized. It is good training to be required to function with a foot in each world, but the navigation can indeed be tricky. Just as in a space around a dying person, delicacy is needed to respond to the higher awareness present.

The elimination of garlic and onions is not this school's practice alone, but is to be found in other spiritual communities. Fundamentally, garlic and onions produce conditions that are counter to clarification of our own atmosphere. From personal experience, apart from the unpleasant smell, they can bring one to the organic from the higher, quickly. When you are working to sustain a high platform for invocational work, such quick triggers to the organic can prove disruptive and destructive of delicate labyrinthine chambers. I've wondered if this property of garlic influenced the myth of wearing garlic to avoid a vampire. A vampire seeks higher being blood, really — transubstantiated blood — but the neck covered with garlic would *as if* ground the victim and disable the atmosphere the vampire needs in order to feed. Interestingly, in the line of psychic self-defense, it is sometimes advised, when one feels under attack, to do something quite mundane. In this way, one removes oneself from the field of play.

Obviously, our work processes will produce in us states of imbalance, and the art of creating balance out of our work life changes, is a fine one indeed. We move toward balance, but not self-calming. Sublimating and distilling the gross and base into the fine and rarefied is at the heart of alchemy. When addressing the topic of repaying our debt to nature to be able to cross streams, we speak of reversing the human reality pump. We thus "realize" the inner world — make real the inner world over the outer. The process of repaying nature our debt, involves voluntarily dying before we die, and with each successive death, the being is distilled.

In the world of plants, the purest and highest distillation of plant matter can be found in its essence. Essential oils are thus good assisting agents for affecting subtle, essential changes within the scope of our work lives. Beyond that, given the knowledge of the creation of atmospheres, aromatics provide key components to a space of invocation. In the establishment of resonance with entities of higher dimension, one must charge up the atmosphere so that there is electrical correspondence, and incense as well as essential oils will help in this necessity. At times the heavy and ongoing use of incense is necessary to create the medium or atmospheric condition required for Angelic Invocation.

The conditions of invocation of the Simurgh, which offers us a prime example of macrodimensional voyaging, included a charged atmosphere that was dense with incense. The complex mix of incense burned that night was comprised of Frankincense, Myrrh, Elecampagne, Blue Vervain, Sandalwood Rue, a little tobacco plant, and trace amounts of other materials. The atmosphere was very carefully created by E.J. and the invocation centered on an experimental performance of *Creation Story Verbatim*. Robbert, playing Gabriel, and I, playing the Lord, sat opposite one another, simply saying the lines without any acting, allowing the movement of the moment to take us. This was after several other experiments that did not quite flow. The audience sat in a semi-circle around us. There were several deliberately-placed elements in the room. A beautiful miniature room, which was an exact replica of a space for invocation at the Cosmo Street center during the earliest times of the Institute for the Development of the Harmonious Human Being, was one of the prominent props. There were large Oriental cushions and rugs that were carefully placed. The drapes were drawn on all the windows except there was one corner of one drape deliberately brought up just enough to expose a little bit of window. I don't have a note of this in my journal, but memory tells me that this was done to represent the void. I also have a sense of it as signifying infinite possibility.

At some point my consciousness was greatly altered and the atmosphere was high-pitched and electric. I could hear a faint buzzing sound that soon gave way to something like a rattlesnake rattle — it wasn't so much that I could hear it, as it was just a part of my morphology which was undergoing change, as I seemed to be traveling through labyrinthine chambers. Then there came a place of stasis from the movement where I could no longer say the lines, all I could do was sit and breathe. With each inhalation and exhalation, it was *as if* the entire space was being inflated with a huge-winged creature that seemed comprised of the folks gathered. Robbert and I were *as if* at the crown of this bird-like creature that had a massive body. It wrapped around the whole of the large room in which most were gathered and then into an adjacent atrium. It seemed to settle down with a massive stretch of its wing. All I did was stay very still and breathe. As I wrote in my journal — "To sit and breathe, at that point when it seemed I could do nothing but sit, breathe and look over at Robbert, that is when the puffing started and the bird grew. Voluntary postures were imperative to the space, voluntary movement maintained the beam, involuntary movement would have caused a loss of track."

It was quite clear that the various elements put into the creation of that intentional atmosphere were vital. Successful invocation requires one strike a balance between keen attention to detail and overview. I will never be able to express the extraordinary aliveness of this magnificent creature, nor the profundity of the feeling quality throughout its invocation. There are more indepth explanations of it to be found in *Life in the Labyrinth* as well As the "Talk of the Month" titled *The Simurgh*. One description is that it is the King that the thirty birds seek in Attar's brilliant allegory *The Conference of the Birds*.

This successful school experiment offered benefits to my work that were far-reaching and demonstrated well the relationship between theater and the creation of intentional atmosphere for invocation that reaches far back in ancient history. Frankincense, Myrrh and other resinous and balsamic ingredients were so highly prized that with the domestication of camels, which enabled travel through the harshness of the desert, they opened trade routes among people of vast distances. The Frankincense trade route is still known to this day and travelers in caravans will be greeted by nomadic campsites with the honoring gesture of throwing a few frankincense tears into the fire.

The gods love fragrance — we offer hospitality to our great Host by clarifying our own atmosphere, distilling our Essential Being. We can use the world of essential oils and work-intelligent fragrance composition in our clarifying processes, inviting essential self dominance into our daily lives. It's been many years and lifetimes since I walked into the very first Perfumerie hours after it was built in Nevada City. I walked in just in time to watch the new shop until E.J. and crew returned from their dinner break and prior to an art opening at the Fifth Avenue Gallery. An incredible generosity continues to flow toward me just from having been willing to walk this fragrant path in faith, stopping to smell the roses along the Way.

The Magician
Grace Kelly Rivera, acrylic on canvas, 36" x 30" © 2011 Grace Kelly Rivera

Topic Ten

The Uses of Acting, Sacred Acting and Theater in the Work

How does one apply theater and acting in transformational work?

An awareness of theater in life and the intentional use of posture and mood dawned on me in this primitive way and remained as an evolving impression long enough to arrive at a school where it has been given the opportunity of refinement.

I had the good fortune of having a tough childhood. That is, in the world of duality, in the world of personal history. Sitting where I am now, here — nowhere — it's all good. But in the world where I have a personal history, there was a lot of stress and difficulty that produced conditions for alternative states of consciousness, provoking an inquiry into God and the nature of personal reality early on.

I remember one day quite vividly when I was in the front yard area of my apartment building in a large low-income housing project in Hyattsville, Maryland, just outside of Washington, DC. I was in second or third grade watching other children play. I marveled at how utterly free they seemed, completely oblivious to the weight that I felt pressing on me all the time — I wondered how in the world they did it, how were they that happy? And then it struck me — I could act that way! I could mimic them and maybe produce the same effect in myself. And indeed, it worked enough to inspire me to walk the path again and again. So an awareness of theater in life and the intentional use of posture and mood dawned on me in this primitive way and remained as an evolving impression long enough to arrive at a school where it has been given the opportunity of refinement.

As with any process of refinement, which in objective art really has no end point, demolition work is involved before the foundation for a new platform can be established. Experienced artists of different disciplines who work with E.J. tend to shed some training at the same time that they are exposed to a new skill set within the art form. Eventually, an important skill developed is that of getting out of the way in order to serve the needs of the invocational space completely.

There are different approaches to the study of acting and theater. When I studied theater in New York, Stanislavski and Method Acting were prominent. Constantin Stanislavski was an actor who studied actors while they were at work as well as within the context of their daily lives. Out of his observations, systems of teaching have been created. He observed certain things great actors seemed to have in common such as a natural tendency to observe many different types of people to gain data. They also dipped into their own reservoir of emotional experience to fuel their characterizations.

Herbert Berghoff and Uta Hagen put emphasis on the development of belief in acting, and the creation of conditions that support that possibility. Meisner's technique on the development of an actor places emphasis on relationship and its expression in present moment. And at the Process Studio Theater, where I studied after studying at the Herbert Berhoff/Uta Hagen Studio, focus was placed on presence and posture leading to mood. One of the things all of these methods have in common is that they are created to address the needs of a Theater that is non-objective in the Work sense. In this kind of theater, skill is developed to replicate conditions for emotional experiences that relate to the reality pump as nature intended it to work. Present moment is addressed, but as it relates to the needs of a theater that is not necessarily present moment-based, expressing the human experience without relationship to voluntary evolution.

It attests to the strength and potential inherent in the theatrical arena that sometimes even this type of theater can take audience and performers to a place of "Everyman" which transcends the ordinary, where the whole becomes larger than the sum total of its parts. The qualities that create ready parallels between the world of Objective Theater and ordinary theater can cause confusion in much the same way that adrenaline-driven sports can bring folks to a false awakening. A necessity to distinguish an evolutionary theater from any other presents itself.

Objective Theater is a product of, as well as aide to the process of, reversing the function of the human biological machine as a pump for making the outer world real. It produces conditions for awakening latent faculties of perception and the invocation of higher dimensional entities which can offer radiations necessary for evolution. One makes voluntary manifestation to this end of using the outer world to feed the inner rather than just for the purpose of entertainment. Mood, the rudder by which we steer in the macrodimensional labyrinth, is exactly orchestrated, while at the same time, there is left enough opening in the theatrical elements to allow for the quality of fluidity that is necessary to invocation. Objective Theater has a broad spectrum that includes all of Life to the Objective Actor.

In Objective Theater, which bears a relationship to Ceremonial Magic, the space of the theater is prepared through banishing first, clearing the space of anything unwanted energetically. There is a form of intention taking place here as one creates the conditions for a fresh invocation, clearing out any density that might occur from residue of previous work, thus setting the conditions for fluid presence. Following this preparation, there will be the evocation, or the "bowl of milk," as it is sometimes referred to, that will be used to feed the entities — electrical configurations being invoked. This special food is gotten by the audience's engagement in the emotional changes they are being taken through as they watch the play's unfolding.

One can't know what is meant by this unless one has experienced it. It is like trying to explain the "such-ness" of sex — it is only in the experience that one can know it. It takes walking a path that will bring about the development of the perceptual faculties and accumulation of experience in dealing with macrodimensional entities. Working alone, a ceremonial magician will evoke out of himself/herself the quality of changing mood that can trigger the production of certain glandular secretions. These are fed upon by higher dimensional entities. Everything in the universe eats, including macrodimensional entities. The kinds of creatures we invoke in school conditions are those that will give in exchange data and radiations that serve our evolutionary work.

Evocation in objective theater is done relative to the audience; the actors work to produce the psycho-emotional conditions that will put them through emotional change — from a sense of wonder to laughter, trepidation and joy. The audience is taken this way, then that, until out of them is evoked sufficient substance to provide food for the entities wanted. This substance is electrical in nature, and is directed to the stage and offered as food. When the entity has been successfully invoked, it descends on the audience, which is visible to one with this quality of vision, and thus produces an emitting Work artifact. This artifact produces, in turn, a striving toward the School, the Dharma, in those exposed to it.

The kind of audience that is present will determine the kind of entities that will be invoked. In a situation where the audience is comprised of people who already have the Work infection, so to speak, that is to say, a developing magnetic center that inclines them toward the Work, the kind of entities invoked will be those providing the kind of initiatory experience needed. Once one has entered the Work, the kind of entities to invoke will be those that can offer real Work. Once evocation and invocation, taken place, one must then banish and close the space.

In the wonderful play *The Dresser*, by Ronald Harwood, which was made into a film with Albert Finney and Tom Courtenay, one of the two main characters, Sir, is an aging Shakespearean actor in an equally aging acting company that is past its prime and trying to maintain afloat during the Second World War. He seems to be losing his mind, and is, in fact, close to death, but doesn't know it yet. In his state he delivers a brilliant Lear, considered by many the most difficult of Shakespeare's plays. The play revolves largely around Sir's relationship to his Dresser, Norman, who has served him for many years. But the extraordinary is hidden within the ordinary, and in these lines we catch a glimpse of how theater can fuel the transcendence.

The Dresser

Sir, "I thought tonight I caught sight of him. Or saw myself as he sees me. Speaking, 'Reason not the need' I was suddenly detached from myself. My thoughts flew. And I was observing from a great height. Go on, you bastard, I seemed to be saying or hearing. Go on, you've more to give, don't hold back, more, more, more. And I was watching Lear. Each word he spoke was fresh invented. I had no knowledge of what came next, what fate awaited him. The agony was in the moment of acting created, I saw the old man and that old man was me. And I knew there was more to come but what? Bliss, partial recovery, more pain and death. All this I knew I had yet to see. Outside myself, do you understand? Outside myself."

(Harwood, *The Dresser* , Samuel French publisher)

It is said that if an actor needs to spit on stage, he must learn to do so theatrically, with elegance, with stage presence. Stage presence is fundamentally the result of accumulated experience in applying one's concentrated attention with presence. The aim of the actor is to breathe life into the character, to awaken the creation that is the play by living that character's life on stage in real time, here, now. An actor with weak attention and presence will not have the ability to transport the audience, to take the audience's suspended state of disbelief and engage them into believing the life they are witnessing. So many acting exercises target the actor's ability to be present and able to harness the energy that is available in the theatrical setting, largely in the form of the audience's attention and the intentional conditions created.

One acting coach I worked with, Jack Waltzer, illustrated well how our psychological and corresponding physical blockages will deflect energy away from the performance and communication of character. He would first have us warm up our bodies to the point that we would call relaxation. As we sat in our chairs, relaxed, he would move the different body parts — like the arm or leg in such a way as to show the level of relaxation we had achieved — and lastly, he would do this with the head. It took a great deal of trust and relaxation to get to be able to allow him full control of the movement. Following this, we were to imagine a number of absurd things going on all at once — having a shower that is first cold then wonderful, then made of warm molasses that turns hot, while stepping on marshmallows…this sort of thing. He would carefully build these scenes in layers and apply them to isolated parts of the body, and thus engage our complete, as well as divided, attention.

Out of this kind of theater game, uncustomary postures were readily adopted — he would freeze us in these postures one by one and ask us to speak as the character they invoked. In this way, we got an opportunity to experience something completely different, and this, for me, served to highlight a route to the voluntary within. Another exercise had us one by one stand before the audience of other students, breaking up the simple song *Happy Birthday to You* into syllables, each single syllable would be sung as a note while making eye contact with the audience, one at a time, a syllable per person. We were to do this as relaxed as possible, meanwhile giving each syllable the fullness of our voice and presence. It was remarkable to watch myself and others in this exercise, even after all the previous work of getting out of our own habitual postures as we would stiffen up unconsciously in one spot or another, but slowly we learned how to have enough Will of Presence to correct these blockages. Jack would walk behind a person and start manipulating their arms while they were singing the syllables to test whether they were genuinely relaxed and present. He explained that wherever we were stiff, it represented blockage of energy, energy that would otherwise be used to communicate to the audience.

This quality of voluntariness and awareness of energy is useful in Objective Theater. With this, it becomes possible to create the necessary mood changes, thus leading the audience as needed. Some data is emotional in nature — there are higher emotional states and nuances necessary to our evolution. We serve the audience as an objective actor by our clarity, our ability to allow the creative force to come through unobstructed.

Life as Theater is the reality, in fact — a huge production of *Much Ado About Nothing*. I'll walk Shakespeare's path a little further here, but with a twist and say all the world is a stage — for the Work. In the context of the school, we will use theater skills in our work, using recall and creative imagination, movement, posture and mood. If we have a sense of Life as Theater, then we have likely begun developing our voyager skills, because the attention to detail, mood, posture, space and movement will have begun to bring focus to a more subtle realm of events, the subtext. Objects take on a new aliveness as props and there is a perfect timing to all that takes place when we can align ourselves well to the present moment's unfolding.

The best acting is of course no acting at all.

We are applying theater skills when invoking presence. Inwardly, we create the correct conditions with our Will to Work, our presence and attention that make for the ritual sacrificing of the outer world to feed the inner. Before we are able to succeed at some of the practices we must do them *as if*. To *as if* is a very important cornerstone practice that serves our work in much the same way a runway serves a jet's flight. To apply the technique of *as if* consciously gives the opportunity to become aligned to the goal and through repeated application done under the right set of conditions "the model becomes the thing itself."

The Magical formula "As above so below" applies to Objective Theater and can be seen as the actors use posture and mood to bring the audience from the known to the realm of the unknown yet familiar. By establishing resonant conditions, creating a close model, the actors, through posture and the intentional creation of mood, can enliven the model to the place of it becoming not only a model, but also a source of transformative energy.

When we operate *as if* our goal is attained, or will be, we are intentionally creating a relationship to that goal, and intention fills a void that accident might otherwise fill. Magical invocation applies the technique in the creation of resonance. We take what is known and springboard into the unknown and tap into an ancient tradition in the process. This technique has been used by many since the earliest of times and is here known as shamanism, there as ancient oracular theater, and still in another place as high mass.

If you examine the general orientation of a church, you will see a close relationship to theater. The audience or congregation sits facing an altar and pulpit from which the head invocant conducts his invocation.

The atmosphere, especially, of a cathedral with its high vaulted ceilings and beautiful stained glass, is a model pointing to macrodimensional atmospheric equivalents. In Catholic Church, prior to high mass, the priest will cense the atmosphere with Frankincense in accordance with certain rites long before established.

Frankincense has been used since ancient times to cense and fumigate chambers because of its many properties that are useful to invocation. The resin, with its essential oils that are released when burned, produces a pleasing fragrance that has a general effect of elevation without excitation — a very good thing for the achievement of a useful collective space. Its antibacterial properties would also serve well, along with its clean fragrance, in offsetting conditions that might have been bacterially compromising. Frankincense is often used in the awakening of the heart chakra, evoking the quality of mood wanted.

I once saw a rare manuscript that described a high mass in its esoteric and more original meaning and intent. It included diagrams that showed how the energy currents of the invoked entities with transformational effect would circulate in the space around the congregation. We see several theater techniques being employed here. Conditions are created that are conducive to the correct quality of attention and mood. As examples, the quality of lighting, the stained glass windows, the gathering of attention, and use of spoken voice between the congregation and the priest, the posture, costume and speech of the invocants, the quality of sound, the singing of the choir to mimic celestial sound — all these elements serve to evoke subtle mood changes from the congregation that generate energy used for the invocation.

Of course, modern day priests do not necessarily have the knowledge and skill to invoke the quality of presence that is useful to Work aims; rather, too often there is a sign that quite an opposite effect is being produced. As the Lord says in *Creation Story Verbatim* "...for which they gather in special houses, Gabriel, some of which are so opulent *we* should only live in them one day each week, actually one small part of one morning one day each week. A day late, I might add."

This is a theater that confronts our situation with an end toward freedom and encourages our voluntary return to the Garden. It sounds quite poetic, this — the return to the Garden, but we must know that it involves a lot of demolition work and the restructuring of our inner selves to re-verse the pump function we were born to fulfill of making real the outer world. We are voluntarily walking back into the Garden, but before this can happen, we need an objective and working relationship with the fac-ulties used to make real the outer world. Our identification, ability to be-lieve, suggestibility, feelings, and most of all, our will of attention must come under our own volition to apply consciously toward Work aims. Theater techniques are largely designed to help the actor do this, gain a degree of mastery over the instrument in order that it may be used to whatever effect called upon by the script.

To do the Invocation of Presence exercise, we create an inner theater or ritual space. We can readily see for ourselves the effect of radiation of presence when this inner work succeeds. Upon our own inner altar we sacrifice our identification of the moment for the invocation of the presence of our presence. Now consider that this is possible on a much larger scale. A group gathering together has the possibility of invoking the presence of something much greater. Sacrifice is needed, and that sacrifice will, in part, consist of individual identity, as the morphology changes.

One of the greatest examples of Objective Theater is found in the school experiment that led to the invocation of the Simurgh, which was spoken of at some length in the chapter on Alchemical Oils. It seems ap-propriate to offer a little background to this big school event. Robbert and I toured with others as The North American Bunraku Puppet Theater troupe. Bunraku puppetry has been called the Art Form of Three as it brings together three elements — the specially made Bunraku puppets, the Storyteller and the Samisen player. In traditional Bunraku Puppetry, which originated over four hundred years ago, the puppets stand about four feet tall and are operated by two or three puppeteers. The puppets have moveable parts, in some cases, even enabling facial expression.

Coordinating the articulation of movement between the puppeteers that is used to convey the traditional stories is an extraordinary thing that requires years of dedicated practice to achieve. I have had the great for-tune to witness traditional Bunraku Puppetry once and can tell you that the audience is riveted to the action up on stage and the level of attention and artistry is remarkable. It is little wonder that this art form is readily adapted into a Work tool.

We modified our Bunraku puppets — these were larger soft sculptures that were operated by three puppeteers dressed in black, including hoods that covered faces, gloves covering hands, played against a black backdrop. The resulting effect was that all attention went to the puppets, and the puppets came to life. It was an extraordinary way of learning about many things, and chief among them, the idea of bringing a creation to life. I was the storyteller, and Robbert was the head puppeteer who operated the right arm and head of the puppet, Brigitte Donvez operated the torso and left arm while Rick Crammond, Mr. Fix It, worked the feet. Parker Dixon and sometimes Menlo played music, and Rose Gander also told stories, but mainly served as business manager.

It was hard work, there in the hot sun, at fairs, at times was grueling, especially for the puppeteers, but incredibly worth the price of admission. When the puppets came to life, it was unmistakable; everyone felt a subtle and sometimes not-so-subtle current of electricity and the audience was completely transported. We watched life-beaten faces momentarily melt into childhood mirth.

There were shared experiences of many aspects of these ideas that were deepened by the fact that together we also maintained school practices. E.J. asked us to quit smoking cigarettes, stating that he could not work with people enslaved to tobacco, at the same time, we were put on the cleansing diet. All of the elements combined to create difficult internal conditions for us — an alchemical fuel. One personal experience here will demonstrate how individual needs are sometimes met within the context of the larger group work.

Many factors contribute to a particular predilection I have to be open to influence. This quality has its advantages and disadvantages considered from the point of view of invocation. On the one hand, there might be readiness to shape-shift, but on the other, without discernment, trouble can ensue from being subject to the wrong kind of influence. I have been given strong impressions and course corrections within the scope of my theater work, and to my view, in hindsight, one repeated lesson has been in this area of discernment. The following is an example of what I think I could call a shock delivered as a means of correction.

I had not been a storyteller long with the troupe when we did a big fair in which E.J. had a booth selling oils and jewelry. We had very little rehearsal for this gig, and given our crazy schedules, it had been next to impossible to put together a cohesive show — a common situation in the school that seems to be cultivated to the effect of forcing improvisation. Improvisation invites the quality of present moment living we aim to have that leads to true spontaneity and response to the Zen of the moment. Here there is the possibility of having what Zen Buddhists might call "naturalness that springs forth from nothingness." Improvisation, of course, can also be a vehicle for the expression of ego, so it is only used in Objective Theater by those, or under the direction of those, well-educated in the practice.

So there I was, a novice in so many respects, and I was directed by the senior members of the troupe to tell a rather risqué story out of the Juan Tepozton collection of stories in which Juan, played by Monty, the puppet, found himself in a rather compromising position with a young lady. This all took place outdoors on a minimal stage area that felt more like a street theater situation. In these situations that are not contained with all the distraction about one, there is a big challenge in getting and keeping the audience's attention as well as harnessing one's own.

I was working with all of these elements along with the other members of the troupe, about to deliver the story and oblivious to the fact that E.J. was frantically gesturing me to stop the story, not to tell it, it took him coming up behind me and insisting I go off the stage while Rose went on to tell another story. I was mortified and felt betrayed by the fact that I had innocently been doing what I had been told to do. My first reaction was internal rage — my chronic defense mechanism against the waking state in full force. I considered running away from the situation, but this was not a real option, as I didn't have two nickels to rub together and the only vehicles we had carried the group and equipment.

With the help of my pal, Parker Dixon, especially, I managed to bring myself to some semblance of functionality. We were due on for another show later that afternoon, and in between we were asked to watch the booth so that E.J. could go do some business within the fair. Hanging out in this situation took everything I had, or so it seemed. When he came back to the booth, the Teacher looked at me and with a serious and kind voice said — "I had to do that . . . it's Theater." I knew exactly what he meant at that moment — there is a sanctity that must remain intact to keep within the lawful bounds of Objective Theater. I got it to my very core, and this impression still informs my theater experience.

I was honored at that moment to be even a novice in the tradition. He explained that there were children in the audience and that the story I was about to tell was not appropriate. Implied also was the fact that I needed to have the discernment to see and respond to actual necessity, not blindly obey a request. In terms of my Bardo movement, there was much to be learned in that I was overwhelmed by the chaos of the space, not seeing or heeding the warning given by my guide until it was too late. I quickly learned that there were new levels of responsibility to assume, and weakness or ignorance was not going to serve as an excuse. As an invocant performer, I had the responsibility to the audience that included taking into consideration who that audience is, taking them on a journey and then bringing them back from that journey intact.

From this exchange with my Teacher, I went on to perform with the group again later that afternoon. We had no idea what we were going to do to fill the now-empty segment of the show where the risqué story used to be. I'd hoped that perhaps Rose would take over again, but it was insisted that I go on. And then it happened — we were taken up by a grace, somehow we managed to improvise a little scene in which Montgomery climbed up on a Harley and went for a ride — a little gem birthed right there after some labor. This little piece of "something born naturally from nothing" actually served for the basis of a new story that we went on to perform during a tour up the West Coast.

The best acting is, of course, no acting at all. In the above situation, I was stripped of my outer theater training and technique, taken to a more essential place. The second time we performed, I was certainly less of an identity than what I started out on that day. And this translated into being more available to address the moment's necessity. A new invocational movement was allowed to take place. We were given the opportunity to respond to the necessity of the moment with its time, place and people.

At one point E.J. gave Robbert and I the *Being* task of playing Gabriel and the Lord in his play *Creation Story Verbatim*. We were given the opportunity to memorize lines, being relieved of our ordinary duties to this end, and at the same time, he would rewrite the play so that this kept us from getting too comfortable with the lines. He gave us very specific direction that was ever so irritating to my New York Method actress persona and all of this in the bubbling cauldron of life in the school. Robbert and I did not get along and often were at odds with each other during the course of our Bunraku work, but over time, during the course of our many long walks we took to memorize lines, after many experiences together in fire and rain, we developed a true Work buddy relationship that lasts to this day. We worked through dry spells where there was no juice to the material, in front of all kinds of audiences, in strange circumstances — even delivering lines while E.J. maintained a separate conversation going with the guest for whom the performance was ostensibly being put on.

On the Thanksgiving Day when we experienced the Simurgh, I remember the feeling of "nothing left to lose". I had done lots of childcare and cleaning and did not have the energy for hope or expectation. I was in the midst of doing something or other to keep myself busy and avoiding folks when I noticed the Teacher come out into the front room with the censer as some of his helpers brought in a model of Cosmo Street. I was told that E.J. wanted us to do a performance of *Creation Story Verbatim*. There was a faint feeling of foreboding of a particular kind — something told my psyche that it was going to have to take a back seat that evening, and fortunately, it was subdued enough not to put up too much resistance. Talk about earth-shattering experiences . . . well, indeed, I did talk about it, and in the process, gained another valuable set of impressions around my unconscious subjectivity to influence.

As previously indicated, the Simurgh refers to the invocation of a very large macrodimensional creature that is both bird-like and serpentine. The Simurgh is the name of the King that the Thirty Birds seek, while at the same time, being comprised of the Thirty Birds in the allegory of *The Conference of the Birds* written by the Sufi mystic and perfumer, Attar, in the thirteenth century.

It was not until the following day that we discussed the event. At some point I'd been asked to describe what I had seen and with the Teacher's prompting, I gave a clear description. Then there was a break in our meeting. During that break, in conversation with other students, it was suggested that this creature invoked might have been the Peacock Angel which is invoked among the Yezidi tribe. By the time we gathered again that evening, I had completely adopted this idea unconsciously, now referring to it as the Peacock Angel without even being aware of the fact that I'd just taken that leap from someone's suggestion.

At the meeting that evening, the event was discussed at length, and I received good cleansing radiations, as it was demonstrated to me how readily and unconsciously I had adopted the given suggestion. Among the things we discovered about the entity that was invoked, which Rumi cites in his writings as being elusive, rare and grand, is that there are likely only about eight or so of these creatures in existence. Another name for this is "Groonk" — Crane — which symbolizes the feeling of spiritual majesty.

When one objectifies one's own character, there is given room for pure Being to stick its hand in the puppet and manipulate its activities with gusto.

These are, indeed, very grand events and ideas, but they are founded on simple basic practices around the development of a Bardo Voyager's attention. Whole body awareness, attention on the natural breath, impartial self-observation, voluntary activity — these serve our life and work in Objective Theater.

Perhaps we have a life situation in which our character responds to another with a repeated pattern of communication or behavior that seems only to serve lunar entities. By lunar entities, I refer to any energetic configuration that feeds the moon, to use a Fourth Way phrase, which I interpret as feeding the reality pump as nature intended, rather than reversing the energetic flow up from density. Chief Feature is one such entity.

With such a repeating life situation, we are given opportunity to try on a different character, or at least gain the impartial vision of our own character reacting in its predictable manner. In *Life as Theater,* we are ever-perfecting our own character, getting to know it in its every facet. In this way we use repetition as a tool that works for our work rather than the creation of unconscious habit.

Enough of this observation, and we may gain the energy needed to try something new and uncharacteristic, but responsible, taking care not to incite the natives to riot. The more we can objectify our own character through impartial observation and voluntary activity, the greater the possibility we have of being able to adopt all the necessary postures that Completed Being is able to assume, indicating the transcendence of typicality. The better the possibility also we have of serving the greater good as we will not be bound to those postures that serve to feed the unconscious aspect of our Being. We must be fluid enough to respond to *this* moment's calling.

Remember, it all starts with remembering, with being voluntarily who we are in the present moment, full embrace. There must be enough faith to allow ourselves to give up our enslavement to habitual reactions that keep us identified with the organic. In order to see that we have existence beyond what our reactions are, we must at some point gain the will and presence not to react with habit, but to have the ability to respond as we choose, in service to work aims rather than the maintenance of our psyche's identity.

It has been said that only indirect methods work in this business of transformation. Considering the tricky nature of the psyche/essence relationship, even just a little, this makes good sense. Actually, getting down to the high wire, so to speak, when we look at the model of the relationship of the Absolute to Creation, the situation we are addressing here for which our awakening is but the first step, it is clear that only indirect methods will apply. As the Lord says in *Creation Story Verbatim* — "I can't intervene in the outcome of creation once it begins. After the first moment of creation, it all runs on sheer momentum, so after that first great big push, that's it . . . . And you angels, you're just the results of one of my earlier efforts to interfere in the outcome of creation . . ." Direct interference or intervention produces a fresh creation. The Creator creates. Any attempt to adjust makes a new Creation to maintain.

Once a creation, always a creation — to my understanding, one of the primary hopes for alleviation of the suffering of the Absolute is that the creation might produce an evolutionary effect on its Creator, that it might come to life enough to do so. The only way out is through the very indirectness of creation — think magic weenie here — I refer to the trick of taking the two pointer fingers, pointing them to one another a couple of inches apart, diffusing the vision. Let's say the left finger is the non-phenomenal and the right the phenomenal world. The magic weenie you will see in the middle, there, not there, that's Being. This is what we are out to substantiate.

Theater works with the illusory to get to the real, thus participating in the natural movement of existence springing forth from nothingness. It is pliable enough to serve the natural flow of creation outward in its momentum, making much ado about nothing, or it can serve the unnatural flow of creation back inward, returning back to nothing the much ado. I'm talking about the reversal of the pump here — taking the outer world to feed the inner instead of using the higher energy to feed the creation of the lower. But you have to get in to that creation to get out.

Just as we had to apply our attention and vision to our hands and fingers in a new way to achieve the magic weenie, in theater we apply our attention on things we may normally not consider, we may indeed take for granted, but in that application of attention are given an opportunity for transcendence.

We see similar trend of movement when we work with the chronic defense mechanism against the waking sate — the energy of the momentum of the chronic can be used toward the very awakening that it is intended to avoid in a form of internal Tai-Chi practice. And like a maturing Tai Chi practice, it involves the development of a particular quality of attention that can stretch beyond the narrow band of awareness to which we are normally confined — a voyager attention. Diffusion of vision, especially with a corresponding undifferentiated awareness — no one thing more than another — can help us access the realm of voyager attention.

In theater, there is a mass of collective attention that is available for the awakening of the creation up on stage. That attention, well-directed by the actors through speech and silence, posture and movement in the created setting can infuse fresh life and meaning to an inanimate object, a prop, or a conversation, or even just a gesture, catapulting the ordinary into the profound.

For the windows of transcending opportunity to be well-used, it usually takes a combination of repetition and the artistic daring that comes with living the moment in truth. Just as we discover when we work with the intentional development of any skill, repetition can helps us grow our Will and allows for a deeper familiarity from which to springboard into the unfamiliar when the moment is present to do so. Some ancient theater was oracular, using the technique of establishing resonant magical conditions combined with repetition of the known to produce a possible window into the unknown so that the actors would start off with a script from which they would then depart into improvisation at a certain point.

> *No matter how many people are out in the audience, we are playing to one — there is only one Being that has taken a portion of itself and put it outside of itself, making it into characters up on the stage so that it may observe and learn.*

The objective actor uses the body as an instrument of communication and invocation of the character. Doing this effectively requires self-knowledge. One's own characteristics need to be known well enough to use them impartially as called for depending upon the character being played. It is the character that needs to be communicated, not the actor. As Rumi would tell us, it is the Musician's breath that makes the sweet music out of the flute — we praise the Musician, not the instrument.

In order for the instrument to come to life like that, hosting the play of breath, it must be clear of any obstruction. Even in ordinary theater, there is a lot of opportunity to make voluntary things that might otherwise be involuntary. This kind of training, well-used for our work, can help in the clearance of our obstructions. When one works in theater or approaches Life as Theater, the intentional allowance of manifestation of what is, given the right attitude of volition, can aid in the objectification of one's own character. The stage expands from the realm of the particulars to the gestalt of the whole. When one objectifies one's own character, there is given room for pure being to stick its hand in the puppet and manipulate its activities with gusto.

In the objectification process is also implied the presence of the impartial Witness. As I write that word — Witness — an association comes up that seems worth telling. Something E.J. said to Robbert and I while working with *Creation Story Verbatim* — "no matter how many people are out in the audience, we are playing to one" — there is only one Being that has taken a portion of itself and put it outside of itself, making it into characters up on the stage so that it may observe and learn.

We are here talking about theater for work invocation purposes, Objective Theater. No matter what kind of theater we are talking about, there is invocation involved and either we are invoking what can be called "lunar entities," which do not serve our work, or we are invoking the "solar entities" that provide transformational effects. In any event, the same basic process of feeding will take place — food is offered in the form of elixir or venom and the corresponding Being will eat and be bound, giving data and transformation or nothing at all. Solar entities will feed, but give in exchange, while lunar entities will only rob us of precious energy, while giving us a sense of exhilaration or pleasure.

The way is not out but through. I am going to paraphrase something I once read Al Pacino was supposed to have said — he is considered by many one of the greatest of actors alive — that "the one thing we all bear in common is our own uniqueness." In sitting squarely in the moment of an ordinary character, he has transcended to the place of *Every Man*. Sitting squarely in our moment here, now, we transcend to the place of all and tell the Greatest Story Ever Told again, as it is most uniquely expressed in us, once more, with voluntary feeling.

Mystical Empress
Grace Kelly Rivera, Mixed Media on Prepared Arches Paper, 14.5"x 11"
© 1998 Grace Kelly Rivera

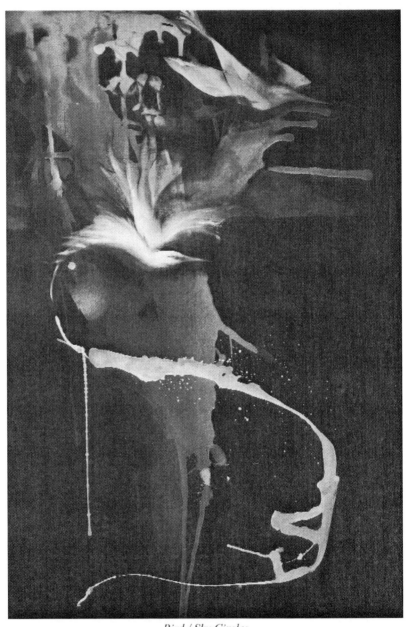

Bird / Sky Circles
Grace Kelly Rivera, acrylic on canvas, 60" x 40" © 2011 Grace Kelly Rivera

Topic Eleven

My Journey to the Heart of the Maker:
The Way of Service

My Journey to the Heart of the Maker
To remember who I am ...
But to lift a soul is not easy,
Some suffering there must be

(IDHHB, *Angel Song Book* — lyrics by Menlo Macfarlane, page 145)

It doesn't really seem likely that the quality of assessment implied here can be readily applied to the realm of one's spirit. Yet we are living under the impression that there is something outside of spirit and with this a natural tendency to want to assess and question. Though spirit will elude any attempt at definition, I enjoy Rumi's take — Spirit is the art of making flow once again what is blocked. Or, Spirit is a delicate girl that comes out to play when one draws the sword of selfless action.

Assessing one's alignment and thus, ability to take the next step on the Spiritual Path, might prove an interesting re-formulation of this topic. Looking at this will bring us into the realm of the question E.J. formulated for the group many years ago — *How do I make my transformation a necessity to the Work?* This is a useful question formulated by a very good question and answer maker.

In the *Creation Story Verbatim* play, which play contains in potential

All and Everything needed to learn how to Work; the Lord tells Gabriel repeatedly that Angels can't evolve. And yet, there is some indication that they do, in fact. Certainly Gabriel's all-centered readiness to take in any data the Lord wishes to offer as a preparation for his imminent succession to the third and highest realm, would imply evolutionary impulse among angels. But the Lord remains steady in her stance — ". . . They can't evolve, that's why it's so important for these stupid two-and-a-half-brained humans to take the necessary steps toward voluntary evolution." After some bantering, Gabriel challenges the Lord, brimming over with his subjective experience of being on the brink of the annihilation into his Beloved for which he longs. The following dialogue ensues:

"Okay, if us angels can't evolve, how do you explain these extra points on my horns? " says Gabriel

"Extra points?" asks the Lord.

"Yes, extra points — indicating evolution to the highest degree."

"Brace yourself Gabriel," she says, "there are no extra points on your stupid horns. Point on your head perhaps, but not on your horns."

A disappointed Gabriel tells her, "It sure felt like I was about to go over the edge."

"...Over the edge?"

"Yes, you know, Lord, over the edge, the great beyond, the land of Nod, the Land of Milk and Honey — you know, over the Edge!"

"You want to go over the edge? I'll send you over the edge you stupid angelic son of a bitch..." she says as she charges toward him in her Divine rage.

(Gold, *Creation Story Verbatim*, unpublished manuscript)

The Lord had indeed provided plenty of opportunity for him to be on the brink of real self-initiation, but the fixation of Gabriel's attention, in accordance with certain angelic characteristics, inadvertently moved him away from the object of his impartial striving. This dance is eternal and fixed. At the same time, this brilliantly-choreographed dance has the potential of evolutionary movement within its model, that is to say, the model of the thing can become the thing itself and yield genuine macrodimensional results as evidenced by the Simurgh experience.

The *Creation Story Verbatim* play served in my alignment process. Repeated exposure to the play, with its obvious data and the transformational by-products of invocational experiences through public and private performance, produced new synaptic connections. All of these synaptic changes took place in and through school conditions within the proximity of a genuine Teacher. But as can be seen by the play — Gabriel is right there with God Herself and yet falls for identification with the less exalted aspect of His Being precisely in his fixation with the evolutionary exaltation in annihilation.

What is this evolution we feel moved to volunteer working towards anyway? Remember at some level, all is an invocation. We volunteer ourselves to undergo evolutionary transformations through our activities, intentions and exposure to school conditions that are designed to help in the removal of impediment to the waking state. Intentional invocation plays a part in this process, starting with our practice to invoke the Presence of our Presence into the Present. Eventually, we call ourselves to the attention of the Agency that brings one to where one is quickened along the path.

On another level, Chief Feature, a creature that opposes our work self, invokes into our electrical field every thirty seconds. By virtue of this invocation, there exists also a thirty-second Moment of Freedom from this invocation. We can learn to be aware of these and to utilize these Moments of Freedom to our work advantage. Every action has an equal and opposite reaction. But there is a way of doing that is not doing. And it seems that this is a way of getting things done along the Way. For these non-doings we will look for Moments of Freedom.

Within the context of this school, the move to evolve is for the sake of something bigger than our own personal enhancement; in part, it is to serve in the alleviation of a particular kind of suffering that is the result of an involuntary creation. Through the bearing of consciousness into greater degrees of awakening and shape-shifting, we participate in cosmic maintenance. Practically speaking, this means clarifying and creating the chemical, biological and radiological factors necessary for transformation that will enable us to function multi-dimensionally. Angelic invocation and corresponding cosmic maintenance work serves this transformational process in its radiological effects as well as the chemical

and biological factors that result in consequence. With on-the-job training, an alignment of sorts takes place. The possibility of being recruited
for more work is enhanced.

Perhaps it is obvious, but nevertheless, I'll say it here — this Work
is all about *service*. The wish to help is a fundamental property of Being.
From one point of view, everything, all of creation, at some level, knows
its origin and everything yields to that knowledge in its own way. We
are not separate from everything, so in a way, service is even a pointless
concept, except to demonstrate a particular quality of movement.

The first taste I had of the concept of *service* outside the realm of my
Roman Catholic-based conditioning was when I was fourteen. I had an
awakening experience in which I saw that my attention, as I usually use
it, did not measure to the potential I'd just glimpsed. Suddenly, I had become the whole and the part within the whole, and the body shimmered
with light — all the rich details of my surroundings were revealed in
their perfection. But most importantly, I discovered attention, though I
didn't name it, I knew there was a quality of consciousness that was responsible for the marvelously rich experience of the ordinary. I'd never
taken into consideration my attention as a separate entity onto itself with
changeable quality.

I sat at the edge of my bed as this event reverberated forward. I knew
I wanted to live with this quality of aliveness more than the shadow life
I normally experienced. At some point, in my contemplation, I asked
myself what I was going to do with my life, what was to be my job?
While I had interests in both theater and art at the time, and I would say
when asked that I wanted to pursue life as an artist and actress, there was
something missing in my conviction. I examined this and other issues
closely.

Three contemplative thoughts presented themselves as I sat. One, as
indicated, was that as I normally existed, I was but a shadow of self —
I was capable of a richer experience of life. The second was that there
was an invisible world in which I held a job, and somehow it seemed
that job had to do with art, though I could not conceive how this could
be at the time. Moreover, relative to this job, I instinctively knew that it
was more substantial than anything based on worldly, physically-oriented
criteria. I knew also that in performing this duty, I would serve the greater

good. It was a new way of looking at *service* outside of the realm of charitable acts, such as volunteering at an orphanage, something I'd done.

The third of these contemplative thoughts was that there were folks on the planet who were intended to bear a particular kind of suffering, and I knew I was one of those folks. When this came through, there was no drama, it was quite matter-of-fact, yet there was overlay that had me making something of this particular nothing. In hindsight, I get a good view of conditioning and its effect on a fresh revelation, catching glimpse of the mechanical triggers stimulated by an objective, impartial and beginning apprehension of the idea of the suffering of the Absolute.

In New York, I worked at the Cloisters Museum, which is part of the Metropolitan Museum of Art, and holds a good portion of the medieval collection. Its structure was based loosely on the layout of a Benedictine Monastery. Portions of ancient ruins of Cloisters in Europe were shipped over to the northernmost tip of Manhattan, overlooking the Hudson in Fort Tryon Park and incorporated into the architecture. A cloister is an area of a monastery that may be open-aired while surrounded by enclosed columned walkways that can also lead to a center where there are often gardens, fountains and statuary that is conducive to the contemplative Christian life. Depending upon the monastic order, in this area of the monastery there would be no talking at all, or it might be the one place where some discussion of scripture was allowed.

There is an ambiance at the Cloisters Museum that lent itself to my burgeoning contemplative life, and artistic inspiration was to be found in the magnificent works of both religious and secular art. In the illuminated manuscripts, the incredibly intricate Rosewood-carved bead where the life of Christ is depicted, the Unicorn tapestries, statuary and magnificent altar paintings, I saw a beginning relationship between art and spiri;, I saw that art could serve spirit. The impressions taken during this time further nurtured this thought of having a job in the invisible world that related to art making and consciousness.

After working at the Cloisters Museum, I worked at Windows on the World at the Trade Center. It was while working here that I met E.J. and attended workshops and dinners. The ideas being presented in talks and the rich impressions taken in were expansive and so incredibly relevant that naturally the impulse to share presented itself. There were so many answers and questions bursting forth from within, I just wanted to take everyone by the hand to E.J. so they could have this quality of experience. I quickly found I was unable to express the ideas and cognition flooding me, and this inability combined with a deeper wish I'd always known, but couldn't formulate, brought me to a place of recognizing the service in Work-healthy communication of these ideas.

Service is a way of life that is naturally aligned to the truth of our existence. "We are one" and to be in a place of service acknowledges this fundamental fact. Much points to our being created to function in some form of service to the Creation and the Creator. We often speak of the idea of the reversal of the reality pump here. Ordinarily, humans serve the function of using finer matter to push reality out into the atmosphere — to make real the outer world. To jump rivers, to serve in a different way, entails paying great nature back what we have been given, or dying before we die. Rumi might say we go from river to ocean, but however it is said, in reversing the direction of energy back toward the finer, we play a different game altogether.

Looking a little at the Angelic model, we will see each Angelic entity has its range of function and characteristics that work together, yet they maintain the integrity of their identity in cosmic maintenance. Seeing that there is good evidence in many writings and visions to support the idea that such a thing as cosmic maintenance and service exist, it might be wise to look at our position from the point of view of what we are serving at the moment, and what we want to serve. Assessing where our alignment is in this respect will yield much more, it seems, than just looking at our individual characteristics alone. With the concept of service, we pull in a greater mass of necessity, a form of energy that can often give us clearer pointing to true north.

Service helps us to break the habit of egocentricity that keeps us bound to our limited morphology.

In any case, we are going to serve something whether we like it or not. Working with this fundamental aspect of things instead of fighting it seems to align us in a work friendly way. A shaman uses whatever tools and conditions are at his or her disposal. Service to the Work can be a way of making voluntary and, therefore, conscious what might otherwise be involuntary and unconscious. Habits built around work intended service help to keep us aligned to that which we would want to serve rather than leaving us open to influences that would have us serving something unwanted.

The first form of service is simply to be present and in remembrance in our life. Making a habit of this will deepen the experience of what it is to be in self-remembrance, in presence and the range of service will open up accordingly. If we feel inclined toward the Work, then we look to hook ourselves into service that aligns us with the Work and that can provide the radiations and impressions we need as nutrients to develop our faculties as well as food for the efforts we must sustain to affect our transformation.

When I first met E.J. in New York and it was clear I would be moving out to work with him in California, I came prepared to stop doing the things that I did — that is, the theater and the art. But E.J.'s encouragement of my work in these areas was clear. He purchased many art supplies for graphic and illustrative work that seemed to be in response to my involvement. When he heard of my plan to go to Pratt Institute for illustration as a means of making money to pay for my other habit of theater, he said to become an illustrator would be the same as waitressing, I should become a fine artist instead. On a couple of occasions he had me sit near him and work on illustrations while he conducted group meetings in New York. When I moved to California I was almost immediately put to work doing illustrations for *Talk of the Month* covers.

But the serious work that I do now in the studio, which E.J. has described as basically voyaging to a space and recording what I see there, this work did not really come about until after I went through a lot of fire. Motherhood definitely opened me up for the quality of pliability and acceptance I needed to be able to see as I needed to see. Then of course, there is the Friend as beautifully played by E.J., who creates conditions that bring us to ripe brinksmanship in our work, opening us, guiding us, to look in a particular direction.

When I worked at the Cloisters Museum, and just prior to my first experience of Dear Oobe, before knowing what an E.J. or Dear Oobe was, I had an awakening experience while shading with a pencil that I have referred to in my description of my first Dear Oobe experience. I was practicing shading, watching my every move and being with my breathing as I gently built up shading areas without forming anything consciously. Suddenly before me, I saw that there was a very clear head of a gargoyle staring back at me from what I had done, my vision had diffused slightly to see this. It was so real and vibrant, it frightened me! I thought it would jump out. But it was an incredibly alive moment and thrilling to experience. This was a taste of what would later develop into a method of service.

Fundamentally, I get into a state of Being that enables me to see certain visions as I stare at a canvas that has been prepared with texture. Most of my work is in getting into the state of Being and then resolving the visual problems that come up when I try to translate what I am seeing such that others can participate. It seems that the process of seeing and the work of executing that vision combine to document something that some viewers find useful to take in. To get me from the place of my early experience at the Cloisters, to the place of having ongoing work in this area that feels viable, has taken a lot of help which I've gotten through experience in and around the school and Teacher.

In New York, because I had not had as much experience as actors Mark Olsen and Jeff Burnett in theater, having only done a couple of Off-Off-Broadway plays along with my studies at the HB Studio and Process Studio Theater, I did not consider myself a theater person, though I really wanted to be. At one point, I remember E.J. looked at me during a workshop and mockingly said, "You do act, don't you?" I said that I'd done a little acting. He said, "A little acting? Ha!" That moment stands out because it seemed as though he was tapping into a vast reservoir of memory and clairvoyance that enabled him to see much more of my experience than what I knew at the time. I am reminded presently of something he has said about his vast knowledge in so many areas, which knowledge is often clairvoyant in nature. What is necessary to the Work of the moment is available to him, no more or less. The knowledge about a particular subject will also have a full scope of depth and range that is instantaneous. I can't claim to know the range of his perception at that moment, but I would venture that at the very least, he saw the work we would be doing together on *Creation Story Verbatim*.

Many rough edges have needed smoothing to bring me to a place where I feel I can work with E.J. on theater material and there is flow that is useful to the process. There have been many occasions of exasperation, confusion, frustration, with heaping helpings of humiliation. Humiliation has yielded to humility, a humility that is more readily accessible now than it was before and which allows for ease of movement, because that is where the Teacher hangs out. He hangs out in a place of humility as he Works. When one is taken up by a mighty force, there is no room for anything but acquiescence. I am still quite arrogant in my way, but this arrogance does not seem to get in the way like it used to.

When we first did *Creation Story Verbatim* at the Nevada Theater, we had a very special knapsack made with these big beautiful puffy wings sewn on it that Robbert, as Gabriel, would use. After the first run of the show, the knapsack was stored in a storage area of Robbert's along with many other things. When we prepared to do the show again at a different theater months later, we discovered that it had been stolen from his storage area.

E.J. was livid — impartially, voluntarily so, but livid. He called a meeting about this and used it as an example of why we as a group couldn't work. He turned to me and very sternly reprimanded me for not having the consciousness to prevent this from happening, not being a good work buddy and leaving the responsibility to Robbert alone for the care of the knapsack. He said that he himself would know where everything is, all the props, if it was for his work.

I cannot tell you how incredibly awful I felt about this. It brought me to the depths of despair and the thought of not being able to work, which is how it boiled down, the possibility that I would lose this opportunity to work was just devastating to me. I was brought to my knees, yet without a ground to kneel, my whole world was turned upside down. And this, too, did pass. But in time, approached from several angles at once, as part of life, these lessons kneaded me into more pliable clay and they were delivered in a way I couldn't have possibly imagined.

School conditions are such that there is created a theater space for evolutionary activity to take place to the greatest possible effect. There is a quality of energy that cannot be manufactured; it is borrowed through the grace of the dharma as it flows through the Teacher, with a line of transmission that goes directly to the Source. In these school conditions, the seemingly small and insignificant can be magnified to great proportions. The potent energy around a real school will elevate people, places and things to an archetypal platform and matters can take on a life or death significance.

A culture is developed among participants of an evolutionary school that maintains the quality of space needed to create these conditions. This is where it gets tricky, because too often cultures are created around the activities of leaders that do not have the quality of transmission found in a real school. A different quality of energy is at source. In the news we have seen the tragic results of this phenomenon of cultures being formed around misguided leaders. The leaders and the folks following are in one way equally responsible for this condition. For this reason, we are encouraged always to maintain enough presence of our critical faculty and our discernment, applying these to our work efforts. We are asked to not blindly believe, but to verify these ideas for ourselves.

One sign that is given of actions that spring forth from our connection to Source is a feeling of peaceful joy. Of course, there are many factors to take into consideration when gauging our actions, and we must know ourselves well in order to discern such a feeling. This holds especially true for our service work.

In any art form practiced around here, one big skill being developed is that of being able to get out of the way so that the creative force can flow in response to the time, place and people of the moment. It so happens that I've always had a predilection toward art and theater. This combination within the context of the school has an intimate, subtle and useful relationship that I couldn't have arrived at on my own. And yet, I was pulled to pursue both even when this relationship was unknown.

There is a combination of skills and tendencies that made it most expedient for me to take up the oils and work with the *Creation Story Verbatim* play. In the process of this work, with a group of about thirty, we served in the invocation of a massive entity called the Simurgh, which, in turn, served to provide radiations and chemical factors that were useful to our transformation.

The range of service and what is needed will vary according to one's morphology and state of Being. The thing is, service is a function of Being. Our focus will be on Being, therefore over any doing. One way in which we assess our state of Being might be in looking where we find ourselves in terms of our service — what are we serving? At some level we are serving something. When we are serving something greater than ourselves, consciously, we might be given good perspective by which to assess our movement. The movement of our work might be seen by the way in which we serve, our transactions with those involved, our focus of attention. I will repeat here, in agreement with Rumi, "The spirit is like a little girl that comes out to play when we draw the sword of selfless action." Service is one way in which such selfless action can take place. Service also helps us to break the habit of egocentricity that keeps us bound to our limited morphology.

Unsurprisingly, service has its traps, not least of which is pride of service. But with a little soul intelligence and experience in the ways of the Work, we can come to either sidestep or relax our grip on what traps us. My experience of service has changed remarkably throughout my years around the school, and even as I speak, undergoes change. But one thing seems consistent, the moment I become aware of being of service, it throws me off — there is no longer a vehicle there for spirit to come out and play. It is one thing to note what action seems to serve the greater whole over another action, to have that quality of awareness present, letting us see how we might better serve. It is another to be aware of one's service in such a way as to take up the breath of purity and blow it into the lungs of our ego. We focus on our Being rather than our Doing.

At the same time, we wish to know what we serve, to some degree, and we wish to be conscious in our choice to serve. When we are using service as a way intentionally and successfully, it truly serves all. When this choice to serve becomes mechanical, we run into the kinds of problems like, pride of service, (like Gabriel's new points on his horns!) that embroil us in the illusion further instead of freeing us, thus hindering us from developing as Beings that can serve the greater needs of the Work.

In order to be able to see the Work, we must be operating through an awakened HBM. We are inviting more electrical input for transformation into our circuitry. Think about it. Have you ever gotten an electric shock? The machine will feel the effects of what are real electrical experiences if not during an invocation, certainly after. When on the job, for example, in an angelic invocation, one is inexorably bound to the situation of posture, light, sound, mood and particular sensation throughout its duration. One will serve the needs of the space selflessly, despite any discomfort that machine reverberations might produce. We develop skill in rendering ourselves useful in this way. We are opening ourselves up to the Divine and turning away from the realm of egoistic identity. We have to be out of our minds to be seeking this out, quite literally.

In a way, alignment happens by a process of seeking out the best means of alleviating, or equalizing, the pressure there is to evolve, which often means removing an impediment. In a school, the presence of the Teacher helps to quicken and create conditions where impediment might be removed more readily, at the point of brinksmanship that makes for the smoothest possible transition. It is all self-initiatory, but with guidance and the opportunity to borrow a higher will. We evolve because it hurts too much not to evolve. Remember, pain is a product of the illusion of separation and sleep. When we awaken, we realize all as spirit and there is no pain in this condition. But just as in death, there is unraveling, so too, the death of the set of illusions that led to pain will require unraveling, and in this process, there will likely be pain felt. In a school we learn to minimize our machine reactions and reverberations, and this is helpful to the process of unraveling to the place of clarity.

While we might have a trace of the angelic character that is "driven onward by a passionate painful ecstasy of hopeless yearning for fulfillment" (from *Creation Story Verbatim*), we also can blow the energy away readily when the lines of tension reach a certain threshold. We don't hold the post of an angel yet, and thus do not realize the level of obligation and necessity they were made to know. Alignment in the Work brings us to a place where we might realize obligation and the need to evolve — so that we might fulfill obligation.

Crossing streams, as it has sometimes been called, will have us change our natural function. I will now refer to the human reality pump idea and work with negative force. Negative force will be created by the human biological machine just by virtue of its planetary arising. Again, to repeat this useful idea — as we are made, we function as a membrane that pushes finer matter out into the atmosphere like a pump that makes real, substantiates the outer world. There is the possibility of reversing this pump, taking the outer world and using it to feed the inner, to make real, substantiate the inner and use the outer as resistance, which pushes the energy in and on up toward the finer. One can see that this would serve to counter the effect of entropy. The automatic movement of inner to outer is referred to as *feeding the moon* in some Fourth Way writings.

Negative force accumulates at various points in the electrical field of the HBM and between these points of accumulation there will be lines of tension. We can learn to get a sense of this phenomenon with practice. Under normal circumstances, the tendency is to reach a certain place of tension and accumulation only to blow off the energy and thus start the cycle again. Blowing off energy serves to disrupt the lines of tension, doing nothing about the accumulation of negative force. The negative force is going to accumulate in any event. We suffer in the worse sense of the word because of our disruption of these lines of tension. If we were to maintain the tension up to a point of stabilization, we would not suffer pain as we do with the constant disruption and rebuilding of these lines of tension. We would energetically bring the machine to the waking state by maintaining the lines of tension and accumulating force. In the waking state there is no pain.

At any point along the line, considering all the factors we've mentioned thus far, and there are more to consider, there may be a calling for movement toward alignment. *Know thyself.*

One product of inner transformation seems to be changed relations.

We are asking for more awareness, which is a form of Suffering in the sense of bearing — one is being asked to bear more consciousness. It seems this is inevitable anyway — all will return to Source eventually; we are asking for a quickening of this process. One gauge for progress might be any movement in this direction of increased awareness, which implies the general, and any development of attention in the more specific, that we might witness. This is one way in which communication with a group of people of different typicality can offer help in feedback. One product of inner transformation seems to be changed relations.

More tolerance, not because one is trying to have more tolerance, but because it just is the only response possible; one has been changed such that more tolerance is part of the make-up. Being on the side of the solution as opposed to the problem comes with the territory of transformation, and tolerance is often a part of this equation.

The mirror quality of the universe might impose itself a little more into our awareness. More tolerance for others also generally seems to reflect a self-exposing process that has revealed to one the demons once harbored and a corresponding patience and faith that sees through their ultimate illusory nature. I cannot truly be tolerant of others if I am not tolerant of myself. And sometimes it takes conditions that bring us up against the wall to get us to the point of need that brings about the quality of self-tolerance that is useful. The person who lifted a bus to save another would not have known his capacity for strength without the great necessity of that moment.

Humility will enable us to move into exalted spaces at necessity without entrapment in their afterglow. With humility, one is compact enough to move from one shape to another in accordance with right action, in accordance with service to the needs of the time, place and people. Thus humility and this quality of fluidity are other useful areas of examination to check out in our attempt to assess the situation.

We will take the next step on our transformational path, or path of service, when all aligns itself such that we have become the one who takes the next step. Really, that is what it seems to boil down to. Sometimes we will consider ourselves ready when, in fact, we aren't, and sometimes we will be thrown into situations where we feel unprepared, but, in fact, are ready. Something E.J. once said to me — he makes mistakes, but he pays as he goes along. His work is objectively too important for him to allow himself to stop. One way I have found this useful is in seeing the importance of obligation. Because he had addressed my tendency at that time to allow disruptions with others to continue stealing work energy through my own behavior, I found in obligation a new use as an anchor. Serving genuine Work necessity clarifies, just as the deathbed perspective clarifies, putting in order priorities and encouraging efficient use of our time, space and energy.

The Deathbed Perspective

"If you can ever really come to know and understand that you must

soon die — and eventually we are all going to lie down on that same couch and wait for the angel of death to take us — you can understand how none of the straws you have been grasping at — are of any real value . . . . Everything comes to nothing in this world; if your body is going to die anyway, and it certainly is, then your attention can lift now from the body, and the things of the body — the material, mental and emotional possessions — and is free to then settle itself onto what can be accomplished that's of any value . . . . It's hard to bring yourself to believe that the body is going to die, isn't it? But if you can, you'll stop wasting your time being impressed with all the things that are going to die with it on that day. The clarity about the life and death of the machine — and the futility of ordinary existence, that is, life without the Work, can be a great cure for intellectual, emotional, material or spiritual grasper's disease . . . . At the end of your life you're going to look back at all those things which so preoccupied you, and you'll realize you could have used the same energy to bring the machine into the waking state . . . Look back over your life and ask yourself how many of your involvements were necessary, how much you could have dispensed with in order to do your Work."

(Gold, *The Deathbed Perspective*, page 1)

We align ourselves to the school influence and at a certain point the culture seems to grow in us like with yogurt. At least that's the way it has seemed to me. At first, these ideas felt so familiar to me, yet distant, and then many synaptic and box-destroying experiences with the guidance of a real Teacher have brought me closer to nearness. Illusion still lures me, hooks me, but I am more willing to suffer its shattering.

Years ago I found myself quite rebellious, and I remember that even preceding that, during one of the very first talks I heard E.J. give in New York, he said that we would undergo phases in our development — just as children do, and that at some point we would be as rebellious teenagers, fighting against him and his influence. At the time he said that I could not imagine this, but sure enough, as with many things he says, this did come to be.

One way that I acted out my rebellion was through a devil-may-care attitude that would have me grab the car and go straight to Starbuck's for a soy latte, then Raley's (a grocery store) for a treat of a Balance Bar. From there I headed for Ross, my church away from home. For those who don't know it, Ross is a store where one can get designer clothing, shoes, luggage and a vast array of housewares, including some furnishings at a discounted price. While standing on line at an L.A. Ross with my friend Angela during my recent trip where I purchased some sheets and bath sandals for myself, she commented on how great it was to have a store like this. I told her that I thought they should have holy water at the front entrance. With that, the woman standing in front of us turned and said "Amen!"

So I would go to Ross to spend hours perusing and escaping the realities of communal life. This indulgence seemed to reach a high-level of intensity and then dropped off completely following the recovery of memory of early childhood trauma. When the unraveling process commenced, the origins of this habit were revealed to me, and with this revelation the need was satisfied. I am reminded of a modality of healing work that involves cellular memory. One of the ideas presented to me is that all experience can be said to want our attention. Experiences of a traumatic nature will often blow the circuitry such that we put up buffers preventing our actual placement of attention on the event. These events and the survival tactics of the ego will gather similar electrical data, forming anomalies that influence our intake of impressions as well as our responses. These anomalies can be accessed as cellular memory. When the attention is placed on an event, it seems to discharge it, and these electrical masses that eat up energy and keep us asleep can thereby be broken down.

But at the point of this story, I was still in the throes of the habit. The coping mechanisms that are developed are done so because the ego wants to survive annihilation into spirit that might otherwise result at a point of shock. Remember, only the essential self can handle intense stress. At a level of the essential self there is the recognition of all as spirit and in this realm there is nothing outside of oneself to harm or not harm, nothing to be done; it's all one big electromagnetic party.

Shopping — you get things, lots of things, you know . . . things — things to further refract the light of Being, to feed the moon, as is said. We can get things to keep us believing in our separate existence, main-

taining the consensus reality show at its top ratings. Communal life in a
school has the function of diminishing. The way things are set up, we
have to rid ourselves of the obstacles to the waking state. Our waking is
closer to the game of finding buried treasure than Monopoly. As can be
seen by the massive collection of art and artifacts and plush toys, and so
on, to be found at the Institute ranch, things are still gotten and used, but
the intent behind their use will bear relationship to this process of diminishment.

Whenever the process of purification reached a place that threatened
the revelation of my secret to myself, as I see it in hindsight, I made my
escape to Ross. In time, even in ignorance, the wind and water way of
the school brought me to the place of seeing I couldn't keep fooling myself. So on this occasion, I decided to begin to impose a certain discipline
on myself. I would go to Ross, yes, but this time not stopping for the
latte and Balance Bar.

From Penn Valley, where I lived at the time, to Grass Valley, my mind
was engaged in the drama of the moment that had pushed me over the
edge and towards seeking sanctuary in the realm of Ross. By the time I
came, to I found myself at the Raley's, Starbuck's parking lot! I was
completely taken by how extreme my sleep had been, how I forgot the
intention to avoid the treats. However, since I found myself there, I fig-
ured to get a Balance Bar, as I was hungry and would not be anywhere
near food for several hours.

No sooner did I walk into the nearly empty store, when I heard the
sound of a toddler screaming the kind of scream that meant real trouble.
My body is programmed to respond to this sort of thing, and I observed
this phenomenon and the accompanying sensations of urgency. The next
thing I knew, a woman came charging through with her cart to the front
of the store, her very unhappy but gloriously beautiful daughter caught
in a miserable position, stuck in the front little carrier seat of the cart.
Her leg was completely and immovably caught in a very uncomfortable
position. A couple of women who worked at the store joined the mother,
and now me, as we gathered around feeling momentarily helpless trying
in vain to comfort the child. Suddenly it struck me — Oil! I went to the
nearest aisle where oil could be found and handed a bottle to one of the
employees who quickly opened it and applied it to the child's leg. With

ease she slipped right out, and we all breathed a united sigh of relief. I didn't bother to get my Balance Bar that day.

The story is a good example of "my habits carrying me through." The body of habits seemed to have brought me to the appropriate place of usefulness despite my sleep. But also suggested by the severity of my rebellion is the fact that living in a school, I had adopted habits that rendered the seemingly harmless act of going to get a treat and coffee and driving to a store as the height of daring. Though I can readily acknowledge times when such an act could have devastating results, at the same time, the contrast to former behavior, which likely would have taken the form of drinking alcohol to some degree of oblivion, is noteworthy.

It seems some of my work has to do with children. After undergoing a bit of a screening process when I first started working with E.J., I was often put to work doing childcare. I do love children, but any parent knows there are big trials we face when working with children; they teach us much about how to genuinely love, if we are open to the experience. One learns how to put oneself aside, yet at the same time, within the context of a work community, one learns how to sustain the conditions that will enable the child to develop their own center of gravity, with impulses that are "essential self friendly."

The kind of training that I underwent under school conditions around childcare has served well in every facet of what I presently consider to be my *service* work. It also seems to have left a subtle mark upon me that invites fairly frequent special encounters with children. Witnessing one such encounter tickled my daughter into calling me "the child whisperer."

We were returning from a wonderful trip we made to New York City. The flight was very crowded, and it felt rather oppressive. This oppression was compounded by the unremitting sound of a toddler crying at full force. Being a mom, I recognize the sound of a child who is crying, but will soon doze off. This was not that kind of sound. That tireless child was giving it her all — must've been for a full fifteen or twenty minutes. The parents had given up trying to comfort her and simply sat there red faced but expressionless. The tension in the cabin was unbelievably high — I would say dangerously so.

Before I knew it — and I mean this literally — before I was aware of the fact that I was going to do something about the situation, my body had already gotten up and was walking the three rows up to where the young family sat. I instinctively reached for the Bach Flower Remedy called "Rescue Remedy," a formula of several flower essences. Somehow I'd been allowed to carry this onboard. My awareness was on and of my energetic body at the moment and with this ever-so-gently, I laid my hand on the shoulder of the father who was sitting at the aisle seat holding Emily. At that moment Emily stopped crying and stared at me. Gently, I asked them if they'd ever heard of Rescue Remedy. No, they hadn't. I started explaining to them a bit about it, meanwhile, using the opportunity to ease myself into Emily's sphere. The mother explained that Emily wanted to be in her crib at home and at this point, I engaged Emily fully, using a soft lyrical voice.

It was clear to me that the Being in that machine was unclear about what was going on, this was a new experience and likely she was picking up the tension of the passengers around her. I let her know that she was right, it was very uncomfortable, but that it was safe for her to just allow herself to rest here with her mom and dad so that when she awoke, she would be closer to or at her home. She listened intently, and I knew communication had taken place. As a final gesture, I took a few drops of the Rescue Remedy under my tongue to show the parents it was safe, letting them know if they needed any, I was three rows back from them. When I took the Rescue Remedy, it was quite amazing, I had the experience of the entire cabin inside my chest and the effect of the remedy was on the entire cabin. The next sound we heard out of Emily took place after we landed and it was the most delicious sound of delightful laughter you would ever want to hear. As I walked out of the plane, one of the stewardesses exclaimed, "Our savior!" I didn't take it personally.

That was a situation where I was taken up by a tremendous force. It was incredibly impersonal. And this is how I think of *service* — it is impersonal, one is merely an instrument for genuine help to come on through. My particular set of skills and inclinations and so on rendered me a good vehicle for the moment's necessity. Of course, we aren't always under such fortunate, obvious circumstances. But situations such as these, where we are clearly taken up by a mighty hand, help to electrically impinge us with information that informs and reinforces our habits of work.

There are questions we can ask ourselves when we are in a "should we or shouldn't we" place. There will be room for questions in this state. When our actions spring forth from pure Being, on the other hand, there is no room for question, there is only completion, we are one with our activity. It serves us well to have some form of ritual or practice that will readily enable us to access the place where a question might find resonance with the answer that lies within. Meditation in whatever form can be the vehicle by which we navigate toward "impartial I" and guidance.

In this same conversation, E.J. told me all that his Teacher wanted from him was the truth, and that is all he wants from us.

When there is a specific question about a next step that one feels might be taken in one's Work, it serves to be aware of where the question resounds within the body, and any immediate indications given by subtle sensing that may come forth with the question. To a question asked sincerely, under the correct set of conditions, responses of clarity will present themselves; the answers are found at the place of the question's origin. One has to get everything still enough within and cease identification with the persona of ignorance, instead identifying with the one who knows. This is a very real thing that was beautifully expressed to me by E.J. He was describing his time as a student with a Zen Master who put to him the koan, "What is the sound of one hand clapping?"

E.J. was given the task of meditating on this koan and then returning with a response. He did this several times over a period of months, each time coming up with a new answer that demonstrated the state of awareness reached, each time being sent away to meditate more. He came up with a full range of answers that went from making a slapping sound on the table before him to, yes, folks, making the slapping sound against the Teacher's cheek! The Teacher's response, as described by E.J., was elegant and appropriately full of the curmudgeon. Drily, he looked at him and said, "No, *that* is not the answer." Finally, his meditation brought him to the place of relinquishing identification with the one that doesn't know and instead, identifying with the one that knew. When he next arrived, after a much longer interval, he replied thus:

Imagine the body split directly down the middle, one half of it is

Being, the other a reflection of that half. The sound of one hand clapping is the sound that is made when creation comes into Being, when Being is met by its own reflection to produce the sound of one hand clapping. With this, E.J. no longer needed to study with the Master as he had and was sent on his way.

In this same conversation E.J. told me all that his Teacher wanted from him was the truth, and that is all he wants from us. In this realm of relativity we inhabit, the Truth of what we are at any given moment can give the appearance of change and needs to be acknowledged as we maintain the constant of navigation toward the knowledge of all as spirit.

We are not always at the place of wishing to Work, above all else. With the appropriate efforts in school conditions, it is possible to condition ourselves such that despite our desire, we find we can't help but move toward Work. Obligating ourselves to the fulfillment of the school's Work, we entrain the body, mind, spirit relationship to function in alignment with Work and Service. This is not to say we will not stray away from the mark, but if we remain within the magnetic center of the Work, which a school with a genuine Teacher can provide, one eventually must yield to the greater force.

Our activities around a school will have us bearing a responsibility to others in a group that will include individuals one would not necessarily want to have any connection to on a personal basis. One is here, given the opportunity to see beyond the narrow strip mall of personal preference to the elegance of function within the larger scope of the school's Work.

But even at that, as indicated by my story, our incompletion will assert itself. Another question we might ask ourselves: what is my truth at the moment? Where is my center of gravity? If we are steeped in desire for chocolate cake and can't get ourselves to the place of wanting our Work energy over the chocolate cake, then perhaps having the chocolate cake and suffering the consequences is in order. Sometimes we need to go down a few floors to get to the side moving car that takes us to the elevator that will go all the way up.

The Lord's big message for humanity in the *Creation Story Verbatim* play is: "Be Who You Are and Do What You Do." This is actually at the heart of the matter. The unique expression we are of the Whole is to be found deep in the present moment. We do well to remember always that in the present moment, if we sit in it completely, our deepest necessity is answered. Let us be clear here — we are likely not going to reach a place of permanent balance on this planet. The sooner we can get rid of the tendency to seek a painless state, the better. At the same time, the sooner we can cease identifying with the sleep that steeps us in our pain, the better. And one way we have of helping ourselves is by dipping into the fresh spring of the present moment. The point of transformative power is in the present moment. Arriving at this moment here, now, opening up in it, if we can get ourselves to cease identification with the one that has a history, that has gone from point A to point B, we stand a chance of walking a path of right action, of breathing as an essential Being in communion with the Beloved. Our journey to the Heart of the Maker is happening right this very moment. In deep stillness, we will feel the pulse that moves us truly.

From **Cetus: The Sea Monster, or Kraken**

I hear nothing in my ear
but your voice. Heart has
plundered mind of all its eloquence.
Love writes a transparent calligraphy, so
on the empty page my soul
can read and recollect

(Barks, *Rumi: The Big Red Book*, page 454)

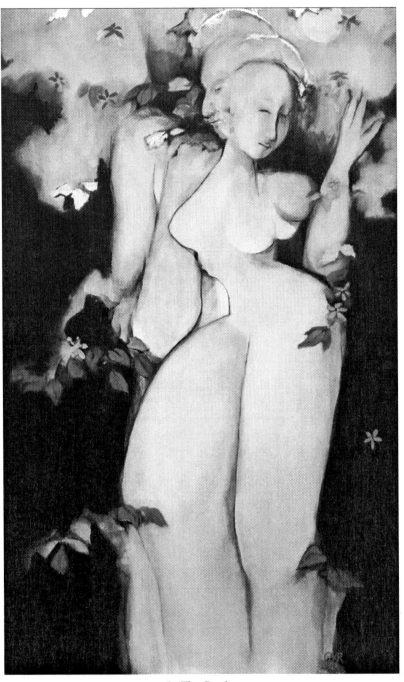

In The Garden
Grace Kelly River, Oil on Canvas, 40"x30", © 2004 Grace Kelly Rivera

REFERENCE

This section provides sources for information on a variety of topics mentioned throughout the book. Most of the resources mentioned here are either in DVD or CD format and are available online at the address given. Written resource material will be found in the Bibliography.

The ABCs of Love: CDT145
This outstanding talk presents love in the shamanistic view, distinguishing it from other meanings of the word love and forms of love in machine life. Information includes opening up to the breath of love, using attention to mold the force of love, non-dependency and risk of real love, differences between love, God and lightning handlers. A revealing and perspective-altering discourse.
Available online at:
http://www.talkofthemonth.com/talkcds/relationships.html

Accessing the Waking State: CDT135
This talk explores the efficiency and consequences of using different methods to achieve the waking state. Adoration of the machine is stressed and students reconstruct instructions given, but not recorded, concerning the Popcorn exercise and the reversal of headbrain/tailbrain functions.
Available online at:
http://www.talkofthemonth.com/talkcds/pwos.html

Alchemical Oils: An Indepth Interview: CDT234
Practical applications of the oils as they relate to work-on-self and learning obligation are discussed. Kelly Rivera has worked with Alchem-

ical Gold oils since 1987 and explains their use as effective tools to translate work theory into work practice.

Available online at:

http://www.talkofthemonth.com/talkcds/pwos.html

Antime Yoga: DVD 192

E.J. Gold describes the antime as your chief competitor, rival. The antime is dedicated to tearing down everything you build up. Gold gives the origin of the antime and graphic examples explaining how to recognize it. He examines the antime in the light of physics and metaphysics.

Gold offers Antime Yoga as in a yoke to take on some kind of work. You must work to free yourself from the domination of this enemy. What emerges is better able to tolerate the waking state. Then you can really understand the pack of green (PoG), and at that point you can do work on yourself and become more able to participate in the Great Work.

Available online at:

http://www.idhhb.com/waking_state_series/antime_yoga.html

Chief feature and Negative Force: CDT 141

This revealing presentation explores the multiple meanings of the term "Chief Feature" and man's choice of whether or not to feed it. Equilibrium of tensions, modern superstitions, emotional bodies as psychic phenomena and feeding a higher dimension are explored.

Available online at:

http://www.talkofthemonth.com/talkcds/transformation.html

Fear and Risk: CDT 162

Lee Lozowick and E.J. Gold talk about dying to ordinary life, overcoming fears and the necessity of risk-taking in the school. New Age imitation spirituality is debunked. The kind of attention needed for work, what it means to be in the Work, and making oneself available to receive the teaching are also discussed.

Available online at:

http://www.talkofthemonth.com/talkcds/moc.html

The Focus of the Work Community: CDT 182

In this birthday question, the direction and activities of the Work community are questioned as well as levels of perfection, the excrement of concentrated attention, cultural imperatives, art as a form of Work, and more adventures in the Gutai school of painting. The question, "When are you Happiest?" is asked of members of the community.

Available online at:

http://www.talkofthemonth.com/talkcds/intro.html

Man on the Cross: CDT105

As any serious seeker can attest, Man on the Cross material is hard to come by. The difficult and esoteric work idea of "Die before you die" is explored within the context of voluntary reascension of the cross. Very esoteric ideas are presented here with full candor. This talk is pan-religious and erases all barriers between oneself and one's cosmic position.

Available online at:

http://www.idhhb.com/talks/moretalks/talk41.html

Objective Theater: CDT 018

This talk examines the function of man on the planet, his involuntary or voluntary feeding of lunar or solar entities, the invocation of entities by actors on stage, and the play as a form of invocation.

Available online at:

http://www.talkofthemonth.com/talkcds/art.html

Out of Body Workshop : CDT 138

Work data on dreaming and sleep states, out-of-body experiences, the Face of God (FoG) exercise and adoration of the machine.

Available online at:

http://www.talkofthemonth.com/talkcds/transformation.html

The Physical Body/The Pump: CDT005

Side 1: A talk on the symbolism of the Tarot as it relates to the science of types and the assimilation of impressions.

Side 2: Reversing the flow of substances so they pass through man from the outer world to the inner world is the subject of this informal

talk to an intimate group.
Available online at:
http://www.talkofthemonth.com/talkcds/moc.html

The Popcorn Exercise: DVD 076

The Popcorn Exercise is a classic at IDHHB. It is one of the tools that E.J. Gold has stated to be so effective that you could work with it alone to gain time in the waking state.

Presented here in DVD format, Gold shows exactly how it is done. He appears with a small group of students and guides them through the process on camera, sharing the benefit of his critique of their efforts.

Available online at:
http://www.idhhb.com/dvds/popcorn-exercise.html

Prayer Absolute and Discipline: CDT 167

What is the relationship of the Voyager to the Absolute? The necessity for discipline and the Creation as a dead lover are explored in this revealing talk.

Available online at:
http://www.talkofthemonth.com/talkcds/moc.html

Presence and Negative Emotion: CDT121

Inner transformation sooner or later comes to address the issue of negative emotions. This Montreal talk with partial French translations explores the nature and arising of negative emotions. Moving center sensations, higher emotions without mental significance, presence of the essential self and banishing negative emotions are presented.

Available online at:
http://www.talkofthemonth.com/talkcds/transformation.html

Relationships: CDT 035

Your partner as the Guide, the Cosmic Computer, soulmates and essence friendships, the Here and Now, the trap of enlightenment and removing the veils.

Available online at:
http://www.talkofthemonth.com/talkcds/alchemy.html

Spirit Dance with E.J. Gold: DVD 177

In our society, there is often automatic and incorrect intertwining of sexual and erotic energy. Erotic energy is a much higher level of energy. ESD properly belongs in the category of spiritual energy. We will be dancing ourselves back into the spaces we have been before, looking to recover the erotic energy incorrectly assigned to them. E.J. Gold gives the means to take back the energy from past events.

Available online at:

http://www.idhhb.com/esd/dvd.html

Theater Absolute: CDT 124

This discussion of ancient theater and the power of manifestations includes a powerful exercise for working with attention and the source of attention.

Available online at:

http://www.talkofthemonth.com/talkcds/art.html

The Way of Right Action : CDT 174

A talk on the difficulties of working with attention in day-to-day life. Moments of being "on," exalted states, phenomenal outcomes, retaining one's Buddhahood, the dark side of the Force and the world beyond illusion are examined with references from the film *The Golden Child*.

Available online at:

http://www.talkofthemonth.com/talkcds/shamanism.html

The Way of the Shaman – Parts 1 and 11

Mr. Gold tells of the shaman's continual efforts to expand his perception so as to include all the details of the so-called "invsible" world, and his shape-shifting way of maintaining his presence in the higher dimensions. He goes on to talk about men and women and how their respective natures are at once well-suited and ill-suited to the Work, and what they must accomplish if they are ever to serve the Work.

Available online at:

http://www.talkofthemonth.com/totm/totm023.html

When the Rapture Comes: CDT 140

This revealing discourse between E.J. Gold and Lee Lozowick begins with a discussion of Roman-occupied Judea and the crucifixion. The universe as a purely decorative object, creation and destruction cycles, the teacher as a guest, conflict management, the danger of harmony and joining the Work Chain outside of Creation are explored in this informative discourse. Not for the timid.

Available online at:

http://www.talkofthemonth.com/talkcds/moc.html

Whole Body Attention: CDT 168

The machine and the electric bubble, expansion of one's own morphology, repetition in beginning work, expansion, contraction, focusing and withdrawal of attention are all explored.

Available online at:

http://www.talkofthemonth.com/talkcds/transformation.html

BIBLIOGRAPHY

---------------Attar, Farid ud. The Conference of the Birds, Afkham Darbandi (Translator). New York, Penguin Classics: 1984.

--------------Barks, Coleman (translator of Jelal al-Din Rumi). The Big Red Book. New York, HarperCollins: 2010.

--------------with John Moyne. The Essential Rumi. San Francisco, HarperSanFranciso: 1995.

-------------The Illuminated Rumi. New York, Bantam Doubleday Dell: 1997.

-------------Soul of Rumi: A New Collection of Ecstatic Poems: HarperSanFrancisco, San Francisco: 2001.

--------------Gold, E.J. American Book of the Dead (30th Anniversary Edition). Nevada City, CA , Gateways Books: 2005.

------------Angels Healing Journey. Nevada City, CA, Gateways Books: 1997.

------------Bardo Stations. Nevada City, CA , Gateways Books: 2005.

------------"Brother Judas: The Compassionate Betrayal" in The Lost Works. Nevada City, CA , Gateways Books: 1994.

------------Creation Story Verbatim. Nevada City, CA , Gateways Books: 1986.

------------Creation Story Verbatim. Play, working script. IDHHB, Inc., Nevada City, CA: 1985.

------------The Human Biological Machine as a Transformational Apparatus. Nevada City, CA , Gateways Books: 2007.

------------The Invocation of Presence. Nevada City, CA , Gateways Books: 1989.

-------------- The Joy of Sacrifice. Crestline, CA, IDHHB Publishing: 1978.

--------------Life in the Labyrinth. Nevada City, CA , Gateways Books: 2001.

--------------Parallel Worlds Explored. Nevada City, CA , Gateways Books: 2009.

--------------Seven Bodies of Man. Nevada City, CA , Gateways Books: 1989.

-------------"Talk of the Month" (Journal, monthly). Issues 6-7 (Life as Theatre, 1 & 2), 34 (The Deathbed Perspective), 38 (The Simurgh Talk), 91 (Learning to Do/Plasma at the Speed of Light), etc. Nevada City, CA: Gateways, 1983-1991.

------------- Macfarlane, Menlo. Heart of the Maker (song lyrics) in The Angel Songbook. Crestline, CA, IDHHB Publishing,: 1987.

------------- Ouspensky, P.D., In Search of the Miraculous, New York, Harcourt Brace Jovanovich: 1965.

Contact Information

We hope that you have enjoyed and drawn inspiration from *Journey To the Heart of the Maker* by Kelly Rivera. For more books on spiritual life and practices, please contact:

Gateways Books
P.O. Box 370
Nevada City, CA. 95959-0370

Phone: (800) 869-0658
       (530) 271-2239
Fax: (530) 687-0317

Websites: www.gatewaysbooksandtapes.com
           www.idhhb.com
           www.gorebagg.com
           www.brane-power.com
           www.yoyodyneindustries.com